Japanese and Americans:
Cultural Parallels and Paradoxes

Published in association
with Grinnell College

Japanese and Americans: Cultural Parallels and Paradoxes

by Charles Grinnell Cleaver

UNIVERSITY OF MINNESOTA
PRESS, MINNEAPOLIS

Copyright © 1976 by the University
of Minnesota. All rights reserved.
Printed in the United States of America at
NAPCO Graphic Arts Inc., New Berlin, Wisconsin.
Published in Canada by Burns & MacEachern
Limited, Don Mills, Ontario
    Library of Congress Catalog Card Number 75-18081
    ISBN 0-8166-0761-3

"Dust of Snow" and the excerpt from "West-Running Brook" are
from *The Poetry of Robert Frost,* edited by Edward Connery Lathem.
Copyright 1928, © 1969 by Holt, Rinehart and Winston, Inc.
Copyright © 1956 by Robert Frost. Reprinted by permission of Holt,
Rinehart and Winston, Publishers. The haiku quoted from *A Chime
of Windbells* by Harold Stewart, copyright © 1969 by Charles E. Tuttle
Co., Inc., are used by permission of the publishers, Charles E. Tuttle
Co., Inc. The excerpts from Bashō's *The Narrow Road to the Deep
North and Other Travel Sketches,* edited and translated by Nobuyuki
Yuasa, are used by permission of the publishers, Penguin Books Ltd.
Copyright © 1966 by Nobuyuki Yuasa. The passage from Kawabata's
Japan the Beautiful and Myself is printed with the permission of Mrs.
Kawabata Hideko. The three poems on page 97 are reproduced
from Great Ages of Man/*Early Japan* by Jonathan Norton Leonard
and the Editors of Time-Life Books, © 1968 Time Inc., by permis-
sion of Time-Life Books; they were adapted from an illustrated scroll,
Nisen-ni ban shokujin utaawase, at the National Museum, Kyoto, courtesy Shizuhiko Kosetu, Osaka.

This book is dedicated

to Moy and Allen

Preface

This began innocently enough as an essay in American Studies. I have suspected my craft of suffering from a weak comparative base, and I wished to strengthen it. We have said this or that about the culture of the United States, but we have seldom asked, compared with what? Rapidly deteriorating relations between Japan and the United States, however, have urged me to hurry up about it: political considerations now crowd in on the academic ones.

My credentials are none too good. I am properly accredited in American Studies, and I trust that my training and practice in interdisciplinary study in this field will be helpful here. I have visited Japan on five occasions, from 1945 to 1972, as soldier, Fulbright lecturer, and grantee. Here's the rub, though: I read and write no Japanese, and my conversation with Japanese people is perfectly satisfactory to me only if they are under the age of five. My dependence on translators in Japan and in my study of Japan at home reduces part of this study, then, to the status of the semipro. But I have collaborated with my good friend Professor Shibata Tokue, formerly a commissioner with the Tokyo metropolitan government, now director of the Tokyo Metropolitan Research Institute for Environmental Protection, on a long essay on Japan. We had hoped to join forces on this study, but helping govern Tokyo is an arduous business.

A comprehensive comparison of the two cultures is obviously out of the question, so I have chosen the method of the prospector after oil, drilling down here and there, where science or hunch suggests that there might be a payoff.

It is my opinion that differences in the two cultures have been emphasized so much that similarities have been overlooked. Further, when differences have been discovered, a moral judgment has often been implied. I hope to maintain a decent cultural relativism, remembering that every culture must make its own kind of adaptations to dizzying change. Cultural relativism rejects one habit of mind which Westerners have found difficult to shake off, the supposition that "progress" is multilinear, and follows the path cleared by France, or Britain, or the United States, or the Soviet Union. If a people chooses to solve a new problem in their own way rather than in the way another people solved it, that of course is their business. When solutions involve racism or militarism, however, a writer may surely be pardoned for abandoning his academic objectivity.

Now, three definitions. We in American Studies use the word *culture* in the manner of the anthropologist: the way of life, the whole fabric of generally "shared significant symbols." We use the word *imagination,* not meaning "fancy," but, following Coleridge and I. A. Richards, meaning that fusion of thought, feeling, moral vision, and one's manner of sensing the world which marks high art, but which all men experience. We use the word *myth* not necessarily to mean falsehood or fiction but to mean explanations of how the world goes, including descriptions of its origins, which many people in a culture share, find important, and react to emotionally, such as, for example, the American schoolbook account of the Founding Fathers, or the official wartime Japanese description of the divine origin of the imperial line.

Readers may wonder about certain of my methodological assumptions. My approach to a culture has been influenced, as I have mentioned, by the interdisciplinary works in American Studies which have been most successful. That body of writing, like anthropology, assumes holistic cultures, paradox and all. The authors place more emphasis than the ordinary anthropologist does, however, on the clues which the arts provide. Certain literary and architectural forms, I believe, lie close to the marrow of a people's imagination, as I have just defined that word. The poet, said Ezra Pound, is the "antenna of his race." This is not to say that my respect for the various social studies is abridged; it will be clear that I lean heavily on them. Aside from these methods, I must confess that I make use of some guesses based upon personal observation.

There is no reason to believe that this attempt to break down stereotypes and rectify misunderstandings will be much of an advance over earlier ones, but one must keep trying. The well-known critic Eto Jun told the 1972 Shimoda Conference (an annual meeting of Japanese and American scholars) that "mutual understanding at this late date is some kind of joke." Yet his whole earnest study of recent American attitudes toward Japan (published in the Winter 1973 issue of the *Japan Interpreter*) belied his conclusion. While my book may help but little to reduce the absurdity of the joke (if it is one), I still entertain fantasies that people will let me know what parts of this analysis seem to be in error, and why, so that later editions can move toward clarity, where now there is cloudiness.

I am grateful to many who made this work possible—many more, in fact, than I will be able to mention. I hope that I have acknowledged most of my learned sources in my bibliographical note. To the anonymous friend of Grinnell College who read the manuscript and then afforded the subvention, through Grinnell, that helped the University of Minnesota Press publish it in these hard times, my thanks. Also thanks to the Ford Foundation, whose grants to my college for faculty research supported two summers of research in Japan as well as many other costs. My serious interest in the Japanese culture began during my year, 1963–1964, as a Fulbright lecturer there.

The following people know that they have helped me, and will not require that I spell out the ways: Professor and Mrs. Yokozawa Shiro; Professor Iwama; the students of the "teru-teru bozu" group; Professor and Mrs. Shibata Tokue; Kojima Ryoichi; the librarians in the International House of Japan; Sara Cleaver, and Anne and William Cleaver; Adena McBee and Mary Beth Roska; Mike Liberman; and Glenn Leggett.

C. G. C.

February 1975

Contents

CHAPTER 1 The Problem: Stereotypes
(Self-Imposed and Otherwise),
"National Character," and Paradox, 3

CHAPTER 2 The Wilderness Zion and the
Land of the Gods, 18

CHAPTER 3 The "Crass Materialists" and
the "Economic Animals," 38

CHAPTER 4 The Old Environment: Nature, 58

CHAPTER 5 Workaday and Holiday, 83

CHAPTER 6 Fiction and the Popular Imagination, 124

CHAPTER 7 Shelter and Symbol, 170

CHAPTER 8 The Nurture of the Young, 203

CHAPTER 9 In Concluding, 231

EPILOGUE: "Same Difference," 244

By Way of Bibliography 247

Notes 259

Index 269

Illustrations

between pages 178 and 179

Prints by the Japanese Hiroshige
  and the American George Caleb Bingham

Hirosaki building

Ise Grand Shrine

The Shokintei Teahouse
  at the Katsura Detached Palace

Frank Lloyd Wright's Falling Water

Kenzo Tange's Yamanski
  Communications Building

Frank Lloyd Wright's Price Tower

Katsura Detached Palace garden

Japanese and Americans:
Cultural Parallels and Paradoxes

Let us stop the continents from hurling epigrams at each other, and be sadder if not wiser by the mutual gain of half a hemisphere. We have developed along different lines, but there is no reason why one should not supplement the other.

Okakura Kakuzo, The Book of Tea, 1906

Lo, soul, seest thou not God's purpose from the first?
The earth to be spann'd, connected by network
The races, neighbors, to marry and be given in marriage,
The oceans to be crossed, the distant brought near,
The lands to be welded together.

Walt Whitman, "Passage to India," 1868

There is a thing which is all-containing, which was born before the existence of Heaven and Earth. How silent! How solitary! It stands alone and changes not. It revolves without danger to itself and is the mother of the universe. I do not know its name and so call it the Path. With reluctance I call it the Infinite. Infinity is the Fleeting, the Fleeting is the Vanishing, the Vanishing is the Reverting.

Laotse, about 650 B.C.

"Speaking of contraries, see how the brook
In that white wave runs counter to itself.
It is from that in water we were from
Long, long before we were from any creature.
Here we, in our impatience of the steps,
Get back to the beginning of beginnings,
The stream of everything that runs away.
Some say existence like a Pirouot
And Pirouette, forever in one place,
Stands still and dances, but it runs away;
It seriously, sadly, runs away
To fill the abyss's void with emptiness. . . .
The universal cataract of death
That spends to nothingness—and unresisted,
Save by some strange resistance in itself
Not just a swerving, but a throwing back,
As if regret were in it and were sacred.
It has this throwing backward on itself.
So that the fall of most of it is always
Raising a little, sending up a little.
Our life runs down in sending up the clock.
The brook runs down in sending up our life.
The sun runs down in sending up the brook.
And there is something sending up the sun.
It is this backward motion toward the source,
Against the stream, that most we see ourselves in,
The tribute of the current to the source.
It is from this in nature we are from.
It is most us."

Robert Frost, "West-Running Brook," 1928

A NOTE ON NAMES

Japanese customarily give their names family-name first. I employ this order to the extent possible, but complications arise. Names such as Kenzo Tange and Daisetz T. Suzuki are so well known in the West rendered in the Western manner that it seems foolish to reverse that order. Then, too, some Japanese writing for English-language publications use the Western order. Finally, some authors have traditionally chosen pen names which they use alongside their family names; they are ordinarily known by their pen names. Natsume Kinnosuke, for example, adopted the name Sōseki, by which he is ordinarily known; specialists have rendered his full name either as Sōseki Natsume (the order I have used) or as Natsume Sōseki.

The Problem: Stereotypes (Self-Imposed and Otherwise), "National Character," and Paradox

Cultural myopia has been severe on both sides of the Pacific, and when that disease has been compounded by xenophobia, as has often happened, the results have ranged from ludicrous to deadly. An ensign on Commodore Perry's expedition, encountering a Japanese bath, "turned away with a hearty curse" because of the "lewdness" of coeducational nudity.[1] Japanese who visited the United States soon after Perry "opened" Japan with his "black ships" reported back that Americans were immoral: they had been discovered to kiss in public. In 1868 a Japanese official found it necessary to declare to his countrymen that they should "give up the ignorant opinion that foreigners are wild barbarians, dogs and sheep; we must work out arrangements to show they are to be considered on the same level as Chinese."[2] Twenty-five years or so later, in his classic *The Book of Tea*, Okakura Kakuzo wrote, "When will the West understand, or try to understand, the East?" He is "appalled" at the "fancies" Westerners have harbored concerning Asiatics: "We are pictured as living on the perfume of the lotus, if not on mice and cockroaches. . . . It has been said that we are less sensible to pain and wounds on account of the callousness of our nervous organization!" He is of course aware that Japanese are just as capable of grotesque error concerning Westerners: "Our writers in the past—the wise men who knew—informed us that you had bushy tails somewhere hidden in your gar-

3

ments, and often dined off a fricassée of new-born babes! Nay, we had something worse against you: we used to think you the most impracticable people on the earth, for you were said to preach what you never practised."[3]

Surely we have improved our understanding of one another during the past century or so. Japanese clearly know more about Americans than Americans about Japanese, but some stereotypes, misinformation, and ignorance still exist on both sides. The amount of space devoted to Japan in the American media, except for wartime propaganda, has simply been very slight—until recently, when American businessmen began to feel the pinch of Japanese competition. (Consequently, most of the news is now about business.) Few Americans have surmounted the formidable language barrier, and, while most Japanese start studying English in junior high school, the inoculations seem not often to take. One Japanese scholar suggests that Japanese don't *want* to be well understood, just as they have traditionally used the *sudaré*, a kind of screen which allows those inside to see out (and also catch the breeze) while outsiders can't see in.[4] I have in fact heard Japanese say that some of their fellows become nervous when a foreigner learns their language too well, although this seems a suspicious theory.

Some improvement, but not enough. A survey of students at Sophia University in Tokyo in the mid-1960s revealed that many of them hold an image of American blacks which is of the kind maintained by the ignorant or the bigoted in the United States.[5] A Harris poll of American attitudes toward Japan in March 1971 stunned a number of Japanese. While attitudes were generally friendly, Americans' ignorance about their richest ally and their strongest outside Western Europe was astonishing. Only 14 percent of the Americans questioned could identify Eisaku Sato, prime minister since 1964; the rate of recognition dropped to 5 percent, 2 percent, 2 percent, 1 percent, 1 percent, and 1 percent for Mishima, Mifune, Yoshida, Matsushita, Kurosawa, and Ozawa. Many Americans, if they had any response at all about Japan, thought first of its products. A sizable minority, however, retained the images produced by America's propaganda during World War II: militarism, "sneakiness," untrustworthiness.[6] Some improvement, but not enough. In fact, about one-third of the essays in the Winter 1972 issue of the *Japan Interpreter*—essays from the 1972 Shimoda Conference—are devoted to four Japanese intellectuals who are worried about the *widening* "perception gap" between Japan and the United States.

Perhaps the most dangerous kind of misinformation comes from people taken to be prophets. Herman Kahn, interviewed by *Asahi Evening News* in April 1971 had this to say: "Japan is neither a shame society nor a guilt society. . . . The Japanese no doubt will continue to be conscious of their defeat in the Pacific War and of the danger of fighting a war with misguided judgement. But I wonder if they have ever been aware that the Pacific War was also wrong from the moral and ethical viewpoint."[7] To this sort of pontifical ignorance, I would prefer complaints about the immorality of mixed bathing.

Perhaps Americans are no less ignorant than most Westerners. In 1969 a Japanese student, barely hiding his perturbation, told me this story. An English housewife had noticed the high rate of exports to Japan of dogs. Alarmed, she asked the authorities to cut off exports of dogs to Japan, on the grounds that the Japanese were eating them. Exotic tastes she must have assumed them to have: what was really happening, of course, was that people in Japan with a considerable amount of spare money were falling in with a fad for high-status name-brand breeds of dogs.

The story only points up anxieties that many Japanese feel about the image of themselves in foreigners' minds (a good many Americans, incidentally, have known a similar uneasiness). This is in part a historical habit of mind, but it has become a practical matter, presently, as debates about power in Asia and about trade agreements become more acrimonious. Slightly less urgent is the annoyance many Japanese feel about the Mutual Defense Treaty and current arrangements on Okinawa. Japanese all know about the maltreatment of Japanese-Americans from their earliest days as truck farmers in California to their suffering in the World War II concentration camps. Clearly, the American disposition of the defeated Germans after the war was different from that of the Japanese. The worry in Japan is that Americans' attitudes as they attack issues in dispute nowadays might be clouded by old racist attitudes. As American anxiety about Japanese competition becomes increasingly greater, that worry seems justified. Images of the Japanese that in fact verge on racial stereotypes begin to appear again in the American mass media. A Japanese told the 1972

Shimoda Conference, "If a certain kind of American feels secure about a small, thinly-protected Japan, smeared with humiliation from defeat of war, that same American feels threatened by a proud and self-confident Japan which is making a successful comeback."[8]

Perhaps what is to be feared most *is* fear—in this instance, of revived Japanese militarism. In China and Southeast Asia, this fear is endemic. The well-publicized interview between Chou En-lai and the American journalist James Reston revealed that the former believes Japan "bound to develop militarism."[9] Already, some Americans are beginning to predict Japan's emergence as a nuclear superpower. Almost every piece of evidence that is available, as I will hope to demonstrate, points the other way.

The common Japanese fear of American militarism is of course harder to allay. Particularly difficult to alleviate is the "nuclear allergy" of the Japanese which makes them believe—not necessarily without grounds—that, for example, nuclear submarines in their waters have dumped or leaked radioactive waste, and that American strategic bombers on Japanese bases are armed with nuclear warheads. America's long involvement in wars against their fellow Asians, and the disclosure during them of lingering racism in many of its soldiers, have naturally aggravated Japanese anxieties.

Stereotypes that feed fear of war are the most dangerous, but others may nettle feelings. American businessmen and the working people who depend on them become testy when they are unable to compete with the Japanese, and immediately conclude that the Japanese worker is exploited. The facts are more complicated than that. I have even heard it said that the Japanese have gained the edge by using child labor. In fact, of course, controls are tighter in Japan than in the United States, where the families of migrant workers are allowed to remain pretty much outside the protection of the law. Conversely, some Japanese of leftish persuasions cannot understand the conservative nature of the American labor movement, and suspect a very subtle form of control over the minds of workers in the United States. What Richard Hofstadter has called the "paranoic style" and Charles Beard has called the "devil theory" exists on both sides, and inhibits clear vision. For example, in an article entitled "The United States Is Disintegrating," published in May 1972, a Japanese political scientist, Yonosuke Nagai, writes, "America teeters on the edge of revolution

and violence led by radical leftists and black nationalists. . . . America has lost its capacity for self-restoration and has
fallen into a vicious circle of frustration and distrust."[10] True, bitter
dissension exists in the United States today. True, the debate among
historians who see American history as conflict and those who see it as
consensus is still a hot one. It seems to me premature, however, to say
that the ball game is over. Is it even altogether clear that conflict, even
sometimes bloody, might not be a sign of health rather than disease?
Stagnation, or cultural entropy, could be more dangerous than the
violence which Nagai reports.

One of the central arguments of this essay is, as a matter of fact, that
both cultures are paradoxical, paradoxical enough to dizzy the observer. I have confessed to a prejudice that, up to some point which I
am unable to chart, paradox is healthy. James Kirkup, the English
poet and aficionado of Japanese culture, has said somewhere that in
Japan contradictions live happily together. (As to the happiness,
perhaps he should check that out with some youngster who lives in a
tiny apartment with parents whose beliefs are polar opposites to his
own.) Paradox, the dialectic between opposites, has been a clear
characteristic of American culture for a long time. Lionel Trilling may
have begun, in 1940, the interpretation of the American culture as one
defined by contradictions: "a culture is not a flow," he said, "nor even a
confluence; the form of its existence is struggle, or at least debate—it is
nothing if not a dialectic."[11] That sort of interpretation was carried on
by Richard Chase, then by Leo Marx, who took it beyond the study of
literature, the exclusive realm of his predecessors.

It may be useful to mention one notion about why these clichés seem
to persist, decade after decade. The idea of "national character" itself
seems to me partly to blame for ill-informed stereotypes on both sides
of the Pacific. The kinds of thinking range from honest, earnest, and
necessary intellectual curiosity to idle chatter by tourists. One is struck
in reading correspondence among diplomatists by the recurrence of
clichés about national character. Such stock phrases as "hot-blooded
Latins," "inscrutable Japanese," and "ugly Americans" tend to perpet-
uate themselves in serious discourse as well as trivial.

My first complaint about the national character game is that it leads
to oversimplification. Here we are dealing with thoroughly cosmopolitan cultures which have received ideas, symbols, attitudes, and ar-

tifacts from the world over. It is hard to imagine a Japanese or an American who has not, in some way, been influenced by African sculpture, Indian philosophy, or Latin American music. The national character way of looking at things leads innocent folk into thesis-hunting and, human ingenuity being what it is, thesis-finding. Nature abhors categories; the human mind adores them.

Even at the level of serious study, oversimplifications become hardened into the language. The national character approach creates a temptation to polarize things. For example, the status of women in Japan is said to be such-and-such, *in contrast to* their status in America. By implication, then—if not explicitly—American women are represented as "free." In fact, the situation is very complicated in both countries, depending on educational levels, social class, and finally individual decisions. Or Japan is said to be beset by vestiges of feudalism—as if the United States were not so as well; indeed, it is questionable whether hierarchical social patterns in either country are explainable by that historical term at all. Or the Japanese are said not yet to have learned how to use democratic institutions. Again, the implication is that Americans, or somebody, somewhere, *have* so succeeded—perhaps a rash notion. Americans are often characterized as "crass materialists," Japanese as "economic animals." For one thing, the facts are not that simple; for another, what culture is so thoroughly high-minded as to scorn all worldly possessions? Or the custom among Japanese men of entertaining away from the home is presented in contrast to the American custom of entertaining in the home; this overlooks the neighborhood saloon which is dear particularly to certain ethnic groups in the United States and the lavish nightclub for American businessmen away from home on expense accounts. Emphasis on the ceremonial and indirect character of much Japanese conversation suggests that American conversation is always frank and direct; yet Kanto people are said to be more outspoken than Kansai people; southern Americans are probably more ceremonial than, for example, western Americans.

As Karl Marx pointed out, similarities between practitioners of given trades or professions defy national boundaries. While geography and history have made of Japan and the United States a particularly severe test of this observation, professors of medicine in the two places are surely more alike in many ways than a Japanese professor of medicine is like a fisherman on remote Sado Island. An American need not be surprised to hear that the violent disturbances at Tokyo University of 1968 and 1969 began in its medical school, where students complained of "feudal" social arrangements and methods of instruction. That's the way medicine is taught, mostly, in the United States, too. Japanese and American workers on tough and dangerous jobs carry themselves with the same swagger and bravado.

Akin to the slipperiness of the idea of national character is another which I believe to be common to a number of comparative studies of East and West: deduction from premises which seem far too simple. The great Arthur Koestler's study of Japan is almost synecdochical. From what he considers to be the decline of Zen, he deduces the spiritual decline of Japan. He declares his awareness that Zen constitutes but a small portion of the Japanese experience, even of its spiritual experience; yet he was willing to publish his conclusions.[12]

A *reductio ad absurdum* of simplistic thinking about national character appeared in print in 1968. The cause of the polar opposition of Japanese and Western character begins at birth, we are told. "In the West, the largest amount of emotional reward is lavished upon the newborn child," as opposed to the "smallest degree" in Japan. In the West, this attention continues, the personality internalizes the sense of "gratification and security," and layers of consciousness are formed, "like a stone and mortar structure." "The outcome is that [the individual] is relatively independent . . . self-reliant, innovative . . . and responsive only to rational-legal authority." He is also "happy and optimistic." The Japanese baby, by contrast, suffers "emotional deprivation" and "frustration." (Could the author ever have *seen* a Japanese mother and child?) Therefore, "emotional deprivation, frustration, and insecurity become major constituent elements of the Japanese personality." No internalization occurs; no layers exist in the Japanese personality. Therefore, the Japanese "has difficulty in setting limits on . . . both positive and negative emotions," and he is "highly sensitive to the extent of gratification in the immediate here-and-now situation." He tries to be cheerful and brave, but "suffers from a fundamental depression, which explains his preoccupation with suicide." Life is not entirely grim for the Japanese, we are reminded: there *are* those voluptuous baths.[13]

In 1952, the *Yale Review* published just as soberly an equally tidy prescription from another authority. "How did it happen that the Japanese changed so radically between, say, 1600 and 1900 A.D.? History offers a dramatic answer. The Japanese of modern times are products of a dictatorship that foreshadowed the totalitarian police states of the twentieth century. Prewar militaristic Japan emerged naturally and without break from this background of three centuries' preparation." He goes on, "If this sketch justifies any conclusion, it is that, in the formation of national character, police coercion shapes and outweighs infant training."[14] Very tidy; very neat. The author refers with decent respect to Ruth Benedict's classic *The Chrysanthemum and the Sword* but prefers to avoid the difficulty of the pure paradox implied in her title: "in the formation of national character, police coercion shapes and outweighs infant training." Anthropologists have subsequently found cause to quarrel with Professor Benedict's 1946 publication, but they don't quarrel with her refusal to resort to a unitary theory in explaining a complex culture.

Japanese scholars can also find relief in simplicity. We read Ajita Ogiwara: "In America, the people believe in a unifying God; while in Japan, the people are submerged by a need for public order."[15] This is the sort of generalization which seems to tell us something, but at the same time leads us to ask "Which American? Which Japanese?" or even "Which American at what moment? Which Japanese under what circumstance?"

F. S. C. Northrop's monumental *The Meeting of East and West* is perhaps the model of comparison which we must take most seriously. Nakamura Hajime, in his various works on Japanese thought, often refers to the book. Briefly (and the short quotations are unjust to him), Northrop contrasts the two cultures as follows. The Anglo-American civilization is chiefly characterized by individualism, grounded in Protestant theology, in the political theory of Descartes, Locke, and others, and in the economic theory of Adam Smith and his followers. "The Protestant factor tended to make the individual the sole cause of any unfortunate economic or social circumstances in which he found himself. Locke's political philosophy made the preservation of private property the sole justification for the existence of government." Three hundred years, says Northrop, have given this conception of the human being as a fundamentally separate and discrete entity a "tremendous hold" on the Western mind. And of the Oriental civilization, he concludes that the idea of the good requires one to "grasp the immediately apprehended factors in the immediately experienced, aesthetic continuum." "This is precisely what the Oriental means when he asserts that if man gives expression only to the differentiated, specifically sensed, determinate portion of himself and of things then he is caught in the remorseless wheel of fate." Only by recognizing "the indeterminate, all-embracing field component of his nature" can man attain freedom and achieve equanimity before the transitory nature of things. Thus, the Oriental is suspicious of determinate, specific moral codes "which must hold under all circumstances," for determinate things in the world are transitory.[16]

Northrop's purpose is to present the cultures in more or less pure and abstracted form, to find essences in order to facilitate the meeting of East and West. In doing so he necessarily understates admixtures in the cultures. Japan, of course, is different from India and China. To begin with, there is little time to "grasp the immediately apprehended factors in the immediately experienced, aesthetic continuum" as one mans the assembly line at Sony. The practical workaday merchant has been important in Japan since early in the Edo period—for over three hundred years. Conversely, the pure model overlooks, for example, the power and persistence of transcendentalism, from Emerson and Thoreau through Frank Lloyd Wright and Robert Frost into what was recently known as "the youth culture"—a culture, incidentally, shared by many Americans and many Japanese. Perhaps influenced by the bustling China trade which filled New England with things Oriental even in the late seventeenth century, all transcendentalism is informed by this central image in Emerson's *Nature*: "In the woods, we return to reason and faith. There I feel that nothing can befall me in life—no disgrace, no calamity (leaving me my eyes), which nature cannot repair. Standing on the bare ground—my head bathed by the blithe air and uplifted into infinite space—all mean egotism vanishes. I become a transparent eyeball; I am nothing; I see all; the currents of the Universal Being circulate through me; I am part or parcel of God."

This brings me back to an earlier point: both cultures are extraordinarily complex. Both are cosmopolitan and both are in the process of constant, dizzying, drastic change. Alvin Toffler, whose *Future Shock* recounts the bewildering tempo of change in the United States, recently reported that he found Japan similar. Probably he was not surprised; his book mentions that doctors who are currently doing work on the effects of change on physical health began their work simultaneously in Japan and the United States.

One further remark about the pursuit after definitions of national character. Among two such intensely self-conscious peoples as the Japanese and the Americans, this process may lead to self-stereotypes that are as warped as those held by outsiders. For example, to consider some easy ones first, Americans very often say of themselves, "We Americans always favor the underdogs," while any casual search of tax laws, or of the history of subsidies to big business or of American treatment of the poor, would indicate that they are uncommonly generous to their most affluent fellow citizens and heedless of those most in want. Japanese are wont to say of themselves that they are inept in the practice of logical thought, though any observer of their skills in the rationalization of industry, in mathematics, or, in the past, in regimentation of the military—those skills which historically have made the greatest demands on rational thought—might well squint in disbelief. One hears constant iterations by Japanese of the fact that they are uncommonly fond of nature, and everybody agrees; yet their ardent love affair with GNP is causing nature to sicken unto death. Anciently fashionable among American intellectuals, and still somewhat so, is the assertion "America has no culture." Sometimes this takes more specific forms: "no art" or "no literature" or "no music" or "no taste." What is rather the case is that many educated Americans learn little of their own culture, preferring instead to honor the stereotype and their European cousins. Many Japanese accept the Western cliché that they themselves are craven imitators; if they are so indeed, why do so many Americans there, struggling to remove their shoes in the newest office building, or sweating through the ceremony of a business discussion, find the going during their first weeks in Japan so gorsy? The Japanese say of themselves that they have no "social morality," to the puzzlement of the visitor who is astonished to find that he can walk the streets of the cities in perfect safety, even at night. (What the Japanese seem really to mean is that the campaign against littering, intensified before the Tokyo Olympics, is not yet totally won.)

And so on. It is no surprise that people immersed in a culture may lack perspective of it. Self-stereotypes only compound the difficult problems of dealing with two cultures that are convoluted and paradoxical. As might be expected, the outsider's myopia may be aggravated rather than corrected by the lenses offered by the insider. For example, Keyes Beech, a journalist with a wide international reputation and audience, recently interviewed Chie Nakane, the anthropologist whose *Japanese Society* has had wide circulation. His report on the interview concluded, "There is no individualism in Japan." France's slick *Réalités* has also based a story on Professor Nakane's monolithic thesis. Meanwhile, Kazuko Tsurumi's *Social Change and the Individual,* which indicates, as the title suggests, that matters are more complex, goes largely unread, at least in America.[17]

In emphasizing the groupiness of Japanese people, as Professor Nakane has done, and as coiners of catch phrases such as "Japan, Incorporated" have done, some part of a truth is probably uttered, comparatively speaking. The problem is not merely oversimplification, however: one senses some covert criticism. American businessmen imply that cooperation constitutes unfair competition. Perhaps a further American illusion. The plea for autonomous individuality, from the days of Emerson and Thoreau through to David Riesman, assumes not only that such individualism is possible but that it's desirable. In truth, the whole habit which opposes the separate self to the social order may be misleading, as the philosopher Oshio Heihachiro, in the eighteenth century, and the psychologist Harry Stack Sullivan, in the twentieth, have insisted.[18] Has anyone ever been distinct and free, in any large sense, of his family or his peers or his government? Are our decisions to behave in this or that manner ever rid of these presences, real or imaginary? It would appear that the whole debate about individuality and socialization can be dealt with sensibly only in very relative terms.

One may wonder how these old habits of polarizing national traits have influenced people, especially cantankerous people who resist being categorized. Weary of continually hearing the charge that they are of an intuitive and instinctual stock, how many Japanese out of idealism or even out of sheer contentiousness have tried to forbid themselves the pleasures of responding to emotion or instinct? Hearing the charge that they are of a conformist culture, how many

Americans out of the same motives have forbidden themselves the comfort of community? How many Americans, believing that Americans are properly for the underdog, have deprived themselves of the pleasure of admiring the old New York Yankees or the young Jack Nicklaus? How many Japanese, hearing that their culture is still blighted by feudalism, have refused themselves the luxury of parental guidelines? This national character game gets sticky.

I have already touched on the trouble which paradox, or dialectic, or counterpoint causes those who wish to study national character. A word more, though, about the sort of paradox which seems to me to enrich the cultures, to charge them with the energy of the dialectic.

Paradox is at the heart of Tao and Zen—and, in fact, of Christianity. Paradox became a central strategy of haiku. The blessed Bashō wrote:

> The snowy lotus-blossom: it does not spurn
> Birth from the mud to which its seeds return.[19]

And that old tradition is as fresh as the metabolist school of architects, led by the great Kenzo Tange: the permanent base of their buildings is constructed of reinforced concrete, like Bashō's mud, while those parts which they assume will be rendered obsolete by technology or other change are often fanciful flowers made of impermanent metals. In fact, ancient Japanese culture—like that of most civilizations—was a blend of two cultures, the earliest Jōmon, a hunting and fishing culture, and Yayoi, an agricultural. Tange believes that the former, fascinated by "the dark pool of nature's secrets," gave Japanese culture its vitality, while the latter, characterized by "stability and fulfillment," gave it its esthetic quality.[20] Finally, of course, is the paradox of the traditional and the modern coexisting with surprisingly little discord.

At the marrow of the American imagination lie Melville's *Moby Dick* and Whitman's *Song of Myself*, both organized around contraries, various dialectics. (It has been said that Locke, the Englishman, is "the American philosopher," but perhaps Hegel, the German, should have that title; notice also the dialectic that informs the greatest American composer, Charles Ives, the greatest American architect, Frank Lloyd Wright, and perhaps the greatest American engineer, the builder of Brooklyn Bridge, Hegel's student, John Augustus Roebling.) The list of polarities that complicate the American culture is a long one. On the one hand, Lord Bryce noticed its legalistic quality: whenever three Americans gather, he said, they adopt Robert's Rules of Order and draw up some bylaws. On the other hand is the antinomian stream, individualistic and rebellious. "That government governs best which governs not at all," said Thoreau. The essential American, said Henry Adams, is a "conservative Christian anarchist," and history bears him out in large measure. The United States honors two sacred writs, the Declaration of Independence and the Constitution; the former is revolutionary, the latter conservative.

Foreign visitors have been puzzled by the mix of individuality and conformity in Americans, and of moral and religious idealism on one hand and pragmatism on the other. D. H. Lawrence saw the hard-working, materialistic, rational, "snuff-colored" Benjamin Franklin as one archetypal American, and Edgar Allan Poe, brooding on death and the mysteries of the subconscious, as another. Black writers from Frederick Douglass through W. E. B. DuBois to our contemporaries have been especially sensitive to ironies in America, and irony is the central strategy of their writing. "Do I contradict myself?" asked Whitman. "Very well then, I contradict myself, (I am large, I contain multitudes)."

Up to this point, I have attempted to locate the snarls and quagmires awaiting someone attempting the job I am setting out to do. I assume, however, that it's not hopeless.

David Potter has examined the whole history of talk about national character, and has shown how it has been beset by religious notions of national "destinies" and "God's chosen peoples," by ill-considered environmentalism, and by racist genetics. Yet national character clearly exists—paradox can be a part of it. The cultures function. Somehow the Japanese power elite and the disaffected radical young accommodate to one another, as do the American establishment and oppressed ethnic minorities. Violence occurs in both cultures, but both survive. Nor is it altogether clear that the violence hasn't in some cases done some good. The fact of survival may indeed suggest accommodation, for the advanced technology of Japan and the United States renders their densely packed urban citizenries extremely vulnerable. The great majority of both peoples behave in ways that their societies require. Thus Potter's cultural and evolutionary definition of national character seems both plausible and usable: "unique circumstances, conditions and experience are apt to produce unique traits and attitudes among the people as a whole." And "the majority of a national population may collectively tend to acquire certain adaptive traits."[21]

One further comment is important. The topics to be studied in these chapters do not especially lend themselves to a consideration of the problem in each culture which seems most stubbornly to elude solution: space in Japan and racism in the United States. The severe shortage of living room certainly has contributed to Japan's militarism of the 1930s and 1940s, to the severity of its pollution problem in more recent years, and, one would suppose, to all manner of personal and domestic difficulties in families who must share tiny dwellings. Americans find it difficult to believe that half the number of people they share their sprawling land with must, in Japan, live together in an area about the size of West Virginia, if one excludes the mountainous regions which are unsuitable to support life. Similarly, the blight of Americans' attitudes toward people with duskier skin colors has contributed to their commission of domestic and international atrocities, as well as, patently, to personal suffering among many, many individuals. Oversimplification here is all too possible: aside from and beyond color, religion has also been the cause of oppression of Roman Catholics and Jews, and national origin, also, among Germans before and after World War I, for example.

Almost every generalization that occurs here immediately suggests a "but." Crowded Japanese have made marvelous adjustments to their situation, observable in birth control, manners, morals, language, and, as I will propose later, perhaps even art. Americans have in fact accommodated themselves in one way or another to an astonishing diversity of skin colors, religions, and nationalities in a very short time. The original Americans—"Indians," the people I will hereafter call "native Americans"—would hold that their courtesy to European intruders has been, for the most part, uncommonly generous. Mostly, Yankee Americans have pressed "Anglo-conformity" on those who differ from themselves, but self-conscious attempts to assert their unique group identity by blacks, Jews, native Americans, and many others have gained gradually more tolerance. These counterstatements do not have the weight of the statements. I will not confront the issues of space and racism directly, but they hover behind almost everything else in the two cultures.

So equipped, I will proceed to dig at a few comparable spots in the two cultures, and see what might be uncovered.

CHAPTER 2

The Wilderness Zion
and the Land of the Gods

That culture should in part obey the political boundaries of the nation-state testifies to the potency of the sentiment of nationalism among many peoples. I wish here to focus on three faces of nationalism, the cultural, the economic, and the political at those times when the political has taken on heavy military overtones. The modern world has generally defined greatness in a nation-state in terms of the success of this military-political union. Japan wasn't *defined* as a great nation in the Western eye until it defeated Russia in 1905. Whoever it was who said that the high voltage of the nationalist sentiment is attributable to the emotional vacuum left by the decline of religion, however, mistook the examples of Japan and the United States. When those nations have been at their sword-rattling worst, religion was used to reinforce the political and military. It is presently Japan's unique contribution to conceive of national greatness unsupported by the crutch of the military. The United States, as we shall see, set out on such a path, but changed its mind at about the same time it also achieved large economic importance.

Both peoples have made cultural and economic contributions which ought to serve as sources of collective pride and cohesiveness. It has been political-military nationalism, however, which has caused Japanese and Americans to breathe hard and commit heroics. The times when a person is likely to say, "I am an American first," or "I am a

Japanese first"—rather than "I am Jones," or "Watanabe," or a Mitsubishi or GM man, or an ikebana master or a jazz buff—would seem to be times when political-military nationalism has burned hottest. This attitude (which hereafter I will simply call "jingoism") has greatly influenced the fact that culture in part follows political boundaries, so it is to this attitude that I will pay most attention, later in the chapter. Since jingoism came rather late in both national histories, however, it seems best to first provide the context for its occurrence.

The initial point to be made is that nationalism in a modern political sense was forced on the Japanese, who recognized the threat to their security posed by Western technology and military might. History destined the United States to be the crucial agent in "opening" Japan. The China trade and the international politics that were related to it were important in this, but so was American "westerliness," the sense that the destiny of the nation-state was to expand always west. At any rate Commodore Perry's "black ships" were awesome; they could even defy the spirit of the wind. Japanese immediately set about seeing which model for the nation-state could be adapted, to achieve as quickly as possible equal power; in the 1890s they finally settled upon the Prussian and shaped it to center around the imperial family. The American brand of nationalism evolved from the Revolution, through the ratification of the Constitution, which in a somewhat bizarre manner recognized the sovereignty of *both* the nation and the several states. Common national ownership of the unsettled western territories helped weld the states together, and the Civil War effectively ended state sovereignty in most matters.

The next point is that both Japanese and Americans seem extraordinarily self-conscious, touchy about foreigners' reactions to their countries. It is rare in England or France, for example, to be asked, anxiously, "How do you like us?" Liking them is taken either as a matter of course or as a matter of indifference. That question is very likely to be asked a foreign visitor to Japan or the United States, soon after the first conversation begins. This patricentricity has, in both cultures, an unusual history. Both peoples have oscillated between, or held concurrently, a sense of their inferiority among the peoples of the earth and a sense of their own superiority—in fact, unique divinity: Japan, "the land of the gods"; Americans, "God's chosen people." This divinity can be extended to imply a divinely appointed mission in order to support jingoism. Such doubleness of vision requires further looking into.

Divinity also implies divine origins. The Japanese tale is traditional, codified—and embellished—by historians in the eighth century in two works called *Nihon shoki* and the *Kojiki*. The grandson of Amaterasu, the sun goddess, descended to earth to make Japan, and his great-grandson became the first emperor, Jimmu, presumably in 660 B.C. The present emperor, according to this legend, is a direct descendant of Jimmu and therefore of Amaterasu herself. Later, intensely nationalistic writers of the period roughly from 1750 to 1850 insisted stridently upon the cultural superiority of the Japanese to the Chinese. Work from both these periods, then, could be adapted to their own uses by the jingoists before and during World War II.

Puritan parsons, early in the colonial period, began to build the American myth of creation. God separated the good wheat from the chaff of Europe, and appointed the good the task of building a "Wilderness Zion," a "City on the Hill," in America. These religious ideas were useful later in spiritualizing the secular Revolution. "We have incontestable evidence," said one preacher-patriot, "that God Almighty, with all the powers of heaven, are on our side."[1] The myth evolved into something like the following, accepted at least in some metaphorical sense: God, disgusted with the fall of man as described in Genesis and perpetuated in the history of European depravity, decided to give mankind a second chance. His chosen ones were transported to the virgin land of America, the new Eden, where the American Adam would sire in innocence a new people. The Founding Fathers, Washington preeminently, privy to divine wisdom, courage, and virtue, first freed Americans from the Wicked King, then set in motion the "Great Experiment," the government which all the world was longing for. The American was destined, duty-bound, to spread this gospel to the world.

The first historic similarity is clear: the mythological past has in both nations been used to legitimize aggression. The second is that the mythologies ricochet off older cultures, cultures which the myth makers surely suspected to be just possibly superior to their own. The myths, in a sense, protest too much. What seems to support this contention is that, while both cultures have puffed their past, neither consistently or thoroughgoingly believed the boast. America's reservations are compartmental, Japan's cyclical.

Very roughly, the Japanese cycles go like this. The Japanese "discovered" Chinese culture in the fifth and sixth Christian centuries. The court intelligentsia made pilgrimages to China, of long duration, and brought back its religion, art, and learning for the enlightenment of their fellows. In the seventh century, self-confidence reasserted itself, and Chinese culture was assimilated into Japanese. Later, there was the flirtation of a number of Japanese with the culture of Dutch traders and Portuguese missionaries, which was almost completely ended in the sixteenth century. News that the barbarians had overrun China reached Japanese leaders even before Commodore Perry opened Japan in 1854. Since then, says Professor Kato Shuichi, there have been three periods when Japan has been "very receptive to Western ideas," each following a major social upheaval: the Meiji Restoration, World War I, and World War II. The period of receptivity in each instance lasted for ten or fifteen years, followed by a period of national introversion.[2]

Court scholars' awe of Chinese culture in the sixth century had been general, ranging over all the ornaments of a high culture. The post-Restoration receptivity to Western ideas was more specifically targeted. The promising scholars who were sent abroad to study went to England for naval training, to Germany for medicine and military training, to France for law, and to the United States for business. Cycles notwithstanding, Japanese leaders urged "Western techniques, Japanese spirit." In other words, while the West was recognized as superior in particular fields of study, Japanese confidence in the essence of its own culture was on the whole maintained.

Not entirely. During the receptive phases of the cycle, some Japanese slavishly copied Western modes—though they were laughed at by more levelheaded fellows. Japanese who were abroad during this period were surprised to learn that Westerners were capable of esthetic sensibilities. Some even imitated their forms, without immediate success. The cultural exchange had another side to it as well. Elitists among the Japanese had maintained a contempt for ukiyoe, woodblock prints, until an American, Ernest Fenellosa, persuaded them otherwise. (They had, of course, preferred Chinese art; at about the

same moment in history, most Americans preferred English books.)
Here all the clichés are short-circuited. The partially educated American, even today, pestered by a sense of esthetic inferiority, almost automatically assumes Japanese superiority in art. That Japanese could feel themselves wanting *even* in the quality of their own art comes as a surprise. When Fenellosa left Japan in 1886, after a long and distinguished career which included teaching at Tokyo Imperial University, the emperor told him, "You have taught my people to know their art."[3] Donald Keene tells the story of the gruff and salty General Grant, lavishly entertained by the Japanese, as befit a former president, admonishing his hosts at a Noh play never to let the form die out.

Professor Kato's cyclical model would indicate that the Japanese are presently enjoying a period of reviving confidence in their Japanese-ness. Many signs indicate that they are. Those signs are not without their ambivalences, however, which we will look at later.

The American sense of inferiority, I repeat, is compartmental, limited pretty much to a sense of deficiency in the realm of the esthetic. History doesn't show any massive American doubt about the rightness of its social and political behavior, except on the issue of slavery. (Most Americans, polls indicate, think that going into Vietnam was an error, but the kind of mass breastbeating which would occur from a sense of national guilt is not apparent.) Americans have prided themselves also on their technological skills, though boasts about "Yankee know-how" are not presently heard in Detroit in the wake of Mazda's and Honda's breakthroughs with pollution-free engines. Americans, however, have always been vexed by the suspicion that Europeans have more refinement in creating and appreciating the arts, and in general more style, more social grace, more "class."

They have been told so often enough. European intellectuals have been fascinated with America, first as a wilderness which seemed to be a laboratory for theories by the Lockes and the Rousseaus about the "state of nature," then as an experiment in democracy, then as an example of mass culture. A whole procession of them have visited the New World, and reported back. Some, such as J. Hector St. John de Crèvecoeur, have been among its biggest boosters; his *Letters from an American Farmer* circulated widely in Western Europe at the time of the American Revolution. More often, however, the reports were like those of Mrs. Trollope, Charles Dickens, and Matthew Arnold, and advertised the vulgar, the noisy, the pushy, and the sleazy in America. In 1820 an English clergyman named Sydney Smith wrote that the Americans "have done absolutely nothing for the Sciences, for the Arts, for Literature, or even for the statesman-like studies of Politics. . . . In the four quarters of the globe, who reads an American book?" That question, passed down through time, may almost equal in sting General MacArthur's remark that Japanese behave like twelve-year-olds.

Reactions of Americans to these charges ranged from anger to agreement. Among those who agreed were the expatriate artists, the Grand Tourists, and the imitators. Benjamin West left Philadelphia before the Revolution and soon became the teacher in London of a good many of the young republic's aspiring painters. Hawthorne, Henry James, Whistler, Gertrude Stein, Eliot, Pound, all found America incongenial to their art, and Europe is still populated with American artists of that persuasion. (Lafcadio Hearn and Gary Snyder chose Japan.) Early in the nineteenth century, people with the means to do so began the fashion of the Grand Tour of Europe, where they were expected to "get culture," and young men of means traditionally spent a *Wanderjahr* in Europe following graduation from college. The stream of American tourists in Europe has, until the recent economic pinch, grown larger every year. Longfellow assumed that American literature should be no different from the English. That form of art at its best, we shall see, escaped mere copying, but painting, sculpture, architecture, and music remained derivative until the late nineteenth century. Of architecture, more will be said later.

The strategy of counterattack by those who were angered was generally to absorb the insult, then put a good face on it. Revolutionists adopted with glee the English term *Yankee,* with its connotations of simple rusticity. The first comedy written by an American for Americans was Royall Tyler's *The Contrast,* in which the unsophisticated, honest, and manly American protagonist is contrasted favorably with a foppish, clever, and dishonorable fellow American who had been corrupted by English manners. This theme, "the contrast," has permeated folk and popular arts ever since, and was transformed into serious literature by Herman Melville, Mark Twain, and Henry James: we might be crude and simple, so it goes, but we are free of the sinister and feudalistic machinations of those arty Europeans. A second phase of "the contrast" pits the simpler western American against the wiles of the eastern American. In both phases, this attitude has been a potent force in domestic and international politics, coloring heavily, for example, Woodrow Wilson's negotiations at Versailles. Mark Twain's *The Innocents Abroad* represents a twist to this strategy: his shrewd and practical protagonist takes the Grand Tour, and instead of the glories the guidebooks describe, he finds decay, corruption, and squalor.

This sense of inferiority in this particular realm of behavior has subsided somewhat in time. The study of American literature in the universities, for example, once about as fashionable as the scholarly treatment of Japanese fiction in the Heian court, is now almost respectable. Europe has put its stamp of approval on a good many American artists, the final test. Now, in answer to Smith, one might say that *everybody* reads American books. Yet, in spite of it all, the suspicion lingers and is very often voiced: here we fail.

So much for lapses among Japanese and Americans in faith in their national cultures. It is time to look at the opposite face, bombastic and arrogant pride. Of what does it consist?

Certainly it includes the sense of mission that has already been alluded to: from the very beginning, a belief that Americans were handpicked by Providence to create, first a religious sanctuary, then a political model, for the world. Further, their duty was to spread the gospel. We must distinguish among definitions of this mission, and, more importantly, the tone of their statement. Such early founders of the republic as Washington and Jefferson believed so strongly in their experiment that they advised the young nation to stay aloof from European political "entanglements," in order to perfect a system which other peoples would find almost irresistible, once they saw it at work. This tradition, which has continued by way of the gentle mid-nineteenth-century poet Walt Whitman down to the present, depends upon the idea that the Founding Fathers had hit upon a scheme that is so perfect and so inevitable in its conception that all the other peoples of the world would sooner or later adopt it. Such revolutionary heroes as Kossuth, Bolivar, and Mazzini have been looked upon as proof of this conceit. A few latter-day votaries of this notion of the American mission like to point out the way in which

Nkrumah and Kenyatta have quoted passages from American revolutionary documents. This peaceful sense of a divine mission to make the world democratic through good example was not to prevail, of course, though vestiges of it remain in Kennedy's Peace Corps and perhaps in part in certain economic and technical-aid programs, and in the ill-fated McGovern campaign of 1972.

Before looking at the aggressive definition of mission, a digression. Perhaps it is of interest that the warrior-hero seems to be more anciently rooted in the Western imagination than in the Japanese. The first epic we know of in the Western tradition is *The Iliad* of Homer, from the eighth century before Christ, a celebration (not without qualification) of a great warrior. Homer's Odysseus preferred craft to the spear, but fought mightily when he did fight. So on through ancient history: Rome had its Aeneas (another somewhat reluctant warrior), the Anglo-Saxons their Beowulf, the French their Roland, the English their Galahad. Perhaps Japan's island security allowed her the luxury of gentler heroes, early in her history, men such as the deeply religious scholar-leader Prince Shotoku and the radiant lover Prince Genji. With the establishment of feudalism about the twelfth century, however, the knight on horseback became a hero, and during the bloody civil wars of the fifteenth and sixteenth centuries, he became firmly established in the popular imagination, where he still lives vigorously.

The West has also anciently celebrated peaceable heroes: Moses, the lawgiver, Jesus, the man of love and forgiveness, the gentle St. Francis. Except for the cowboy, whose role in the popular imagination is similar to that of the samurai, and the gangster, whose counterpart is the yakuza, killer-heroes do not have much place in the American imagination. Certainly *political* killer-heroes do not. In this respect, Americans differ from their European antecedents. Practically speaking, of course, Americans followed the Europeans in equating military success with national greatness.

The American government, of course, was based upon successful military revolution, and its first president—"The Father of his Country"—was the commander in chief during that conflict. Military heroes of all of America's wars except World War I (General Leonard Wood narrowly missed nomination in 1920) became presidents of the United States: General Andrew Jackson, General William Henry

Harrison, General Zachary Taylor, General Ulysses S. Grant, General Rutherford B. Hayes, Colonel Theodore Roosevelt, and General Dwight D. Eisenhower are among the war heroes who became presidents—eleven, in all, of thirty-eight presidents, not counting a few others who were nearly elected. All the presidents except one from the end of Lincoln's administration until the beginning of the twentieth century had been officers in America's Civil War.

The militaristic streak in the American culture manifests itself today in many ways. The lawns of what must be thousands of county courthouse squares are decorated with some artillery piece from some war. Many also boast a piece of sculpture depicting a soldier. Veterans organizations are among the most powerful lobbies in Washington. Many television channels sign off at night with images of the American flag and military jets while the national anthem plays on the soundtrack. The American flag as symbol still contains enough military overtones for many people so that a standard protest against peace marchers is to wave the flag at them.

But notice this: just as the samurai, whose image informed the role of some of the jingoists during World War II, were in fact often scholars and skilled bureaucrats as well as warriors, and just as Bushido, the ancient and honorable "way of the warrior," originally had deep moral and religious implications, so most American military heroes had other dimensions and embodied moral beliefs that were not merely military. One popular image of Washington was that he was a farmer among a nation of farming people who, like Cincinnatus, left his plow to fight the tyrant British, then further sacrificed his own pleasures in order to launch the republican experiment, before returning happily to his farm, his duty done. Jackson was seen as the man of the people, the antiaristocratic frontiersman who appeared out of the forest with his backwoods hunters to beat the vaunted British at New Orleans. Harrison was popularized, with some violence to the truth, as another product of the log cabin who rose to lead his people in battle. Grant corresponded to an image dear to the popular imagination, the social misfit, the "loser," until plain duty raised him to fulfill his potential. The smiling Eisenhower was hardly warrior: rather, he was the affable, homespun organizer of the military bureaucracy. Military men like Patton and MacArthur, whose mien comported more closely with the stereotype of the warrior, have never had so wide a public following as those soldiers who could be more clearly associated with the democratic virtues.

The peaceable face of the American culture has been evident in its late and reluctant entry into the two world wars; the bellicose face has most often shown itself against a darker-skinned enemy—Indians, Mexicans, Spaniards, Asians. Japan's many centuries of peace, and its pacifism today, tell one story; the Pacific war told another. History isn't kind to any great power. The two faces of these two great powers, however, may be unusual. We may as well look, now, at the ugliest expression on each, where we will discover a grotesque mirror image.

The first great expansion of the infant United States came peacefully, with Thomas Jefferson's amazingly cheap purchase of the immense Louisiana Territory. The War Hawks of 1812 were the forerunners of the influential muscular expansionists. Their cries were echoed more insistently and more successfully during the mid-1840s and in the closing years of the century. It was the "manifest destiny" of the United States, said the editor John L. O'Sullivan, to reach to the Pacific, "the manifest design of Providence." His phrase gave a name and a rationale not only for the land the United States took from Indians and Mexicans, but for demands that it take Cuba, Canada, perhaps all of North America. Not only was expansion of the "Anglo-Saxon" "inevitable," as the argument went, but he had a duty to fulfill, a duty to spread free and democratic institutions.[4]

The thrust beyond the continent during the late 1890s retained the racist and Christian arguments—missionaries preceded soldiers into Asia—and added arguments from the pseudoscientific social Darwinism. A Christian minister, Josiah Strong, paved the way in 1885. The world had been "lifted up," he wrote, by "spiritual Christianity" and "civil liberty."

The Anglo-Saxon, as the great representative of these two ideas . . . is divinely commissioned to be . . . his brother's keeper. . . . Does it not look as if God were not only preparing in our Anglo-Saxon civilization the die with which to stamp the peoples of the earth, but as if he were also massing behind that die the mighty power with which to press it?[5]

The unoccupied areas of the world are filling up; soon the pressure of population, said Strong, will force Anglo-Saxons to fight for subsistence:

Then will the world enter upon a new stage of its history—*the final competition of races for which the Anglo-Saxon is being schooled.* If I do not read amiss, this powerful race will move down upon Mexico, down upon Central and South America, out upon the islands of the sea, over upon Africa and beyond. And can anyone doubt that the result of this competition of races will be the "survival of the fittest"?[6]

The rationale was there, for Presidents McKinley and Theodore Roosevelt, when they needed it. Perhaps it was sweetened further by a Harvard professor of philosophy, John T. Fiske. "The language of Shakespeare will ultimately become the language of mankind," he wrote. And the beauty of it is that American expansion will occur as a part of the world's inevitable evolution toward peace: "Thus we may foresee . . . how, by the gradual concentration of power into the hands of the most pacific communities, we may finally succeed in rendering warfare illegal all over the globe."[7] In the name of peace, then, American soldiers massacred Filipino revolutionaries in 1899 as they have massacred Indochinese since. Notice that what once was an *American* mission became a mission for white Anglo-Saxon Protestant Americans.

The United States, except for the stalemate with the British in 1815 and with the Koreans and Vietnamese more recently, has "won" all its wars (and ordinary school textbooks claim victory in 1815, as well). Japan had, too, until 1945. All Japanese school children know of the miraculous repulsion of the invading Mongol armies of the Kublai Khan in 1274 and 1281—in the latter case, victory was aided by *kamikaze,* the "divine winds." Actually, those were the only wars with external powers in all of recorded history until Japan defeated China in 1894–1895, then won its membership in the fraternity of great powers through its surprising victory over Russia in 1905. That feat so impressed President Theodore Roosevelt, former colonel of the Rough Riders in the Spanish-American War and energetic advocate of "the strenuous life," that he persuaded the other Western powers to reverse a policy which had hitherto treated Japan as an inferior at the treaty-making tables. So the paths of two comparative newcomers to the game of imperialism crossed.

Military success added to the prestige of the military clique in Japan, but not until twenty-five years later, with Japan beset by depression and overcrowding, could they crowd out liberal factions in government. People in such times could easily be seduced by the idea of expansion into lands that were as ill-governed as the Mexican territories that the United States took a century earlier—after all, it is the duty of more vigorous powers to bring order to lawless places, or so went the argument in both instances. The "incidents" in Manchuria escalated much as America's Indochina wars did later, and the Japanese public slowly and relentlessly found itself committed to an ever broader and ever more disastrous war.

They were not unprepared, mentally, for military adventure. Much teaching in the public schools had already been militaristic in its bent, and an Imperial Rescript on Education in 1890 was such that it could later be used by the war party to link the fate of the citizen to that of the emperor, and both to divine will. By the mid-thirties, after a series of political coups that included assassination, the military factions had removed liberal influences from effective power. In 1937, the year of the Peking "incident," the Japanese Ministry of Education published *Kokutai no Hongi* (Fundamentals of Our National Polity), a manual for teachers. This document brewed together a mixture of precepts from, among other sources, State Shintoism, Confucianism, and Bushido, now corrupted by its context. Designed for the moral training of the young, it concludes with this charge: "Our present mission as a people is to build up a new Japanese culture by adopting and sublimating Western cultures with our national entity as the basis, and to contribute spontaneously to the advancement of world culture." The "great . . . historical significance" of the mission is that, just as Japanese evolved "original creations" from Indian and Chinese influences, so the "sublimation of Occidental ideologies and cultures," in the process of "clarification of the national entity," would help to give "full play more than ever to our way which is of the Japanese people." Reminding us of Northrop's formulations, the document warns that without such a sublimation, the clarification is "apt to fall into abstractions isolated from actualities"—cultural actualities, one presumes. Japan's contribution to the world has been and will be to remain "independent" while at the same time being "comprehensive."[8]

I find it difficult to quarrel much with this idea of what Japan has contributed and can contribute to the culture of the world. However, jingoism follows: "The people must more than ever create and develop a new Japan by virtue of their immutable national entity which is the basis of the State and by virtue of the Way of the Empire which stands firm throughout the ages at Home and abroad, and thereby more than ever guard and maintain the prosperity of the Imperial Throne which is coeval with heaven and earth. This, indeed, is our mission."[9] In fairness, another part of the rationale of the military party seems more sensible. Who in Asia *but* the Japanese were strong enough to rid Asia of the "white peril"—European and American imperialists? How else could Asians reap the benefit of their own labor? Would the Westerners be likely to leave Asia to the Asians voluntarily? Subsequent events indicate otherwise. Reason, however, did not play the major role with the militarists.

The providential nature of the American "mission" was advertised to a nation already overwhelmingly Christian. Perhaps to buttress the sense of divinity behind the Japanese idea of mission, *Kokutai no Hongi* taught the legendary ancestry of the imperial family as though it were fact. Other faces of Japanese expansionism, however, resemble America's more exactly. A paragraph on "The Martial Spirit" says it "is not for the sake of itself but for the sake of peace. . . . Our martial spirit does not have for its objective the killing of men, but the giving of life to men."[10] A sign at Marco Polo Bridge, site of the Peking incident, read "Birthplace of Peace in East Asia." Something of the Young America spirit of the O'Sullivans and even of the social Darwinists who saw the United States as the proper heir of a fatigued Britain is apparent in the following excerpt from an interview of 1939 with Matsuoka Yosuke, soon to be foreign minister:

China and Japan are two brothers who have inherited a great mansion called East Asia. Adversity sent them both down to the depth of poverty. The scapegrace elder brother (China) became a dope fiend and a rogue, but the younger (Japan), lean but tough and ambitious, ever dreamed of bringing back past glories to the old home. He sold newspapers at street corners and worked hard to support the home. The elder flimflammed the younger out of his meager savings and sold him out to their common enemy. The younger in a towering rage beat up the elder—trying to beat into him some sense of shame and awaken some pride in the noble traditions of the great house. After many scraps, the younger finally made up his mind to stage a showdown fight. And that is the fight now raging along the North China and Shanghai fronts.[11]

Finally, American racism reversed appears in the Pearl Harbor Day poem of Takamura Kotara, but not without some backspin on it.

Remember December the Eighth!
This day world history has begun anew.
This day Occidental domination is shattered,
All through Asia's lands and seas.
Japan, with the help of the gods
Bravely faces white superiority.
All Japanese are soldiers now,
Ready to fight
Until the enemy corrects his way.
World history has begun anew.
Remember December the Eighth![12]

The almost unanimous celerity with which the Japanese people adapted themselves and committed themselves to the ways of peace in 1945 is a familiar story. There is presently no discernible evidence that any considerable group wishes to diverge from that path. Continual fierce debates in the Diet about the size of the growing defense budget still involve a small military force, from an international perspective. Many Japanese worry about the growing munitions industry: the sale to Sweden a few years ago of some submarine spotters—an event which hardly struck fear into the hearts of the ordinary citizen of the world—occasioned a public outcry in Japan. Public opinion polls constantly indicate that the Japanese people are almost unanimous in opposing the building of nuclear potential or indeed any offensive weaponry. No political party advocating nuclear armament could stay in power, opinion is so forcibly opposed to it.

The symbols of bellicose nationalism are simply not to be seen. One rarely sees the national flag flying. The national anthem is heard so seldom that one little boy called it the "sumo song," since he heard it only on the occasion of the wrestling matches. Some Westerners may have read too much into the suicide of Yukio Mishima and the drama that accompanied it: thoughtful Japanese seem to see his little army and his final gesture as quixotic behavior by a great writer who was complex and eccentric. When in the early 1970s Yokoi Shoichi, the old soldier, was found on Guam, twenty-seven years after Japan's surrender, still uttering wartime precepts, he was like a ghost out of a past which had been hidden away in a dark closet of the mind.

A much more concrete cause for fear in the world is the power of the American Pentagon. One of the ways in which the American democracy had been successful, before the Cold War, was the manner in which civilian power always governed military power. Harry Truman's decision to fire General MacArthur was the most striking contemporary example of that. In recent years, Congress has had little success in fighting the Pentagon, and the presidents since Johnson have shown little inclination to do so.

The peaceful face of the United States has not disappeared, however. The small band of men in the Congress who demanded American withdrawal from Indochina for many years eventually had their way, mostly. The presidential campaign of Senator Eugene McCarthy in 1968 showed surprising strength, based as it was almost solely on the issue of war. The ruthless manner in which McCarthy's followers were clubbed off the streets of Chicago almost seemed to have smothered the movement for peace. The astonishing campaign by Senator George McGovern in 1972, however, surprised all the political experts. Practically unknown when he began his campaign, he became within three months a national figure. His appeal to the voters cannot be attributed entirely to his long and steadfast record as a dove, yet that was much of the appeal. His dismal showing at the polls in November cannot be attributed entirely to his peace platform.

Military success has often cemented individuals who feel powerless in themselves to the powerful nation-state. The obsolescence of that national function seems clear to most Japanese and many Americans. Economic nationalism has served a similar purpose. The rhetoric of this form of national pride is seldom as bombastic: it can hardly arouse religious frenzy or heat the blood. But the aspiration to grow in economic power as a nation has functioned to unify both cultures.

It may be that this aspiration has operated rather differently in the two cultures. When, partly as a result of World War I, the United States gained supremacy as an economic power, what was applauded was generally the payoff to the individual citizen. True, many fewer citizens benefited fully in the general prosperity of the 1920s than was generally recognized. True, the triumph of the economy was also seen as the triumph of an abstraction, laissez-faire capitalism. (Never mind here the fact that the United States government has never espoused the practice of laissez faire: it has espoused the *gospel* of laissez faire.) True, Christianity, often before the 1920s mentioned in conjunction with American capitalism, was also popularly believed to share the triumph: a best seller through the decade was Bruce Barton's *The Man Nobody Knows,* which made the case that Jesus was essentially a businessman—a salesman and organizer. Nevertheless, the cause of all that prosperity was generally held to be what Herbert Hoover called "rugged individualism," and its purpose was held to be the happiness and well-being of the individual family. The nation was believed to be a gentle and not-too-insistent go-between.

Japan's amazing economic growth, partly abetted by the Korean and Indochinese wars, has been accompanied by far less payoff to the individual Japanese. Most Japanese do live far better than they did in 1950; and real wages for both white-collar and blue-collar workers have increased steadily. Still, the fact that the nation that ranks third in the world in GNP ranks about thirteenth in average income—and with relatively weak socially subsidized welfare benefits—suggests the extent to which economic nationalism in Japan has emphasized national growth at some sacrifice to rewards to individuals. Demands are being made that this balance be shifted. Time will tell that story.

Economic nationalism has succeeded as a cohesive force in both cultures, it is said, because both are composed of unusually materialistic people. Are the Americans merely "crass materialists"? Are the Japanese simply "economic animals"? That will be the subject of the next chapter.

The children of affluence, if I can judge from my experience with college students in Japan and the United States, care considerably less about money than the children of poverty. If we can assume that the people running the United States in the mid-1970s are aged between 55 and 60, that means that they were aged 15 to 20 during the depths of the depression. Some sectors of the Japanese economy (as, in fact, of the American) were already depressed when the international depression hit in 1929. People of 55 or 60 in Japan might have experienced the privation of that international depression as well as even more desperate poverty during the years from 1945 to 1950. It is not surprising, then, if GNP holds more charm for the older than the younger generations in both lands. Let's deduce that economic nationalism will provide weaker glue in the future for cultural cohesiveness. I understand that this thesis is weak as well, but—postponing for a few pages the *cultural* question about the clichés "crass materialists" and "economic animals"—I will use it to excuse getting on to a more interesting question, cultural nationalism.

Assuming that the old jingoist model for nationalism is obsolescent, given present weaponry in the world and the present awareness of its consequences, and assuming that beyond a certain point in affluence economic nationalism loses its power to attract, what kind of glue can hold a people together? Perhaps a feeling for the culture itself, "shared significant symbols," recognition and approval of qualities which unite a culture and set it apart from other cultures. Here we are surely in the realm of the imagination, as that term was defined in my preface.

We mustn't overlook the importance of the word *significant* in Clifford Geertz's phrase "shared significant symbols." Some of the old ones don't pack much of a wallop. For many Japanese and Americans the flag fails to evoke much emotion. Both national anthems were ersatz in the first place, the Japanese having been orchestrated by an American bandmaster and the American being a graft on a German drinking song. Certain public rituals, such as the Emperor's Birthday and the Fourth of July, seem to have lost their emotional voltage. (Have the sumo tournaments and the professional football Superbowl replaced them?)

Old symbols can, however, be refurbished. Affection has replaced awe for the imperial family, and that affection increased when they accepted the charming commoner Shoda Michiko as a daughter-in-law. The bicentennial of the American Revolution may bring to Americans not only nostalgia but a renewed interest in the ideas of the revolutionists, ideas which could still be fruitful: "All men are created equal." The significance of some symbols is difficult to ascertain. Each year thousands pay homage to shrines such as Ise and the Lincoln Memorial; it's difficult to see how a certain shared refreshment of the spirit would fail to take place during such pilgrimages. How about the enormous popularity of those uniquely national heroes of fiction, the samurai and the frontiersman? Books, movies, and TV never seem to exhaust interest in these figures. Is this merely escapist nostalgia for days when nature was unsullied and the lone man could count for something? Or does some significant nourishment of the soul occur when people see these heroes' display of courage, independence, and dedication to duty? A student has told me that he does in fact think of Miyamoto Musashi, the archetypal samurai, as a model. The names Prince Shotoku and Abraham Lincoln continue to appear when Japanese are polled about people in history whom they respect.

Generally, America's shared symbols seem abstract and sparse compared to Japanese. Sparse, naturally, with so little time to develop. Their abstract quality has a historical explanation. Puritanism rejected church ornamentation and all but the plainest music as the work of Satan, reminiscent of Roman Catholicism, so that the "plain style" itself became symbolic. Once the Revolution was a *fait accompli*, national symbols had almost to be manufactured out of whole cloth. The United States rejected the traditional kinds of devices, a monarchy and a national church. It was born, moreover, during the Enlightenment, a period of uncommonly abstract, legalistic, and rationalistic thinking—which in fact rejected the symbolic mode itself in its fullest sense. Washington, the Adamses, and Jefferson established the pattern of plain style for the presidency. Americans have not enjoyed a particularly rich symbolic diet.

Conversely, Japan had an ancient history lush in pageantry and symbolism. Renunciation in 1945 of many of the symbolic meanings of the imperial family meant renouncing much but not all of that symbolism which was specifically national. Local Shinto festivals retained their vitality for many people. (Americans cannot expect *kami* to visit their villages annually, though certain Bostonians are said to believe that the Protestant God took up permanent residence in their city.) Besides these rich and vibrant occasions, the Japanese have the opulent iconography of Buddhism. The Tokyo and Sapporo Olympics and Expo '70 were shared significant symbols of enormous importance, indicating Japan's recovery, its national pride. Notice that the old plain style, shaped by ecological interests, reasserted itself in Denver's *refusal* of the 1976 Olympics.

Arts that are particularly associated with a national culture can provide a source of collective pride. The list of uniquely Japanese forms is an extensive one: ikebana, Noh, Kabuki, bunraku, various forms of landscape and tray gardening, of music, of dance. Okakura Kakuzo wrote of the cult of tea, "No student of Japanese culture could ever ignore its presence," and Kenzo Tange of the best of Shinto architecture, "The form of Ise partakes of the primordial essence of the Japanese people."[13] The list of arts which have been born in America is not unimpressive for a young culture: jazz, the skyscraper, musical comedy of the *Oklahoma* genre, blues, rock, the particular deadpan mode of narrating a tale perfected by Mark Twain and William Faulkner, and, again, various forms of the dance. Yet it seems doubtful that any considerable number of Americans take special pride in that fact.

Here, two differences in the cultures seem important. First, as has often been pointed out, America's was the first mass society without a strong folk tradition and without a strong tradition of its own in the high arts. It is not surprising, then, that it should excel in arts with a broad popular appeal. Second, Americans—feeling the cultural deficiency we have noted—tend to define "art" in a manner which excludes all but high art. "Art" is what the academically trained experts, who have tended to be very deferential to European opinion, *say* is art. That art tends to be almost completely insulated from ordinary experience—played in concert halls, hung in galleries, explicated in the university classroom. Notice how many of the Japanese arts evolved from folk arts that were actings-out of ordinary everyday experience: drinking tea, gardening, setting out a meal, harvesting rice or fish, arranging flowers. The form of Ise is simply an elegant adaptation of the form of a grain storehouse. Americans without specific academic training in the arts claim an inability to enjoy them. Social class seems still to inhibit widespread appreciation of the arts in the United States more than in Japan.

Similarly, the work of literature which is *Japan's* work of literature is *The Tale of Genji,* a fragile and highly sophisticated narrative, while the only counterpart one can imagine in the United States is not Mark Twain's best work, *Huckleberry Finn,* but his more widely read *Tom Sawyer,* a boy's book. The epic *Moby Dick,* possibly the greatest long narrative in English, is not an artifact that is a source of general national pride, as is *Genji.* Or: Kawabata was almost a national treasure; his counterpart, Faulkner, had nothing like that status in the public imagination. The American writers who have achieved a sort of laureate status are men like Twain and Robert Frost, who *personally* projected a folksy image.

National arts, then, appear less likely in the United States than in Japan to serve as a magnet for national culture. Are *any* of the "shared significant symbols" we have looked at culturally operational in any important sense any more? Or must we look only at Disneyland, and the Miss America Pageant, and their equally vulgar Japanese counterparts? I will try to tackle that question in my concluding chapter. Before leaving the subject, however, a final point must be made.

In one important sense, we are almost certainly answering the wrong question in all this discussion. Culture has always had dimensions other than the national. Bright young Japanese and Americans emphasize two other dimensions: they are showing a renewed interest in traditional *local* folkways; and, in their dress, their music, and their demonstration against the structure of authority, they are dramatizing the international scale of culture. If these signs are portentous, then the whole national dimension of culture may be increasingly unimportant.

Fifty years ago, in *A Passage to India,* E. M. Forster had his English schoolmaster, Fielding, lament the loss of his Indian friend Aziz, separated from him by politics: "India a nation! What an apotheosis! Last comer to the drab nineteenth-century sisterhood! Waddling in at this hour of the world to take her seat! She, whose only peer was the Holy Roman Empire . . ."[14]

CHAPTER 3

The "Crass Materialists"
and the "Economic Animals"

An almost unchallenged opinion in many parts of the world holds that all Americans are rich and that they are so because of their single-minded pursuit of what used to be the "almighty dollar." The economic miracle which Japanese have wrought during the past quarter of a century has resulted in their being stigmatized, around the world, as "economic animals." *To the extent* that these international stereotypes fairly represent the Americans and the Japanese, they were come by honestly.

The land of Japan is lovely to the eye but niggardly in natural resources. Historically, it has offered a living to all, even a lavish one to some, if everybody works arduously. At the end of the war, with the economy nearly at point zero, ancient habits of hard work, ingenuity, and thrift reasserted themselves. Practically everybody over thirty in Japan remembers dire want, during the war and during the very lean years of the Occupation, until about 1950. An "onion existence" they called it, from 1945 to 1950, peeling off layer after layer of one's possessions to sell or barter for food. Little wonder that the Liberal Democratic party has stayed in power almost continuously since the war. It has placed its priorities on increasing the GNP and on retaining close ties with the United States, which has greased the wheels for the hard push upward to relative prosperity. The "economic miracle" of postwar Japan is widely acclaimed—and perhaps envied. Perhaps it is only economic *success* which causes certain peoples to be tagged as merely materialistic: one recalls that the English were once ridiculed as "a nation of shopkeepers."

David Potter has argued rather persuasively in *People of Plenty* that the central theme of American history has been the quest after abundance. Most of the Europeans and Asians who chose to make the difficult journey to the United States (and that of course excludes the African immigrants, who were not consulted on the matter) were dazzled by the prospect of owning land. In the places of their origin that in itself yielded high status and wealth: we tend to forget that fact. Many immigrants have told us how rumors of wealth in America reached the most remote corners of Europe. People literally believed the old saw about the streets being paved with gold. The disappointment many immigrants met in "the land of opportunity" did not deter what one historian has called the greatest mass migration in history.

The industrial frontier opened well before the geographic frontier closed, roughly in 1890. Agents of factories replaced agents of land companies in searching Europe for workers, and added a new folklore of success in business to the old stories of "the garden of the world." Andrew Carnegie emigrated to America a bobbin-boy and became a tycoon. Much late-nineteenth-century folklore was of success stories. Horatio Alger, Jr., wrote dozens of best sellers about poor boys whose clean habits (and good luck) rocketed them to wealth. There is no need here to recount the sequel: after World War I, the United States became the richest country in the world, and while its prospects seem a bit shaky as this is written, it remains so.

So the sources of wealth were vastly different—skimpy resources ingeniously worked, and lavish resources which in fact were wastefully exploited. But the moral status of materialist values has been suprisingly similar. Both peoples, for example, are instructed by religions and literatures which are ambivalent on the subject of materialism, some voices castigating it, others honoring it.

Whatever other emotions contribute to Japan's "economic animal" image—anxiety, or envy, or national embarrassment—surprise must be one of them. When the "sword" image in Ruth Benedict's formulation seemed inapplicable, the "chrysanthemum" took over. Until recently, the word *Japan* would most probably have evoked fantasies of cherry blossoms, graceful geisha, and meditative monks. Now, polls show, the word suggests products. The fact is that the Japanese as a people have seldom been as otherworldly, as thoroughgoingly esthetic or spiritual as their Asian neighbors are said to be, or as many Westerners have assumed the Japanese to be. Maybe travelers notice exotic differences more than pedestrian similarities. At any rate, some Japanese teachers, religious and otherwise, have traditionally spoken their approval of worldly pursuits.

Professor Nakamura Hajime, who is deeply learned in Indian and Chinese Buddhism, tells us that that religion had to adjust to the stingy land of Japan when it was imported from lusher lands. Religious teaching that one should "take good care of economic products, the fruit of human labor," he says, is not uncommon in the world, but in generous climates where a little work can gain man the necessities of life, wastefulness is less severely condemned.[1]

Professor Byron Earhart, who emphasizes the manner in which the various Japanese religions—Shinto, Buddhism, and Confucionism—have become functionally interrelated, reminds us that from ancient times the "Japanese religion" has had economic functions such as blessing the rice crop and the fishing fleet.[2] (Watching that latter ceremony at Shiogama is not so different from watching a Roman Catholic service for the same purpose in Louisiana.) Advice of later teachers sounds for all the world like the kinds of accommodations certain Christian ministers made to Christianity. For example, the following sounds like the "Christian" idea of "the calling": "Not of his own will is a man born in a family and succeeds to its trade, whatever it may be, agriculture, industry, or commerce. Because his trade is acquired by happy chance, it should be taken as Heaven's decree. Therefore, his neglecting it even to the slightest extent means he is going against Heaven's decree and committing a great crime."[3] As in Christianity, pursuit of wealth was never taught without qualification: Said Ninomiya Sontoku, a Tenrikyo Shintoist, "Keep your heart pure, busy yourself with your profession, and be true to the mind of God."[4] Many of the newer Shinto sects follow this pattern. Dogen, founder of Soro Zen, was a "practical Buddhist." A teacher of the Tendai sect wrote: "Property is a means to help us do altruistic deeds. Business is a form of asceticism and a way to enlightenment. 'The work of the peasant, the anvil of the blacksmith, the plane of the carpenter—all are essentially expressions of Buddhist teaching. Consequently men's activities are regarded as entrances to the Doctrine.' "[5] The final fusion of the spiritual and practical was accomplished by the Zen monk Suzuki Shosan: "Every profession is a Buddhist exercise. You should attain to Buddhahood through your work. There is no work that is not a Buddhist exercise."[6] According to another writer: "A merchant puts the following question to me. Though I was fortunate enough to receive the gift of life, engaged as I am in the humble way of trade, I am entirely preoccupied with the thought of gain. How sad that I cannot make efforts to attain enlightenment! Please show me how to attain to my end. My answer is this. Those engaged in trade should first of all learn how to make as much profit as possible."[7]

Max Weber and R. H. Tawney have established the close relationship in Western Europe between the rise of Protestantism, with its "economic virtues," and the "spirit of capitalism." The theocrats of New England, unfettered by opposing traditions, could if anything tighten that connection. "A true believing Christian," wrote the preacher John Cotton, "a justified person, he lives his vocation by his faith. . . . He would have his best gifts improved to the best advantage." One must love the world, however, with "weaned affections."[8] The Puritans insisted on this paradox: keep one eye on your work, the other on heaven. But by the late nineteenth century, when capitalism in the United States ran unreined, the ministers of "the gospel of wealth" had all but forgotten the second half of the paradox. "Get rich, get rich!" advised Russell H. Conwell in his famous "Acres of Diamonds" sermon—then he added, "but get money honestly." "God gave me my money," claimed John D. Rockefeller, a Baptist Sunday School teacher.[9] The late nineteenth century in America was the moment of triumph for what the philosopher William James called "the bitch-goddess success."

It is surely unnecessary to point out counterstrains in Buddhism and Christianity, strains which condemn such worldliness in the strongest terms. Both literatures, too, contain contradictory advice. Benjamin Franklin—the "practical prototype" of the American, D. H. Lawrence said—grew up in Cotton's Boston, but became a very secular product of it. Fascinating parallels exist between two documents: Franklin's widely circulated *Poor Richard's Almanacks* (one of which hung in Lawrence's boyhood home in England), finally collected in 1774 in *The Way to Wealth*; and Ihara Saikaku's *The Eternal Storehouse of Japan: The*

Millionaire's Gospel, first published in 1688.[10] Both emphasize relentless thrift, minute attention to detail, and severe asceticism. Fuji-ichi, one of Saikaku's protagonists, has been entertaining guests all day. A salted bream hangs before the God of the Kitchen Range, so that they "may get the feeling of having eaten fish without actually doing so." At the end of the day, he tells his guests, "Well, now, you have kindly talked with me from early evening, and it is high time that refreshments were served. But not to provide refreshments is one way of becoming a millionaire. The noise of the mortar which you heard when you first arrived was the pounding of starch for the covers of the Account Book." "A fat Kitchen makes a lean Will," said Poor Richard, and "Fools make Feasts, and wise Men eat them."

It was Fuji-ichi "who first started the wearing of detachable cuffs on the sleeves. . . . His socks were of deerskin and his clogs were fitted with high leather soles, but even so he was careful not to walk too quickly along the hard main roads." "Of what Use is this *Pride of Appearance?*" Poor Richard asked:

> *What is a Butterfly? At best*
> *He's but a Caterpillar drest*
> *The gaudy Fop's his Picture just.*

Fuji-ichi "never passed by anything which might be of use. Even if he stumbled he used the opportunity to pick up stones for fire-lighters, and tucked them in his sleeve. The head of a household, if he is to keep the smoke rising steadily from his kitchen, must pay attention to a thousand things like this." " *'Tis easier to build two Chimnies than to keep one in Fuel,"* said Poor Richard. Franklin, in his *Autobiography,* chides his wife for buying silver spoons when pewter would serve as well; Fuji-ichi starts the New Year with fat chopsticks, which can be shaved down from time to time.

We wouldn't wish to be guilty of missing the satire in these works: Franklin finally hid behind two masks, that of Richard and that of somebody named Father Abraham. Further, Fuji-ichi, like Richard, claimed not to be a miser, but only an exemplar. The examples, it is clear, were taken seriously in the two cultures.

Franklin, incidentally, was the American character who, along with Washington and Lincoln, occurred most consistently as a model for young scholars in both American and Japanese textbooks of the nineteenth and early twentieth centuries. As, following 1903, the Japanese books became more nationalistic, and as foreign models generally began to disappear from them, mention of Franklin persisted longer and more frequently than that of Washington and Lincoln. The attributes of Franklin's which the authors praised were his self-reliance and his zeal for the common good. An accurate picture: on his own, he made a tidy fortune; then at a fairly early age he retired from business to devote himself entirely to the public welfare. The pattern is typical enough so that when the novelist Henry James created his protagonist for *The American,* the aptly named Christopher Newman also made a fortune early, abruptly dropped his business career, and went to Paris in search of beauty and a perfect wife.

If Franklin and Saikaku represent one extreme attitude about the pursuit of worldly goods, Thoreau and Kamo no Chōmei represent the opposite. Neither pole could be considered typical, but the poles help define the mean. The gaunt asceticism of Thoreau and Kamo reminds us of Franklin and Saikaku, but this style of living is intended not to help accumulate wealth, but to dramatize its frivolity. Thoreau in *Walden* and Kamo no Chōmei in "An Account of My Hut"[11] retired to their humble huts for similar reasons, recognition of the vanity of ordinary life. Thoreau retired there early in his life, though, as a two-year experiment; Kamo no Chōmei was sixty when he made the move, permanently. Each built his shelter by hand, carefully. Kamo no Chōmei's hut measured ten feet by ten feet; Thoreau's modesty was slightly less spectacular, his hut measuring ten by fifteen. The dwellings of course symbolize larger lessons the men wish to teach: live simply and quietly in nature.

Both satirize even the concept of ownership, the notion of possession itself. "When the weather is fine, I climb the peak and look out toward Kyoto. . . . The view has no owner and nothing can interfere with my enjoyment." So writes Kamo. Thoreau: "I even had the refusal of several farms . . . but I never got my fingers burned by actual possession. . . . I retained the landscape, and I have since annually carried off what it yielded without a wheelbarrow. . . . I have frequently seen a poet withdraw, having enjoyed the most valuable part of a farm, while the crusty farmer supposed that he had got a few wild apples only." Nature can supply practically all of a man's needs, if they are simple enough: "I eke out my life with berries of the fields and nuts from the trees on the peaks. . . . The very scantiness of the food gives it additional savor, simple though it is." "I have made a satisfactory dinner, satisfactory on several accounts, simply off a dish of purslane . . . which I gathered in the cornfield, boiled and salted."

The work ethic, so dear to the entrepreneurs of Japan and the United States, the first of the "economic virtues," failed to impress these singular fellows. "If I do not feel like working, it does not upset me. . . . My body is like a drifting cloud—I ask for nothing, I want nothing. My greatest joy is a quiet nap; my only desire for this life is to see the beauties of the seasons." "There were times when I could not afford to sacrifice the bloom of the present moment to any work, whether of the head or hands. I love a broad margin to my life. Sometimes, in a summer morning, having taken my accustomed bath, I sat in my sunny doorway from sunrise till noon, rapt in a revery. . . . I realized what the Orientals mean by contemplation and the forsaking of works."

Thoreau's balance sheet, a spoof on the very idea of economy itself, reads like this: "My whole income from the farm was

$$
\begin{array}{lr}
 & \$23.44 \\
\text{Deducting the outgoes} \ldots \ldots \ldots & 14.72\tfrac{1}{2} \\
\text{There are left} \ldots \ldots \ldots \ldots \ldots & \$\ 8.71\tfrac{1}{2}
\end{array}
$$

. . . All things considered, that is, considering the importance of a man's soul and of to-day, notwithstanding the short time occupied by my experiment, nay, partly even because of its transient character, I believe that that was doing better than any farmer in Concord did that year."

Kamo no Chōmei and Henry David Thoreau are extreme examples of the revolt against materialism. The number of heroes of the imagination in both Japan and the United States who are outside the economy, however, is remarkable: the saintly Bashō, wandering through his beloved island in search of purity, the impoverished samurai moving from village to village doing good deeds, even the yakuza, and the dissolute characters of Dazai Osamu's fiction; Cooper's Leatherstocking, Huck Finn, Melville's Ishmael, twentieth-century wandering bards such as Woody Guthrie, who refused jobs that paid too well. We will look further at both nations' literary traditions in a later chapter: let me assert here that they are in general antimaterialist.

If religious advice on the pursuit of wealth is ambivalent, and if literary traditions tend to satirize or ignore preoccupation with money, the two traditions of political philosophy sometimes encourage it—indeed, even to relate materialism of one sort or another to national identity. This seems more persistently to be the case in the United States, but it isn't absent in Japan.

Late in the Tokugawa period, a number of scholars, wholly dependent on books available at the Dutch trading post at Nagasaki, began to chafe under isolation, and urged their fellow citizens to begin to emulate the Europeans—as they understood them. Some of the advice encouraged economic development. In 1798, for example, Honda Toshiaki called for a government fleet of ships, colonization of nearby islands, and creation of a national treasury of precious metals, for use in international trade. Also before Perry's visit, as the foreigners' ships became more and more in evidence around Japan's waters, the versatile scholar Sato Nobuhiro published a comprehensive scheme for nationalizing and strengthening Japan's economy. Two of his three "essentials of economics" sound like Jefferson's, formulated a few years earlier: "To be well versed in agricultural management, to bring all products under a simple control, and to endeavor to spread education. . . . Production will increase greatly, there will be a flow of money and wealth, the whole country will prosper, all the people will be rich and happy, and suffering due to poverty will be unknown."[12] What is *not* Jeffersonian, of course, is the total nationalization: Jefferson wished as much local control as possible. Sato's expostulation, "Ah, how boundless have been the blessings of the creator on our Imperial land!" sounds Jeffersonian enough, though Sato's comparative base was slim.

The great Tokugawa scholar-nationalist Motoori Norinaga considered otherworldliness a Chinese affectation. "Confucionists of the world," he wrote in 1812, "regard not worrying about being poor and humble and not wishing for or delighting in prosperity as a virtue, but it is not one's true feelings. . . . What's good about it? . . . There is," he insisted, "no impiety worse than ruining oneself and impoverishing one's house."[13]

As the extent of Western economic and military power became

clear, economic nationalism became more urgent. "Enrich the country, strengthen its arms," became a slogan of the Meiji period. Economic individualism was in the bag of Western ideas opened during Meiji, but generally leaders emphasized economic nationalism. As nationalism became ultranationalism, and official doctrine in 1937 crystallized into the aforementioned *Kokutai no Hongi,* economic individualism became linked in evil with communism: "The beginnings of modern Western free economy are seen in the expectation of bringing about national prosperity as a result of free, individual, lucrative activities." That was beneficial to the extent that national wealth increased, the document argued, but on the other hand a free economy led some people "openly to justify egoism." Further, the resulting "chasm between rich and poor" led to class animosity, then to communism, with its "erroneous" theory that everything centers on the economy. "Healthy economic life" is possible "only where the people one and all put heart and soul into their respective occupations . . . with their minds set on guarding and maintaining the prosperity of the Imperial Throne."[14] By contrast, the slogan behind the prosperity of recent years implies individual reward: *akarui seikatsu,* "the bright new life."

America's reputation for wealth has not always or in all places been pejorative. People with land to sell began in the first decade of the seventeenth century to circulate through Europe the image of the land of plenty. Crèvecoeur, who came to America from France in 1755, had no vested interest, but with his *Letters from an American Farmer,* widely circulated throughout Europe after 1782, he established one stock image:

Here are no aristocratical families, no courts, no Kings, no bishops, no ecclesiastical dominion . . . no great manufactures employing thousands, no great refinements of luxury. . . . But a pleasing uniformity of decent competence appears throughout our habitations. . . . Wives and children, who before in vain demanded . . . a morsel of bread, now, fat and frolicksome, gladly help their father to clear those fields whence exuberant crops are to arise to feed and clothe them all.[15]

A famous French visitor of different temperament, a half a century later, saw the same thing, but reacted differently:

In America the passion for physical well-being is not always exclusive, but it is general; and if all do not feel it in the same manner, yet it is felt by all. Carefully to satisfy all, even the least wants of the body, and to provide the little conveniences of life, is uppermost in every mind. . . . I never met in America with any citizen so poor as not to cast a glance of hope and envy on the enjoyment of the rich, or whose imagination did not possess itself by anticipation of those good things which fate still obstinately withheld from him.[16]

Alexis de Tocqueville made his report on the American democracy at the same time Emerson, Thoreau, and the other transcendentalists were also complaining of stultifying materialism among their fellow citizens. Tocqueville, too, saw counterforces in the culture—the idea of the perfectability of man, for one.

It is not incongruous, then, that some of the nineteenth-century political leaders who are among America's most beloved cultural heroes placed at the center of their creeds the idea that America is the place where one could "better one's condition." The political thrust of Thomas Jefferson, Andrew Jackson, and Abraham Lincoln was to extend to more and more elements of the society the possibility of "bettering their condition"—the phrase is insistent. In Lincoln's early campaigns for the Senate and the presidency, one of his most effective arguments against the extension of slavery was that it was a threat to the free workers' economic opportunity. Speaking before some shoemakers on strike, he said,

I don't believe in a law to prevent a man from getting rich; it would do more harm than good. So while we do not propose any war upon capital, we do wish the humblest man an equal chance to get rich with everybody else. When one starts poor, as most do in the race of life, free society is such that he knows he can better his condition; he knows that there is no fixed condition of labor, for his whole life. I am not ashamed to confess that twenty-five years ago I was a hired laborer, mauling rails.[17]

In an earlier senatorial campaign, speaking to a gathering of workingmen, Lincoln emphasized the importance to immigrants of a system of free labor:

Now irrespective of the moral aspect of this question as to whether there is a right or wrong in enslaving a negro, I am still in favor of our new territories being in such a condition that white men may find a home—may find some spot where they can better their condition—where they can settle upon new soil and better their condition in life. I am in favor of this not merely (I must say it here as I have elsewhere) for our own people who are born amongst us, but as an outlet for *free white people everywhere,* the world over—in which Hans and Baptiste and Patrick, and all other men from all the world, may find new homes and better their conditions in life.[18]

American labor leaders, incidentally, have mostly taken exactly this line; its popularity is a partial explanation for the failure of radical labor movements in the United States. Samuel Gompers, for decades America's most important labor leader, when asked his philosophy for labor, replied, "More."

By the late nineteenth century, with America's industrial revolution far off the ground, this concept of economic democracy had become a grotesque caricature of itself. The "gospel of wealth" which I have mentioned before was reinforced by the version of social Darwinism which stressed individual rather than group survival, and seemed to sanction the "robber barons" (or "captains of industry," depending upon one's predisposition) whose careers flourished then with a good deal of governmental aid and very little governmental restraint. During Theodore Roosevelt's and Woodrow Wilson's presidencies, some restrictions were placed on them, in part removed during the 1920s, when President Calvin Coolidge proclaimed that "the business of America is business." It must be recalled that reformists such as Franklin Roosevelt and Harry Truman wished in no wise to undermine capitalism—rather, merely to distribute its fruits more equitably.

Of the men who have formulated political attitudes among the two peoples, a few, beloved of memory, advocated wisdom and virtue as the bases for national character. Prince Shotoku's famous Seventeen-Article Constitution, for example, was really a set of ethical precepts. Thomas Jefferson advocated an "aristocracy of talent and virtue," placed free public education at the center of his system, resisted industrialism, and advised a nation of independent freeholders, none really rich. Few political thinkers of either culture, however, have advocated going slow in the cultivation of wealth—certainly not in recent decades.

Advice from their spiritual and temporal leaders has been contradictory, but both peoples have, after all, busied themselves with extraordinary zeal at the production and consumption of material goods. One result has surely been collective pride in their economic achievement, although that pride has not been unmitigated. Another result has been profits to the bosses.

Since the 1920s, roughly, in the United States and the 1960s, roughly, in Japan, emphasis in production has clearly changed to goods for mass consumption, so that the bosses have had to persuade mass audiences that their personal well-being depended upon possession of particular items of merchandise. Therefore, elaborate bureaucracies of advertisers, industrial and package designers, and market researchers have developed to encourage them so to believe. The question that is central to our purposes is one to which no clear-cut answer is possible: to what extent have the advertising men succeeded? Proportionate to other goals in life, how important is the ownership of things?

It might be interesting to compare attitudes toward buying goods at a time when products intended for mass consumption first began to crowd the market. Robert and Helen Lynd did their original study of Muncie, Indiana, in 1923; Ezra and Suzanne Vogel did their study of the Tokyo suburbs of Mamachi in 1959 and 1960.[19] Despite obvious differences in the studies, they were undertaken at times when a very broad market was necessary to the two economies. Both studies show that the business of making a living was uppermost in the minds of most families in both places—hardly surprising, since neither economy could be called one of affluence for most people by present standards, though large pockets of affluence existed in both places. Most families had to sweat over budgets; yet these budgets bought more than almost any people has ever known. What was the struggle for?

I would like here to urge the argument that at these periods the human desires being met by material possessions were less marginal than, for example, the desire for a vacation home in both cultures today. In Muncie, the desires focused mainly on better homes, a car (which could cost a worker one-fourth of his pay), central heating, a radio, and such appliances as vacuum cleaners and washing machines which demonstrably ease the drudgery of the housewife. In Mamachi, the hankering was after a home (an enormously larger expense in Japan), and such appliances as rice cookers, refrigerators, washing machines, and—corresponding to Muncie's radios—TV sets. Cars were as yet hardly contemplated.

In both lists, the radio and TV point to one quality of the new mass culture: a person is simply, for better or worse, an outlander of sorts if he is totally ignorant of what is cast abroad by those media. The ownership of a car in the United States in the 1920s was something of a nonessential necessity as well, but it also meant some other things. First, it reflected the traditionally notorious American wanderlust: "Middletowners" confessed that they would make great sacrifices—new clothes, for example—in order to gain the freedom of motion afforded to them from time to time by their car. Second, it seemed to reflect a new restlessness about leisure, perhaps in turn reflecting an increasingly boring nature of work. As the Lynds studied records of the same city in 1890, they found that most workers were skilled, and most recreation more relaxed and communal. Third, according to popular sociology, the "parlor on wheels" suggested a new sexual freedom among the young, increasingly impatient with parental restrictions. The status to be achieved from owning a car ranged from that granted by Ford's Model T, intended for the masses, to that of the gorgeous Rolls Royces and Cords. (Let it be said that nobody then could have foreseen how inextricable is the web of troubles a people can get into through such pious devotion to automobiles. Unable to see any way Americans can get out of the ecological, economic, moral, and esthetic tangle, I do not cheer growing signs that the automobile is becoming more and more a symbol of status in Japan.)

In neither Muncie nor Mamachi was the ownership of objects the only motivation for hard work. In neither place did an adequate system exist to ensure a decent life after retirement, so security in the future was perhaps an even more urgent motive. Two differences exist here. First, the chronic unemployment in Muncie exacerbated the worry about security while, second, as early as this credit buying began to erode habits of saving, which even today are exceptionally strong in Japan. To the extent that a fear of poverty in old age is a spur to earning, it would probably lead first to saving for a home.

Perhaps, then, a cluster of related motives all contribute to materialism and the appearance of it: insecurity, anxiety about status coupled with a wish to keep more or less on a par with one's peers, boredom on the job and frustration with the restrictions of an industrial bureaucracy, and more simply, the wish for more spacious living quarters and less drudgery for the housewife of those quarters.

If these are the values and the drives which contribute to what appears to outsiders to be mere materialism in the two cultures, contrapuntal forces work, as we have begun to note, with almost as much strength. The opposition isn't always sharp. For example, interest in the arts in both places ordinarily costs money—sometimes, plenty of it. This interest is lively in both cultures, though conventional wisdom that it is stronger in Japan seems to be accurate. Westerners are often surprised and delighted to notice the care most Japanese devote to arranging their daily lives esthetically. James Kirkup, though, reflecting on dinginess in the public sphere, says that the Japanese have a better eye for beauty than for ugliness. Beauty, in this culture where the private is so greatly respected, is the responsibility of the individual, the in-group.

In 1968, the number of parties advertising in the business pages of the Tokyo telephone book that they offer instruction in the various arts were shown in the following list—the figures are rounded off.

Tokyo		*New York*	
Painting	630	Art	40
Calligraphy	450	Ceramics	10
Dancing, Western and Japanese	1030	Dance	50
		Drama	40
Flower arrangement and tea ceremony	1050	Floral arrangement	5
		Music	80
Western music	800	Photography	10
Japanese music	570	Sculpture	10

In 1970, the business pages of the five boroughs of New York offered the accompanying comparison. These comparisons are misleading in several ways. First, the New York business pages clearly do not include in their groupings very small schools or part-time teachers, while I guess that the Tokyo directory might. Second, the Japanese clearly have both worlds of art to choose from, while the Americans do not—three ikebana schools in Manhattan excepted. Third, art is more completely centralized in Tokyo than in New York—the United States has a number of regional art centers which thrive, I am told, in a way that Japan's do not. Many Japanese schools of the art cater to young women preparing themselves for marriage; but I know elderly Japanese businessmen who work actively at their arts after hours. During the nineteenth century, manly men in the United States were expected to be about the business of attacking the geographic or economic frontiers, while arts were left to the women; this situation may pertain somewhat more in Japan presently than before, and somewhat less in the United States now than before—men of affairs, perhaps emulating Winston Churchill, find it socially acceptable to study painting and the like. The "salary man" of Japan, unlike his high-bourgeois predecessors, is expected to be too busy, though he never denies the importance of art, as many American men of affairs certainly did during much of the nineteenth century.

Religion, or at least church- and synagogue-going, is an active concern of a majority of Americans. While American Christians have been notoriously unsuccessful in following Jesus' example of poverty, many churches and synagogues, and such organizations as the National Council of Churches, have nevertheless in recent years compiled a notable record in fighting various social injustices. Religious activity in Japan is of a different sort—not a Sunday by Sunday matter, but rather when the occasion warrants it, such as when a child reaches three or five or seven years old, or when one is married or dies. The importance of religion to both peoples is real, and the fact must mitigate the seriousness with which we view them as merely economic animals.

Noticeable cracks have appeared in the American work ethic itself, and signs of their appearance have been remarked in Japan. This is part of the subject of a later chapter, but if people tend increasingly to work in order to play rather than to store up possessions, it should be mentioned here. Some religious spokesmen in both cultures, as we have seen, have taught the doctrine known to Christians as "the calling," which identifies the individual with the work he is destined to perform. I believe I observe accurately that Japanese with some leisure tend more consciously than Americans to specifically choose an avocation as a part of their self-identification. That curiosity in world history called "the leisure crisis" seems likely to encourage this further. Again, such a fact might explain hard work on the job in a way that puts in question the notion of the merely economic man in either culture: one must earn a considerable amount of money to afford a boat or ikebana lessons, but the goal is not simply materialistic.

In both cultures, people seem to worry considerably about their status in the community. Roles are not ready-made as they are in feudal cultures. A good deal of disagreement exists about the extent to which consumption is tied to concern about the opinion of one's peers in both Japan and the United States. David Riesman and William H. Whyte, Jr., made the case in the 1950s—now widely accepted as conventional wisdom—that suburbanites' decisions to buy this or that article were dictated almost entirely by the urge to conform, the delicate calculation of what friends or neighbors might think about making or neglecting to make a certain purchase. Herbert Gans, reporting on Levittown, New Jersey, and referring also to Levittown, New York—two communities in which blue-collar workers out-number white-collar workers—emphasizes individual choice as the more important determinant.[20] Concerning the Japanese, Ezra Vogel says: "In contrast to what William H. Whyte has called the 'inconspicuous consumption' of the American organization man, the Japanese salary man and especially his wife would like to imitate the richer classes in their conspicuous display of wealth."[21] He points particularly to lavish weddings, expensive kimonos, and the prestige of labels such as those from the Mitsukoshi Department Store (corresponding to less frequently lavish weddings, fur coats, and Brooks Brothers labels, I suppose). He also recognizes that one shouldn't go too far: the industrialist Matsushita, once highly regarded because of his rags-to-riches career, has fallen from popular favor because he has gone too far; his accumulation of wealth seems now merely selfish.

Both Gans and Vogel point to the paramount importance of acceptance by the group. "*Social isolation is the main source of stress*," Vogel says.[22] The ancient value of loyalty to one's group persists in Mamachi, he continues: the old habits of etiquette that are designed to maintain harmony within the group. Wouldn't one be safe in guessing, then, that pressure from peers to buy this commodity and to resist buying that one works in similar ways among most Japanese and most Americans? Nobody wants to be a cheapskate, nobody wants to be a show-off. An occasional splurge indicates generosity, day-by-day thrift shows one's devotion to traditional virtues. And—to return to the fact that many people in both cultures who are of an age to be parents remember privation or poverty—the temptation to provide for the children what one was denied himself is a strong one. For both Vogel and Gans report on the centrality of the family in people's vision of life; in Japan recently, fathers feel less pressure to work long hours at the office, and more desire to participate in what is called "my home-ism."

In fact, the most telling conclusion that one gains from these two splendid studies—Gans's and Vogel's—is that the basic value systems in these modern suburbs are very traditional. In Mamachi, loyalty and competence, two old samurai virtues. Gans concludes:

It is striking how little American culture among the Levittowners differs from what De Tocqueville reported in his travels through small-town middle class America a century ago. Of course, he was here before the economy needed an industrial proletariat, but the equality of men and women, the power of the child over his parents, the importance of the voluntary association, the social functions of the church, and the rejection of high culture seem to be holdovers from his time, and so is the adherence to the traditional virtues: individual honesty, thrift, religiously inspired morality, Franklinesque individualism, and Victorian prudery.[23]

In both cultures, some of those virtues—competence, loyalty, thrift—can involve economic payoff, but that payoff is incidental to more complex value systems. Any stereotypes about "economic animals" and "crass materialists" must be seen in that context. An *Asahi Evening News* poll shows that most Japanese parents wish for their children "a life according to their tastes." A study of American automobile workers indicates that while they themselves feel little expectation of better jobs, they hope for better things for their children—a hope, incidentally, dramatized by Arthur Miller in *Death of a Salesman*.[24] The Japanese have developed a body of humor about their own unprecedented roles as consumers. A series of current jokes refer to the sanctity traditionally ascribed to three national treasures, gifts of the gods to the imperial family: a mirror, a sword, a jewel. Of even more ancient and sacred origin, so the joke goes, is the gift to the Japanese people (in, let's say, 1965) of the washing machine, the vacuum cleaner, and the refrigerator. As, later, a new round of goods were pushed by the Japanese advertising men, the three sacred treasures became a cooler (an air conditioner, that is), a car, and a color TV. At present writing, the three treasures, attributed to the very ancientest of gods, Izanagi and Izanumi, are *Kotteji* (a summer cottage), *Kukka* (an electric oven), and—here a breakdown in alliteration occurs—central heating.[25] Apparently they overstate their own preoccupation with these matters. Japan's National Statistical Research Center, which makes a careful study of the attitudes of the public every fifteen years, aimed some of its questions in 1968 at testing the "economic animal" image. It asked, "Name the one thing which you consider most important." Only 12 percent of the people who were questioned gave answers such as "money" or "property"; larger numbers said "health," "life," "happiness," and "love." A number of other questions, some of them cleverly trapped, failed to give any evidence of the primacy of merely economic drives. They were asked to choose among six life styles:

1. To work as hard as I can and get rich.
2. To study hard and become famous.
3. To live according to my own tastes without thinking about getting rich or famous.
4. To live each day in a carefree way without worrying.
5. To reject the temptations of the world and live as purely and properly as possible.
6. To forget myself and give my all for the good of society.

In 1968, 32 percent of the people chose option 3, 20 percent option 4, 17 percent option 1, and 17 percent option 6. Options 5 and 6, reflecting Buddhist and Confucian teaching, were chosen by 57 percent in 1931 and 71 percent in 1940.[26]

In 1959–1960 Ezra Vogel found the lives of the "salary men" in Mamachi very clearly defined by their vision of security and what Tocqueville called "physical well-being"; he revisited Mamachi in 1968 and found that that drive had diminished. "Excitement about acquiring new material belongings has begun to fade, but it has by no means ended; anxiety about material welfare has almost disappeared," he says. (This does not represent total net gain, however: "no new clear vision has emerged to compare with the clarity of the vision of the salary man a decade ago.")[27]

Evidence that materialism has declined in potency as a mover of Americans is somewhat less conclusive, perhaps because it has been studied less carefully than in Japan. Among young people, a change is clear. It is unnecessary to cite that small group in the prestigious colleges and universities who wish to signify, by dress and style of life, their affinity with the poor. In a recent Gallup Poll of a random sample of all college students, which would necessarily include representatives of institutions more often identified with the mainstream of the American culture, only 8 percent indicated that they wished to go into business management in their future. Thirty-eight percent wished to go into teaching, social work, and the clergy, all notoriously unremunerative lines of work. Of the 7 percent who wished to become lawyers and doctors, it must be said that those professions are increasingly seen as ways of seeking justice and health rather than money. Another recent Gallup Poll indicates that 80 percent to 90 percent of Americans are satisfied with their salaries. Among "serious problems" that the pollsters try to get their subjects to identify, economic ones were in the 1960s rarely said to be as important to them as such matters as law and order, the rebellion of young people or minority groups, the fact of poverty or the fact of war. In 1973 and 1974, inflation and recession in both countries quite understandably changed the findings of pollsters: family budgets again seemed to people their most serious problem. Reduction of one's standard of living is a notoriously bitter pill to swallow; it might be doubted, however, that Japanese and Americans will therefore get much sympathy from the poorer peoples of the world.

Japan's relatively short history of prosperity seems not to have resulted in an irredeemable preoccupation with heaping up worldly goods; recession in both countries, if not too severe, could conceivably direct both peoples' attention toward other sources of satisfaction. At any rate, neither culture was ever fully committed to "the way of wealth" as a complete way of life. Both can afford to be high-minded about such an obsession now. Neither the Nixon government nor the Sato government seemed to understand the changing mood of their people; both seemed to assume the continuing primacy of this drive in their constituency. The early popularity of former Prime Minister Tanaka, however, apparently was in part influenced by his interest in ecology. For a new fact of life is forcing a reconsideration of materialistic attitudes in both "post-industrial" societies. Until very recently, the pleas of ecologists, down through the years, fell on deaf ears among both of them. Cataclysm has now begun to follow the warning of cataclysm, however, on our "only earth," and thoughtful people begin to conclude that production for production's sake, the religion of GNP, must necessarily give way to more temperate relations with that earth. The decision by the United States Senate not to build the SST and the passage by the Diet of some fifteen antipollution laws testify that notice of that necessary change has even reached the attention of people in public places. Fortunately, both cultures contain strains that have always run counter to the rapine streak, strains which the lust for possessions has almost hidden. What is the nature of these contrary attitudes?

CHAPTER 4

The Old Environment: Nature

Most Japanese and Americans dwell in two environments, the old natural one of legend and recent memory, and the new one of their own making, cities and machines. Much of the wisdom of the two peoples, and the symbols by which they order their lives, derive from their close communication through the years with nature. That relationship recedes from the day-by-day consciousness of most of them. In 1930, half the Japanese were still farming and fishing and lumbering; now about 15 percent of them are. Half the Americans were in nonagricultural pursuits in 1870; now 90 percent of them are. The old voice of nature still speaks with authority, however, as TV advertising men, travel agents, entrepreneurs in the leisure industries, producers of samurai movies and westerns, goldfish salesmen, and poets well know. She will not be silent. I have not wisdom enough in me to know whether to agree or disagree with those who assert that some atavistic instinct in humankind requires that we hear that voice; I do know that it is still heard in these two industrial cultures. I am aware that much of our wisdom is also urban, as old as the Athenian agora and the Heian court. Further, many denizens of Tokyo and New York seem to flourish in the rough and tumble of city life and thrive on bad air and water and an absence of daisies. (I think Americans have no word parallel to *Edo-ko*, the canny and confirmed citizen of Tokyo. "Gothamite," referring to New Yorkers of similar stripe, is not in general use.)

Yet the magnet that pulls most city dwellers to nature (or at least to the baseball "park") on good Sundays is visibly powerful.

The historical differences are obvious. The Japanese have had many centuries to make their peace with nature, despite her frequent tantrums—typhoons, earthquakes, and tidal waves. They have molded and sculpted her gradually and painstakingly. They are scholars of her waters. Hardly a nook or cranny is without its legend, its spirit, *kami*. The native Americans, too, had learned to live with the land in harmony, but to the Europeans who invaded that land, nature was both a wilderness to be conquered and, following that, the source of bounty. To the Africans they brought with them, she was a strange and alien prison.

The geographical differences are just as significant. The north-south dimensions of Japan and continental United States are almost exactly the same, from about 45° longitude to about 25°. Almost every conceivable kind of landscape exists along the sprawl of the Japanese archipelago, but the arable areas could just about fit into West Virginia. One finds the fisherman's culture, the mountain man's culture, and the rice farmer's, almost arctic and almost tropical, all in close quarters. The space is small, so the sense of space is small. Conversely, the Europeans who became Americans were conscious of vast space, uncharted space. Some of the shrewdest of the early American "futurologists" predicted that generations into the dozens or even hundreds would be required just to settle the West. That consciousness was enlivened during the nineteenth century by countless travel books and by traveling panoramas, and it's kept alive today by wide-screen western movies. Onto this sense of open space, a fact of geography and a fact of the collective imagination, one must juxtapose the grid. Almost the first men to "conquer" the land west of the Appalachians were surveyors sent there by the Land Survey of 1785, who established a rectangular system of political boundaries, roads, and even farmers' fences, regardless of topographical truths. This geometry has influenced Americans' sense of their wide space in ways that are incalculable. (Chinese Buddhists prescribed to the Japanese that temple grounds be oriented on strict north-south, east-west axes. Often the Japanese dutifully obeyed; but more often they slipped into a more comfortable asymmetry.)

Here is a curious bit of historical continuity. The grid system, whatever its esthetic shortcomings, served well a people in a big hurry to sell and settle land. The Old Testament Jehovah created the earth in six days. The gods of the Japanese myth of creation, on the other hand, took a very long time of it, being often jealous, capricious, sulky, and full of pranks—like human beings, in other words. The point is this: no one in the history of Japan knew a land that was not yet tamed, storied, blessed by the *kami*, while Americans saw their land as a wilderness to be subdued, and one of their most insistent boasts has been that they did so in a very short span of time.

That westward movement was an acting-out by tough and practical men and women of a host of theories dear to the minds of European intellectuals. And that introduces the central spiritual difference, the different mode in which Americans and Japanese have communicated with their land. "One . . . of the most fundamental differences between the East and West," writes the Nobel physicist Yukawa Hideki, "is that the Western mind emphasizes the dualistic aspect of reality while the Eastern mind basically tends to be advaitist." He distinguishes between advaitism and monism: the latter settles the philosophical question, the former leaves it open and "simply asserts that reality is non-dualistic." "It is not-two, which is not the same as one. It is both yes and no, yet it is neither the one nor the other."[1]

Another formulation apparently skews this model somewhat, but makes it more concrete for our purposes. Fosco Maraini, who seems to me to speak more intelligently about Japan than most Westerners, posits a triangular model of final reality which most Westerners work from, with God, man, and nature at the three angles. The Japanese are bipolar, he suggests, with people at the one end and the gods *fused* with nature at the other.[2] The Western triangle which Maraini posits seems more persuasive to me than his bipolar model. Westerners *do* seem to me to speak of nature as something separate from themselves; some religious teachers have thought it inimical to otherworldly godliness. But I suspect that the Japanese, in religion, philosophy, and thus psychology, have tended more to a stance which doesn't feel clean categories even between man at the one pole and gods-nature at the other. A Japanese theologian writes that Westerners immediately react to a situation by analyzing into a "subject-object-predicate relation." "The Japanese seem to direct their interest more to the domain of immediate experience."[3]

To the Westerner, Paul Shepard says, nature is something "out there," separate from oneself. Even Ralph Waldo Emerson, whose seminal essay *Nature* is suffused with Oriental wisdom, makes this distinction: "Philosophically considered, the universe is composed of Nature and the Soul. Strictly speaking, therefore, all that is separate from us, all which Philosophy distinguishes as the *Not Me*, that is, both nature and art . . . must be ranked under this name, *Nature*." Shinto, originally almost empty of intellectual and moral content, involved a sort of prayerful stance before nature in which one hoped to be joined by the *kami* of a particular bit of nature. Buddhism, writes the renowned Professor Suzuki, recognizes, through mere reason, distinctions among objects, but strives for the intuition which sees the unity, the wholeness of all.[4]

The Japanese language itself facilitates this sense of unity. "Suppose a man is taking a walk in the countryside of Japan," writes Professor Kishimoto. It is autumn. "Some sentiment comes to his mind. He feels it and wants to express the sentiment. He would say, 'samishii' (lonesome)." The single word can make a complete statement. "It is not necessary in Japanese to specify the subject by explicitly stating whether 'I' am feeling lonesome, or 'the scenery' is lonesome. Without such analysis, one's sentiment can be projected there in its immediate form." Both subject and object participate in the "collaboration." The language thus enables one to "project man's experience in its immediate and unanalyzed form."[5]

If the pure experience of Japanese in nature has religious and esthetic overtones, such an experience for the American is likely to have symbolic *meaning*, moral and intellectual, and that meaning may be a lens interposed between man and nature. Some of those lenses are as old as Christianity. I know of no Christian interpretation of reality which does not distinguish between the physical and spiritual world, to the disparagement of the former. Shinto assumes that the earth as given is finally good. Certain forms of Christianity would agree to that: the earth may be a manifestation of the mind of God, full of lessons for the pious reader. But the permanent lessons for the mind that the stately oak might teach are more important than that stately but decaying oak. In no wise is it a good bet to commit oneself wholly to this earth, this temporary "vale of tears." Traditional Christian readings, then, shade off into absolute hostility to nature, the tempter. The garden, for example, as Paul Shepard says, may be "a hedonistic affront to ascetic moralism and Christian virtue, full of reprehensible pleasures tempting the pilgrim away from the steep and stony path of righteousness." He tells of an eleventh-century manuscript illustration showing monks on the ladder to heaven. One of them has leaned out too far, attracted by a flower, and he is falling off. Saint Anselm, Shepard says, specifically warned against the "duplicity of the garden," where the enjoyment of the senses was sin.[6] Most of the American Puritan Fathers believed the wilderness to be peopled by Satan, unredeemable heathens, and possibly witches.

Some secular interpretations of nature from the Greek and Roman Heritage have served Americans as alternative lenses. Virgil, for example, celebrates *tamed* nature, the pastoral, the life of the shepherd. More immediately, Americans received rather thoroughly secularized theories from the French and English Enlightenment of the seventeenth and eighteenth centuries. More than "received": it must be remembered that part of the attraction America held for many thinkers during those years stemmed from the fact that the New World was a stage upon which their theories were being acted out. If Rousseau told them that civilization corrupts, they could look to that stage to see the "noble savage"—if not the native American, at least the happy yeoman who went there to share his land. If Rousseau and Locke posited a state of nature in which people drew up their social contracts, there was the Mayflower Compact and others like it. If French physiocrats spoke of the primacy of free farmers, Jefferson could try to build a nation on that thesis. The "stages of civilization," from hunter to herdsman to stationary farmer to city dweller, were visible along lines of longitude moving west. Most important of all, the eighteenth-century idea of progress became, to Americans, synonymous with their history. The landscape would yield to "progress."

Enlightenment *ways* of thinking were as important as specific theories: the increasing tendency toward abstraction, category, philosophical law. Newton's tidy watchworks universe was a secular version of the Christian notion of nature as God's mind manifest, but less mysterious, less complex—reducible to a few static formulas which any reasonable man could grasp. Landscape, as I have mentioned, could be reduced to grid. Man became increasingly "economic man," land one of three sources of income, a natural *resource*. Time as well as space could be rationalized in the name of efficiency.

Americans were, they felt, the new prophecies fulfilled, so they were all the more eager to cut themselves off from older traditions, and translate the new ones into action. Progress on a national level was equated with success on a personal level, in the land of opportunity. The definition of the national mission, as we have seen, was spelled out in large part in Enlightenment language. Their sacred documents, the Declaration of Independence and the Constitution, leaned heavily on Locke and Montesquieu.

But then it wasn't as unanimous as that. Which "stage of civilization" should the culture aim for? Early on, the wilderness held fewer charms than it did in retrospect, after it began to recede. Crèvecoeur, that eighteenth-century booster of the American garden, warned his readers of Americans beyond the line of settlement. He assumed them to have been driven there by misfortune, greed, idleness, or debt; the society of such men, then, was predictably friendless, drunken, lazy, contentious, and wretched. In short, such people "appear to be no better than carnivorous animals of a superior rank, living on the flesh of wild animals when they can catch them."[7] Some of Mark Twain's sketches of the frontier West a century later bear Crèvecoeur out. But before Twain wrote them, easterners had already begun to romanticize nature, perhaps to sentimentalize it.

The gentleman farmer James Fenimore Cooper was one of the chief formulators of the American myth of the West, through his long series of Leatherstocking novels. The idea of stages of civilization presented him with problems he never solved. First of all, what of the Indians? His solution was really no solution: he always presented friendly and honorable Indians on the noble savage model, but also fierce and treacherous Indians, on the Puritan model. The noble ones helped the protagonist, Natty Bumppo, learn the mysteries of the universe which the wilderness unfolded. Yet the wilderness could also make men savage, as Crèvecoeur said. What ordinarily occurred, as Natty was pushed farther and farther west by the encroachment of civilization, was that Natty, a sort of Boy Scout leader, taught promising lads from the settlements his mysteries, then sent them back to help keep their homes free from the decadence of European tastes. For that image of

Europe, which I also mentioned as contributing to American national-ism, influenced American\ attitudes toward the stages of civilization.

It generally led Americans to prefer what Leo Marx calls "the middle landscape." Thomas Cole's rather pretentious series of five paintings entitled "The Course of Empire" gave clear pictorial prefer-ence to the third, the pastoral, stage. So did most of the landscape painters of the nineteenth century, and they were imitated by the popular engravers and lithographers. "The garden of the West": we have already touched on the importance of this myth to the American imagination. Notice that farmers have believed the theories about their own virtue and independence, and that this belief has had many political consequences. (Both American and Japanese farmers are subsidized by their governments, but, so they say, not adequately.) Thomas Jefferson, who envisioned a nation of educated, freehold farmers, felt that cities were "running sores on the body politic"; let decadent Europe be America's workshop.

Alexander Hamilton challenged this vision of an agrarian civiliza-tion. Practically speaking, his plan for a managed and balanced economy which would encourage manufacturing was the one Ameri-cans adopted from their political beginnings. Yet enough of the Jeffersonian vision remains as a deposit of sentiment so that, for example, the process of giving city dwellers an equal vote to that of farmers has not yet been completed (nor has it in Japan). "Progress" defined in Hamilton's way has been Americans' primary faith; so the "middle landscape" falls relentlessly into corporate hands.

A cluster of attitudes different from Jefferson's also continues to challenge the Hamiltonian system. Its source, as Perry Miller has taught us, is in American Puritanism. Jonathan Edwards, the great-est of the Puritan divines, speaks several times in *Personal Narrative* of the mysterious feelings which accompany—he hopes—a sense of being one of the few elected for salvation. They always happen when he is alone in nature, in a pasture praying, or in a meadow meditating. The landscape is full of "images or shadows of divine things," which, when meditated upon, can help a man toward that mystical experience which shows salvation. The American transcendentalists of a century later were in many ways more secular. The central figure of their movement had resigned his Christian ministry. But Emerson's image of some churchless form of regeneration lies at the core of the richly influential transcendental movement. I have quoted from his *Nature* before, to indicate a difference from Japanese thinking and feeling. The following image seems to me close to some Japanese experiences which have been written about: "Crossing a bare common, in snow puddles, at twilight, under a clouded sky, without having in my thoughts any occurrence of special good fortune, I have enjoyed a perfect exhilaration. I am glad to the brink of fear." Nature rejuvenates man. Within the "plantations of God, a decorum and sanctity reign." "Standing on the bare ground,—my head bathed by the blithe air, and uplifted into infinite space,—all mean egotism vanishes. I become a transparent eyeball; I am nothing; I see all; the currents of the Universal Being circulate through me; I am part or parcel of God."

The transcendentalists have been influential far beyond their numbers. The insights of Emerson, Thoreau, and their fellow traveler Walt Whitman illuminate some of the greatest American artists: composer Charles Ives, architects Louis Sullivan and Frank Lloyd Wright, and many authors. The tradition is as alive today as the so-called youth culture. Their influence has been most profound as unspoiled nature receded, however. Looking at ordinary Americans working at the time the transcendentalists were writing, the shrewd Tocqueville reported a different attitude: "In Europe, people talk a great deal of the wilds of America, but the Americans themselves never think about them; they are insensible to the wonders of inanimate nature, and they may be said not to perceive the mighty forests which surround them till they fall beneath the hatchet."

All of this barrage of theory about nature would seem to require of Americans a considerable flipping around of lenses. Individual Americans, I take it, really choose from the supply according to individual preferences or needs: "vale of tears," "garden of the West," "images and shadows of divine things," or, perhaps, for the denizen of Chicago or New York, a mosquito-infested nuisance—Langston Hughes's Harlemite "Simple" found it so. If a parallel catalogue of theories seems unnecessary in discussing the Japanese, it is because, as I have suggested, Japanese generally seem to have been less theoretical about the subject. Certain imported Buddhist philosophies have of course the otherworldly overtones of Christianity, but it seems safe to say that "Japanese religion," seen holistically in the manner of the aforementioned Professor Earhart, has celebrated an intuitive sense of the unity of all. Thus far I have emphasized differences, in history, geography, and spirit. I wish now to begin to show how most people in both cultures share, after all, a love of nature, though they have employed different means of making love to her.

In English, *natural* is about the most honorific adjective that can be applied to a range of nouns from *character* to *cosmetics*. The adjective has been turned into a noun, as in Bernard Malamud's fine novel *The Natural*, to denote a man so completely fitted for his vocation or a thing so abolutely appropriate for its use as to be matched by some elemental law—*natural law*, perhaps. *Naturally* is the adverb which characterizes one's immediate and total acceptance of a statement made by another: "You assert such and such? Naturally, I agree." The elemental quality is present also in its Japanese version. "The first character of the term meaning 'nature,' " says the author Takenishi Hiroko, ". . . may be read either *onozukara* or *mizukara* when it stands alone. The former means 'naturally' and the latter means 'oneself.' To me, Japanese patterns of thought are symbolized by the versatility of meaning in that character. 'Naturally' is at the same time 'Oneself,' and vice versa. . . . The fact that nature is self and self is nature is central in traditional Japanese thought."[8]

Professor Nakamura Hajime affords us a bridge from the language to the arts, folk and "high": "Generally speaking, the Japanese are inclined to search for the absolute within the phenomenal world. . . . [They] tend to esteem highly man's natural dispositions . . . to accept man's natural desires and sentiments just as they are." Professor Nakamura calls our attention to the prevalence of love as a theme in Japanese literature: "The acceptance of love as it is may be taken to be a unique characteristic of the Japanese"—as compared, that is, with other Asians. Donald Keene believes that the eroticism of much Japanese literature is attributable to the fact that in sexuality one finds nature in all its moods most intensely focused. Kenzo Tange says "the essence of Japanese culture as compared to Western culture . . . [is] the contrast between an animistic attitude of willing adaptation to and absorption in nature and a heroic attitude of seeking to breast and conquer it."[9]

The seasons in Japan are for the most part very regular, very predictable, and the poets and the folk have had a long time to detail precisely what and when certain sights and sounds and smells will reach the senses from the iris, the cicada, the frog, the cherry blossom. Proper haiku must contain a tag indicating which season they refer to. Traditionally, Japanese housewives display only one painting at a time in their tokonoma, the little alcove provided for that purpose, and these paintings, too, have seasonal tags which dictate at what time of year they're to be hung. A cyclical sense of the day, the year, and the lifetime informs all subjects and all moods among the folk and among the learned. Back to the unity of man and nature: when Yasunari Kawabata, the Nobel prize-winning novelist, tried to express this in an essay entitled *Japan the Beautiful and Myself*, here, very briefly, is how he went about it. He first quotes a poem by Dogen and another by Myoe.

> In the spring, cherry blossoms,
> in the summer the cuckoo
> In autumn the moon, and in
> winter the snow, clear, cold.

and

> Winter moon, coming from the
> Clouds to keep me company,
> Is the wind piercing, the snow cold?

Then he gives his assent to a sentence from Yashiro Yukio: "One of the special characteristics of Japanese art can be summed up in a single poetic sentence: 'The time of the snows, of the moon, of the blossoms—then more than ever we think of our comrades.' "[10] Such a manner of putting the thing makes even this exercise of abstracting out "nature" as a subject seem very artificial indeed.

Again, however, this caveat: Japan has its urban tradition in the arts—the Tokugawa fiction about life in the gay quarters, the ukiyoe showing actors and wrestlers and geisha, and so on. And so does the United States. Irving Howe has somewhere pointed out that one distinction between American and English literature is that the former has a much stronger urban tradition. This began with Whitman and Melville, and continued through Henry James and William Dean Howells, and became almost the dominant setting—and theme—in post–World War II literature, so much of which is the work of city-bred Jews and blacks. Nevertheless, nature has been the usual setting for most American writers, probably, and for the landscape painters who dominated the nineteenth century and continued to work in the twentieth. The canon of American literature, the "classics," most often portray the individual protagonist more or less alone in nature; a standard survey of American fiction would very possibly include the following works: a Cooper Leatherstocking novel, Thoreau's *Walden*, Hawthorne's *Scarlet Letter*, Melville's *Moby Dick*, Twain's *Huckleberry Finn*, Toomer's *Cane*, Faulkner's *The Bear*, and Hemingway's *The Old Man and the Sea*. In each of these works, nature is at the core, setting and theme. But then, the old contrast reasserts itself: nature is setting against which the protagonist proves himself. It is still "out there," either as friend or as antagonist. Thoreau tries to merge with nature, but compared to a Japanese writer he always seems theoretical, even masked in his ironies. Toomer's unschooled southern blacks come closest to a unity with their setting, but his educated blacks can't manage it. Ahab's whale, Faulkner's bear, Hemingway's big fish are all antagonists. Yet an important qualification must be made here. Striking the bear and the fish has more of love and respect in it than of hate. The confrontations are presented as fated events. The man proves his manliness. So goes the American tradition, to which I believe there is no counterpart. One isn't surprised to learn that the leading American conservation groups enroll large numbers of dedicated hunters and fishermen.

As a test case, we might look now at travel books by the two writers most beloved of their people, Bashō and Mark Twain. Both are archetypical characters, embodying in their writing much of what is best of the imagination of Japan and the United States. Their travel books would serve as models to their readers, of what to experience and how to experience it. (Being an American, I almost wrote, "what to *see* and how to *see* it.") Both peoples are energetic travelers, and their writers, too, tend to be a peregrinating lot.

In Bashō's *Narrow Road to the Deep North*[11] and Twain's *Life on the Mississippi*, the movement is from settled places, Edo and Hartford, Connecticut, toward unsullied nature. They paid homage to other than natural things—shrines and temples in Bashō's case, cities in Twain's—but the movement north and west is symbolically telling. The two centuries which separate the books, 1689 to 1883, seem to me less important than what the authors mean to their people, and what their pilgrimage into unspoiled landscape therefore signifies, as models for the Japanese and American imaginations. Twain's readers were predominantly eastern and urban, Bashō's urban as well: going west and going north was movement toward simplicity and purity.

Both books are first-person narratives interlaced with haiku, in Bashō's case, and stories and sketches, in Twain's. Each traveler makes his purpose clear. In earlier sketches, Bashō had told of his desire to "shake off the dust of the world," to become a "weather-exposed skeleton," to discover his "everlasting self which is poetry." In this one, his Buddhistic piety is also evident. Having arrived in the North, he writes that "for the first time, my mind was able to gain a certain balance and composure, no longer a victim to pestering anxiety." Twain's first lines are these: "The Mississippi is well worth reading about. It is not a commonplace river, but on the contrary is in all ways remarkable." Characteristically, he begins with statistics proving it to be not only remarkable, but big. As the book proceeds, however, other purposes become evident. The river that Twain is chiefly concerned with is the river of his boyhood and of his early days as steamboat pilot. He is creating legend about a historical situation in nature after that situation had radically changed. His job is both easier and harder than Bashō's: he must make the river symbol in the minds of readers who thought it perhaps only river; but he needn't work with a symbolic tradition already in the minds of his readers, as Bashō did.

Just as natural objects had long been tamed in Japan, so also had they long been storied. Bashō must see freshly places that had been seen previously by skilled poets.

I went to see the willow tree which Saigyo celebrated in his poem, when he wrote, "Spreading its shade over a crystal stream." I found it near the village of Ashimo on the bank of a rice-field. I had been wondering in my mind where this tree was situated, for the ruler of this province had repeatedly talked to me about it, but this day, for the first time in my life, I had an opportunity to rest my worn-out legs under its shade.

> When the girls had planted
> A square of paddy-field,
> I stepped out of
> The shade of a willow tree.

But then sometimes, in all modesty, he would refuse to try to outdo a predecessor. He visits a famous pine tree:

The entire beauty of this place, I thought, was best expressed in the following poem by Saigyo.

> Inviting the wind to carry
> Salt waves of the sea,
> The pine tree of Shiogoshi
> Trickles all night long
> Shiny drops of moonlight.

Should anyone dare to write another poem on this pine tree, it would be like trying to add a sixth finger to his hand.

(Seemly modesty in the man we think of as the greatest of the haiku poets; similarly Mark Twain asks George Washington Cable "to see" New Orleans for him.)

Occasionally Twain's comments ricochet off earlier ones, but mostly those are from European visitors, as often as not uncomplimentary. Twain, who *knew* the Mississippi Valley as perhaps no other man has, corrects the record which he believes others have skewed. He hasn't many sympathetic *printed* observers to work from. The fraternity of affectionate travel authors, past and present, that Bashō could assume was very much larger than Twain's.

Twain was working with traditions, too, but oral ones, old stories and modes of speech which he wishes to make legitimate through publication by a well-known author. That is aside from our concern, except that the occasional snatches of river scenery gain respectability, too, by the same stroke. Twain shows a somewhat embarrassing tendency, on occasion, toward the prettiness of description of the standard nineteenth-century travel book. Twain's lampoons of taste-less southern mansions and ersatz castles, and of drunkenness and violence along the river, prevent sentimentality. Nor can Bashō be accused of that emotional sin:

A storm came upon us and I was held up for three days.

> Bitten by fleas and lice,
> I slept in a bed,
> A horse urinating all the time
> Close to my pillow.

Bashō knows that nature can be vile and violent—but maybe hu-morously so.

A scene before my eyes:
>Roses of Sharon
>At the roadside
>Perishing one after another
>In the mouth of a horse.

Yet nature is never felt as adversary in Bashō's books. The inconven-
ience it sometimes causes is to be expected—travel was travail in those
days. It is quite another thing with Twain, necessarily. His central
purpose is to evoke the steamboating days of twenty years earlier, and
particularly to recount his own role during those days, as famous
steamboat pilot. Serving as pilot required amazing skills. He had to
learn to read the signs of all the hidden hazards—the snags and
sandbars along a twelve-hundred-mile stretch. Then, since the river
changes constantly, to reread them constantly. That he did so is
understandably a source of pride. He is aware of the cost these skills
levied on his sense of beauty, however. Here, I ask the reader's
indulgence of a long passage from this work, not only to let Twain
demonstrate that last point, but to make two others as well. First,
please notice, as he describes a sunset, that his images are almost
entirely visual, and arranged in the perspective that a landscape
painter would have used. Emerson, when he spoke of the curative
powers in nature, in the passage cited a few pages ago, made one
reservation: a person's eyesight must be good. I believe Bashō to be
less exclusively visual—but then so is Mark Twain in *The Adventures of
Huckleberry Finn*. This leads me to the second point. *Life on the Mississippi* was aimed at a genteel audience, and in such company a respectable nineteenth-century author maintains a certain conventional
stance toward nature. Notice the bookish diction of the passage, to be
contrasted later, as Leo Marx has done, with the diction of *Huckleberry
Finn*. The landscape painter and the travel-book writer seemed in
league to train us to respond to nature in an approved manner.
Something of the old American ambivalence toward nature is surely
involved. A half-educated boy of the lower orders such as Huck, or
perhaps Crèvecoeur's barbaric frontiersmen, could indulge themselves in nature with a sensory immediacy which was not granted the
polite and well-schooled. So to the long passage.

Now when I had mastered the language of this water, and had come to know every trifling feature that bordered the great river as familiarly as I knew the letters of the alphabet, I had made a valuable acquisition. But I had lost something, too. I had lost something which could never be restored to me while I lived. All the grace, the beauty, the poetry, had gone out of the majestic river! I still kept in mind a certain wonderful sunset which I witnessed when steamboating was new to me. A broad expanse of the river was turned to blood; in the middle distance, the red hue brightened into gold, through which a solitary log came floating, black and conspicuous; in one place a long, slanting mark lay sparkling upon the water; in another the surface was broken by boiling, tumbling rings, that were as many-tinted as an opal; where the ruddy flush was faintest, was a smooth spot that was covered with graceful circles and radiating lines, ever so delicately traced; the shore on our left was densely wooded, and the somber shadow that fell from this forest was broken in one place by a long, ruffled trail that shone like silver; and high above the forest wall a clean-stemmed dead tree waved a single leafy bough that glowed like a flame in the unobstructed splendor that was flowing from the sun. There were graceful curves, reflected images, woody heights, soft distances; and over the whole scene, far and near, the dissolving lights drifted steadily, enriching it every passing moment with new marvels of coloring.

I stood like one bewitched. I drank it in, in a speechless rapture. The world was new to me, and I had never seen anything like this at home. But as I have said, a day came when I began to cease from noting the glories and the charms which the moon and the sun and the twilight wrought upon the river's face; another day came when I ceased altogether to note them. Then, if that sunset scene had been repeated, I should have looked upon it without rapture, and should have commented upon it, inwardly, after this fashion: "This sun means that we are going to have wind to-morrow; that floating log means that the river is rising, small thanks to it; that slanting mark on the water refers to a bluff reef which is going to kill somebody's steamboat one of these nights, if it keeps on stretching out like that; those tumbling 'boils' show a dissolving bar and a changing channel there; the lines and circles in the slick water over yonder are a warning that that troublesome place is shoaling up dangerously; that silver streak in the shadow of the forest is the 'break' from a new snag, and he has located himself in the very best place he could have found to fish for steamboats; that tall dead tree, with a single living branch, is not going to last long, and then how is a body ever going to get through this blind place at night without the friendly old landmark?"

No, the romance and beauty were all gone from the river. All the value any feature of it had for me now was the amount of usefulness it could furnish toward compassing the safe piloting of a steamboat.

Necessarily, the river was adversary.

Yet in one extremely important way, Twain underrated himself. He couldn't, to repeat, find his proper voice as respectable author writing about the haunts of his younger days. But he was in the midst of a long struggle with *Huckleberry Finn*, at the time *Life on the Mississippi* was published, and in that book Twain saw the river through the eyes of Huck, perhaps an alter ego. If the Twain of *Life* seems conventional and a bit uncomfortable in describing his experiences in nature, his persona Huck does not. Huck's famous sunrise "poem" comes at a time in the narrative when he and his friend the runaway slave Jim are temporarily free of all the troubles the shore people have made for them.

Two or three days and nights went by; I reckon I might say they swum by, they slid along so quiet and smooth and lovely. Here is the way we put in the time. It was a monstrous big river down there—sometimes a mile and a half wide; we run nights, and laid up and hid daytimes; soon as night was most gone we stopped navigating and tied up—nearly always in the dead water under a towhead; and then cut young cottonwoods and willows, and hid the raft with them. Then we set out the lines. Next we slid into the river and had a swim, so as to freshen up and cool off; then we set down on the sandy bottom where the water was about knee-deep, and watched the daylight come. Not a sound anywheres—perfectly still—just like the whole world was asleep, only sometimes the bullfrogs a-cluttering, maybe. The first thing to see, looking away over the water, was a kind of dull line—that was the woods on t'other side; you couldn't make nothing else out; then a pale place in the sky; then more paleness spreading around; then the river softened up away off, and warn't black any more, but gray; you could see little dark spots drifting along ever so far away—trading scows, and such things; and long black streaks—rafts; sometimes you could hear a sweep screaking; or jumbled-up voices, it was so still, and sounds come so far; and by and by you could see a streak on the water which you know by the look of the streak that there's a snag there in a swift current which breaks on it and makes that streak look that way; and you see the mist curl up off of the water, and the east reddens up, and the river, and you make out a log cabin in the edge of the woods, away on the bank on t'other side of the river, being a woodyard, likely, and piled by them cheats so you can throw a dog through it anywheres; then the nice breeze springs up, and comes fanning you from over there, so cool and fresh and sweet to smell on account of the woods and the flowers; but sometimes not that way, because they've left dead fish laying around, gars and such, and they do get pretty rank; and next you've got the full day, and everything smiling in the sun, and the songbirds just going it!

Huck's "gars and such" correspond to Bashō's lice: these men tell the truth. And the truth for people closely acquainted with nature may be animistic.

> The passing spring,
> Birds mourn,
> Fishes weep
> With tearful eyes.

Or:

> Red, red is the sun,
> Heartlessly indifferent to time,
> The wind knows, however,
> The promise of early chill.

Huck, somewhat corrupted by a bit of schooling early in his trip down the river, relaxes into Jim's more familial relationship with nature.

It's lovely to live on a raft. We had the sky up there, all speckled with stars, and we used to lay on our backs and look up at them, and discuss about whether they was made or only just happened. Jim he allowed they was made, but I allowed they happened; I judged it would have took too long to *make* so many. Jim said the moon could a *laid* them; well, that looked kind of reasonable, so I didn't say nothing against it, because I've seen a frog lay most as many, so of course it could be done. We used to watch the stars that fell, too, and see them streak down. Jim allowed they'd got spoiled and was hove out of the nest.

Yet a difference still exists. One reason for *Huckleberry Finn*'s great importance to American literature is that it fused the vernacular landscape with vernacular language. Previously, American nature poetry was ordinarily handled in a bookish way; only a heightened poetic diction was considered appropriate—Twain himself occasionally lapsed into such language in *Life*. Twain in *Huck* is linguistically wed to his landscape. Yet the separation that we noted earlier still exists. " 'Scenery,' " Paul Shepard tells us, "comes from the Greek word for 'stage.' . . . The history of scenery is the history of painting and tourism. . . . Modern scenery-tourism has been the attempt to apply the esthetic learned from art to the landscape as a whole."[12]

Sentences such as the following pepper *Life on the Mississippi* (italics mine): "The scenery from St. Louis to Cairo—two hundred miles— is varied and *beautiful*." "We were approaching Hickman, a *pretty* town perched on a *handsome* hill." The landscape is *scenery*; appreciation of it is primarily visual, "out there," with only a hint of the observer: "I stood bewitched." Even Huck's description of the sunrise, quoted above, is arranged with the great care about perspective which we have noticed; in that passage, however, the sounds and smells appear as well, and Huck's relationship with nature is much more closely felt.

The form of the haiku limits Bashō to only a few images, of course, compared to Twain's freedom to use many. The gap between "scenery" and "painter," however, is hardly perceptible, the range of senses is broad, and the relationship between image and thought about the image is very close. (I switch here to translations[13] which I personally prefer to the foregoing.)

> Over the summer moor my horse would stroll:
> I find myself inside a landscape roll.

Or:

> O brightest mood of autumn, all night long
> I've strolled around the pond, in search of song.

The following is chillingly subjective at one point; then the subject is suddenly diffused into—what?

> Forgetting my umbrella, drizzle fell
> Upon my newly shaven head: Ah, well. . . .

Out of deference to the idea of literary form, perhaps one should compare these attitudes as they appear in two short poems, one by Bashō and one by Robert Frost. The subject is crows.

> Though usually hateful birds, the crows
> Are lovely, too, amid the morning snows.

Visual imagery and feelings about how that image transforms feelings, even moral feelings, all fused: outside and inside are one. Frost's poem is quite similar, but becomes a bit more conceptual.

> The way a crow
> Shook down on me

> The dust of snow
> From a hemlock tree
>
> Has given my heart
> A change of mood
> And saved some part
> Of a day I had rued.[14]

The rocky hills of the New England landscape have produced nature poets besides Frost whose terse and elliptical style resembles the Japanese; better than Emerson and Thoreau, Emily Dickinson can merge image and thought and feeling in a few words.

> A toad can die of light!
>   Death is the common right
> Of toads and men,—
> Of earl and midge
> The privilege.
>   Why swagger then?
> The gnat's supremacy
> Is large as thine.[15]

Isn't that rather close to the Japanese sensibility?

Back to travel books. Umemoto Seiichi's *Japan Here and There*, written for Westerners in 1959, could include not only haiku by Bashō but reproductions of paintings and photographs as well.[16] The United States has gradually compiled a large enough literature so that photographic travel books may contain bits of poetry as captions. The photographer seems to have pretty much taken over from the poet as guide in both cultures. In the United States, where grandly published books with line drawings once were displayed on the parlor table for all guests to see, now one finds beautiful photographs particularly of wild nature on the coffee table. An ecological message is hinted at, but the statistics, the boasts, the accompanying legends are missing. Japan, too, has its gorgeous books of nature photography.

Domestic tourism in Japan follows Bashō's model closely. The old meccas are still attractive, Kyoto, Nara, Ise, Kamakura, Matsushima, and of course Mount Fuji—every Japanese is expected to climb Fuji at least once in his lifetime. Those apparently remain the favorite goals for the countless official school trips, the company tours, the tour clubs of middle-aged ladies. Because of the Japanese practice of selecting beautiful natural sites for shrines and temples, one visits nature at the same time he is visiting a shrine or a temple. The size of the United States almost requires the vacationing family to choose between nature and national shrine. If shrines are the choice, the family heads for Boston, Philadelphia, and Washington. If nature is the choice, the chances are that the family will choose the farther West of Twain's *Roughing It* instead of the Mississippi. Sentiment for his old steamboats keeps a few families still on the river, though, and some people pay the equivalent of a trip to Europe to retrace his old voyages. (Donald Keene has retraced Bashō's routes, and found the memory of his visits very much alive in remote mountain villages.)

The occasional tour in Japan or family trip in the United States is one way in which old attitudes toward nature find expression nowadays. But during the rest of the year, day by day, Japanese of modest means live with their gardens and similarly situated Americans live with their yards. All kinds of evidence—research, the careers of real estate agents—demonstrate that most Japanese and most Americans are strongly driven to surround themselves with soil of their own, unlike some English and Scandinavians who do not spurn multifamily dwellings. It seems safe to assume, then, that these gardens and yards are practical statements of the going attitudes toward nature in the two cultures.

The first glimpse of a Japanese family garden is of something small and enclosed, of an American yard of something spacious and open. Outrageous land prices restrict the Japanese to a few square meters of shrubs, rocks, and plants outside their homes and inside their fences. A middle-class American can afford a lot from three thousand square feet to over ten thousand.

For the American, the rectangle of grass, with shrubs at the foundation of the house, two or three trees, and a circle or rectangle of flowers in the summer, is the norm. The Japanese garden should have all the ingredients of the larger landscape, rocks, water, trees, shrubs, flowers; the householder arranges them carefully in order to suggest the larger landscape. (I do not speak here of the work of professional gardeners, who may specialize in just rocks and sand, for example, in a flat garden, or the features of a mountain landscape.) The wall not only effectively closes out the turmoil of the city but emphasizes the *composition* of those elements. Emulating, I believe, the grounds of an English estate, and unwalled, the American lawn suggests space. The usual taboo against walls, which an ordinance in my little city makes official, leaves an American's front lawn contiguous with his neighbors', therefore compounding the sense of space.

If the American model is probably English, the Japanese is Chinese. As usual, Chinese concepts became very Japanese. The symmetry the Chinese insisted upon slipped off into a more comfortable form that honors movement, surprise, process. One important Chinese conception remained: gardening is a fine art. It has never ranked high among the arts in the Western hierarchy. Perhaps for this reason the appearance of an ordinary Japanese garden suggests that its owner has taken more care in arranging its elements than an American has.

Perhaps another ancestor of the American yard is the New England commons, where all the townsfolk's livestock grazed in common. For there is a social dimension to the American yard. As the English have used that word, it has suggested an enclosed place, such as a winter deer park. The absence of fences in the United States leaves the yard open for public scrutiny. High status is accorded not only to the neatness of the rectangles of grass—an astonishing number of Americans handle the chore of keeping them tidy, even on lots of sixty feet by sixty feet, with big power mowers—but also to their expanse. Little difference can be noticed between the style of architecture of the millions of postwar middle-class suburban homes and that of many very expensive dwellings, but the much broader stretch of lawn the rich can boast tells the difference.

If American yards are public, Japanese gardens are familial. Zen models for domestic gardens were for meditation. Elements were selected and composed to interpret nature. Space permitting, parts of a garden are always hidden from view. Well designed, it suggests more and more, just out of view. The American yard tends toward symmetry and tends to be all there, in full view. Americans, incidentally, begin to see the beauty of rocks, and use them more in landscaping, without, however, a sense of the mystique of rocks. "Man," writes Tange, "trembled before the incomprehensible forces (ke) that filled primeval nature and space." These forces were thought to "permeate" matter and space. "Driven by the compulsion to make the invisible, mysterious forces of nature and space tangible, man saw one particular substance stand out in the gloom of primeval nature—solid, immovable rock."[17] Rock, then, is a visible and palpable embodiment of mysteries and powers in nature—one could hardly imagine a more incontestable symbol.

Americans use the word *garden* to mean that part of the yard set aside for growing flowers or vegetables, or to mean the big, showy estates—sometimes now commercial—which self-consciously follow European precedents. In both instances, the organizing ideas seem to be symmetry and plenitude, as opposed to Japanese asymmetry and ellipsis. American owners of even modest homes may have both flowers and vegetables, probably in rectangular patches. As a student has pointed out to me, Americans grow their flowers in rows to be harvested. The "harvested" flowers, taken into the house for "bouquets" bear no resemblance to Japanese flower arrangements: the former are relatively unstudied and again, plenteous, while the latter are very carefully composed and spare. Again, the latter suggest landscape: the *relationship* of the flower to the rest of nature is insisted upon, while the American composition of flower, leaf, and vase is isolated out from their origins. The Japanese prefer buds— process?—the Americans full bloom—perfection?

Since popular sociologists began writing earnestly about American suburbanites in the 1950s, conventional wisdom has held that they tend their yards only to conform to their neighbors' expectation, and that they find the chore a nuisance. Herbert Gans learned that a good many Levittowners find pleasure in working in their yards, particularly those who had moved out from the city. Furthermore, he says that neighbors' demands are minimal, only requiring that the yard is respectable—in fact, *too* much work in the yard is frowned on. My own observations bear out both his findings. Many people simply enjoy growing things. Still, the social dimension of the yard presents some complicated cultural questions. Is it a vestigial puritanical insistence on following one's fellows' actions or a democratic pressure for conformity? The large "picture window," *facing the street*, that is stock in postwar houses reinforces the gesture of appearing open before one's neighbors. Do they say, "We are open for all to see?" The forerunner of the picture window was the broad and open front porch. Before radio and television dragged people inside, Americans could sit there to chat with passing neighbors—very public, again, but also sociable. In Japan where the inside of the house is composed with the order of the garden, the wall emphasizes the organic relationship of the family order and nature's. Would it be reaching too far to conclude that if Japanese housing arrangements dramatize the order of the family in nature, American arrangements dramatize the social importance of shared space? The Japanese tendency is to relate the building to nature, the American, at least until recently, to wall out nature. For a change does seem to be occurring, and this change is signaled in architecture, perhaps influenced by Frank Lloyd Wright's affection for Japanese architecture.

In any case, the models described seem to be those in use where space and money permit Japanese and Americans of moderate incomes to practice them. Even in the denser portions of their cities, where many families must share a building, both peoples have been adept in importing nature into the inner cities. Casual observation hints that the population of songbirds, potted plants, and aquariums is slightly heavier in Japanese danchi than in American apartment buildings, but few Americans deny themselves some natural object in the home. The balconies that are standard in the former are useful not only for airing bedding but also for sunning the geranium. That seems small compensation, since the appalling rise in land prices in Japan threatens to drive more and more people into multifamily complexes. Very high on the list of political complaints by the Japanese is that so little space in Japan's major cities is devoted to parks and playgrounds. Then there is periodic flight—the rush to the countryside of urban people in both places on weekends and during holidays. It's becoming difficult to flee far enough. In the United States, the motorized camper business was over a billion dollars in 1972, and these vehicles park hub to hub in the great national parks of the West—if computers have given them reservations. Flight into nature for regeneration has always been a central theme in American literature: the protagonist of Saul Bellow's *Henderson the Rain King* has to go all the way to Africa, and that's where Kenzaburo Oë's "Bird" longs to go, in *A Personal Matter*. Bellow's intent is in part comic, working off the old tradition. Oë intends Bird's dream to be fantastic. To what extent has the potent old emotion about nature been reduced to mere sentimentality or fantasy or even bitter humor? One could as well read Bellow's and Oë's books as complaints that Henderson and Bird had to stretch their imaginations so far.

I have mentioned that in some way, however, attitudes at least in the

United States seem to have changed. This may be a case of the reverse of the "convergence theory" which holds that industrialized nations become more and more alike, so that Japan would increasingly resemble the United States. Instead the United States may increasingly resemble Japan. If Christianity is losing its proscriptive influence in American life, any suspicion of nature which it may have imparted would be dying out; and of course the frontier—nature to be "conquered"—is now only a few small patches in the West and in Alaska. In fact, some Americans have lost even a sensible awe of nature. Perhaps confusing cute cartoon bears with real bears, people are mauled in national parks nearly every summer. Prideful of the power of their automobiles, Americans every winter ignore blizzard warnings and find themselves buffeted about by nature's ferocity, not infrequently fatally. The Japanese mountaineers who die seem a different matter: mountaineers calculate risks and take them anyhow. At any rate, some of the historic ambiguities in Americans' attitudes toward nature seem to be resolving themselves: their affection for nature, the profit system permitting, seems unencumbered.

The bitter irony in all this is apparent to everybody. Now that more people have the leisure to enjoy nature, it is disappearing before them, and the industrial system which is apparently necessary to provide that leisure was chiefly responsible for spoiling it. As registered by political pressures, the public sensitivity to outrages against the environment is stronger in Japan than in the United States at this moment. The variables are different. Japan's industry and its cities are more densely packed than America's, so pollution is more densely concentrated. Nobody in the United States, so far as is reported, has suffered a fatal illness as a result of an overdose of air or water. Then, Japan needn't worry much about certain higher priorities in the American culture: war, racism, poverty (people *do* suffer incurable illnesses from an underdose of food in the United States). The Japanese can afford to put nuisances at the top of their public priority list, alongside peace. Even so, progress is very slow in Japan, despite numerous laws on the books. Slower in the United States. Automobiles are the prime offenders, and Detroit seems to respond to the Mazda and Honda engines with propaganda rather than engineering skills.

The Japanese marriage to their homeland has lasted for a long time, and their infidelities, their flirtation with gaudier mistresses, have been of relatively short duration. Yet their wife is frailer than the Americans'. The Americans' land is robust, but their attentions have been rapine, and their affection has never been unambiguous. And they seem less eager to swear off dalliance with shiny profits. Both peoples must necessarily change their ways, or their old wives will curl up and die.

CHAPTER 5

Workaday and Holiday

The fact that most people in Japan and the United States, so deeply immersed for so long in nature, have adjusted to the vertiginous changes required by their new "secondary environment" surely testifies to the marvelous adaptability of the human animal. The difficulties in making the change have been, as one would expect, similar in many respects. The timing of their preparation for change differed, however. Urban life on a scale which bears some resemblance to the contemporary is older in Japan: Edo and New York were founded at about the same time, early in the seventeenth century, but the former had about a million residents by the early nineteenth, when New York had about one hundred thousand. Many of those nineteenth-century New Yorkers, however, had already had a century's preparation for life with industrial technology, having long known about spinning and knitting machines, for example, and division of labor in manufacture. (Their European forebears, Lewis Mumford says, learned about routine very early, through the example of monasteries.) It is to that aspect of the secondary environment that I will particularly address myself here. Perhaps it is the most difficult. Urban problems today are certainly different in degree from those of old Edo or London. But where they differ in kind, they do so, I believe, because of technology, often industrial technology.

The demands that industrialization makes on a culture include the rationalization, fragmentation, and regimentation of much of what people do, particularly at work. The time they measure out their lives by is no longer biological time, or cyclical, the kind that matters to people close to nature. The efficient industrial man ought even to suppress psychological time, with its whimsical leaps into the past, future, and fantasy. Rather, time becomes "public," as Isaac Newton put it, "mathematical" and mechanical. Industrial workers in America quite understandably focus many of their animosities on the time clock and its minion the conductor of the time-motion study, the machine and the man who are both arrogantly disrespectful of their felt time. Laurence Sterne dramatized modern man's incredible enslavement to the clock by creating a character who made love to his wife only at a given hour on a given day of the week. Space is no longer personally sensed surroundings, with their mnemonic and symbolic meanings; it becomes charted, mathematically labeled, walled in as factory or office for the sake of efficiency. A woman is to sit just here, a man just there, for reasons deduced from management theory. Telescopes, micro-scopes, maps, transform it to abstraction. The movement of a worker's hand is dictated by the calculus of its relation to the speed of the assembly line belt, however inimical that might be to the normal functioning of the nervous system. Ordinary social relationships are subordinated to the demands of the job. More and more communica-tion is electronic, devoid of the look on the face of the speaker who is giving instructions. One might still work communally as before, but under constraint to speak only about the business at hand. The Sony factory is no place for work songs, nor is the General Electric plant any place for harvest dances. In fact, as Marx remarked long ago, the individual worker probably never even sees the harvest.

The ledger which is at the center of the operation reduces the concrete world of steel and men to abstractions, yen and dollars neatly in a row. The whole bureaucracy which springs up to serve these abstractions compounds them. The white-collar workers in the banks, the insurance companies, the reinsurance companies, the advertising agencies, the legislatures, the corporation law offices, the maritime law offices, the tariff law offices, the accounting firms, the cost analysis firms, all the various consulting firms—how removed they are from the primary world of pigs, coal mines, and rice plants. There is an accompanying abstraction of human relationships as well. What an array of faceless people is responsible for electricity, or mail, or Brazilian coffee arriving inside a home in Chicago or Osaka! One might pass a subway ticket taker three hundred times a year, and never acknowledge his face. Who are those people who handle a city dweller's government, his health, his savings account?

The farmer is a jack-of-all-trades, skilled in many crafts. The city and the factory demand a division of labor. When the latter is at its worst, in the form of the assembly line, the only part of a worker's total person that is required may be an arm skilled in one motion only. The whole man is reduced on most jobs—typist, file clerk, steel puddler, riveter. Perhaps the only large groups of people in Japan and the United States whose jobs require a wide range of skills are the housewives.

Division of labor fragments the whole person, the industrial city fragments traditional social arrangements. Mobility of workers is breaking up the extended family in both countries, with results which we can't fully see yet. Both cultures more and more abandon their old folks. Margaret Mead believes, furthermore, that the alienation of young people is a result in part of their having grown up without grandparents: in the old days, children always had allies around in their grandparents, while now they remain defenseless until they are old enough to form strong peer groups.

This old Western habit of abstracting experience had to be learned quickly by the Japanese. That they accomplished this puzzled Westerners, according to Fosco Maraini. Wasn't this possible only to heirs of a long Western tradition? "Japan," he says, "is the country that disturbs Things in General. . . . Things in General are blatantly ridiculed."[1] That the Japanese learned these lessons, for better or worse, in less than a century after 1868 seems to me as miraculous as their post–World War II economic boom, based as it was on that feat.

The English yeoman who emigrated to America may have had a longer preparation for submitting his labor to the dissection of reason, but the newly initiated Japanese laborer had a different kind of advantage, in getting used to change. The Englishman had, typically, been an independent freeholder, but the Japanese farmer had necessarily learned how to cooperate. Rice farming depends upon a very careful communal use of water, historically coordinated by a local leader who was prosperous and persuasive. One easily sees how these old habits translate into factory work. But then there is another twist: apparently some time in America made a worker easier to manage than his newly arrived English cousin. An important lieutenant to Andrew Carnegie in his steelworks said in 1903, "My experience has shown me that Germans, Swedes, and what I denominate 'Buck-wheats'—young American country boys, judiciously mixed, make the most effective and tractable force you can find. . . . Welsh can be used in limited numbers. But mark me, Englishmen have been the worst class of men I have had anything to do with."

Those who were to man the factories had to make adjustments in their lives. Similarly many leaders of both cultures entered into industrialism with a good deal of reluctance. That it was necessary to do so, however, was readily apparent. Only some 17,000 British and French soldiers were required to subdue the entire Chinese Empire (and sack some treasured bits of it) during the Opium Wars of 1845–1857. When this news reached Japan, one of its leaders conclud-ed, "bravery is not enough."[2] Perry's visit clinched it: in order for Japan to survive, it would have to adopt the techniques of the West, including the industry which Meiji leaders hastened to introduce. The slogan *sonnō jōi*, "Revere the Emperor, Repel the Barbarians," was soon replaced by *fukoku kyōhei*, "Enrich the Nation, Strengthen Its Arms." When, soon, the implications of swallowing the latter slogan hook, line, and sinker became apparent, Meiji leaders began to preach, *Toyō no dōtoku, Seiyō no gakugei*, "Western techniques, Japa-nese spirit," or "Eastern ethics, Western science."[3] The Meiji period was busy with debates about how to retain the Japanese spirit in the face of the necessity for Western techniques. As the century moved toward its close, intellectual leaders placed an increasingly greater emphasis on the achievements of the Japanese spirit, as they became increasingly disenchanted with what industrialism and imperialism had done to the Western spirit. Yet even late-century slogans such as *fukko*, "Restore the Old," failed to slow the industrialism which neces-sarily underlay the strong military required for survival.

The development of manufactures, as recommended by Alexander Hamilton during the first American presidency, involved a number of public goals, but a central one was, as in the case of Japan, national defense. The young country was, after all, weak and vulnerable; its very existence as a republic seemed a threat to the European monarchs. Even the agrarian Jefferson finally gave in to the necessity of industry when it became clear to him during the Napoleonic wars that a British embargo had a devastating effect on the American economy. The pressures on the United States to encourage the growth of industry were less dramatic than those on Japan, but they were not dissimilar. The governments of both countries, then, threw their weight behind manufacturing. Yet there have been traditions in both cultures that have opposed industrialism, as a calling unworthy of the best in the two peoples. Practically, this sentiment has been generally ineffective, but it has nevertheless tinted people's attitudes toward the mill and the factory. Both countries began, classically, with textiles. The English had a law forbidding the emigration of technicians of textile machinery, but the United States smuggled some such men onto its shores and others used their own initiative to go there. Japan simply invited technicians to come to teach its people, and sent its own bright young men abroad to learn. Perhaps some clue to the two peoples' idea of the status of the industrial worker at that time can be deduced from the fact that in the textile industry both hoped to use the daughters of poor farmers to operate the machines. The young women were willing enough to enter the mills, in order to save money for dowries, and to help their families—in New England, those farming on the rocky soil needed all the help they could get, as did Japanese tenant farmers. Mill owners in both countries assumed that these young women would work for only a few years, so they needed simple machinery suitable for a quick turnover of labor. Women in both countries lived in dormitories and underwent moral and cultural training after their weary work hours were done. In Lowell, Massachusetts, the boss looked after the young woman's religious observances; in Japan, he helped arrange her marriage. Perhaps it is indicative of the two cultures that soon American factories moved away from a paternalistic system, whereas in Japan such mills still persist in little cities. Almost immediately, the American worker was left to his own devices after hours, while some paternalism remains in most Japanese enterprises.

Other important differences in the early organization of factory work must be mentioned. In Japan, men who had mastered skills for which Japan had no precedent, like metal shipbuilding, were of course very scarce. Since that particular industry was imperative to a strong Japan, these men were granted high status. Ronald Dore sees in this scarcity the source of some of the more benign aspects of contemporary factory organization, such as lifetime job tenure and automatic raises for the industrial elite. Furthermore, fewer than 5 percent of the Japanese were wage workers in Tokugawa Japan. The Western market mentality concerning labor, then, had but a slight chance to gain favor, particularly given old Confucian patterns of mutual personal obligation between employer and employee. In addition, some international standards of decent working conditions had already been established by the time Japan opened its first big factories. This is only one of many advantages that Dore sees for "late developers." They need not repeat the mistakes of the groping pioneers in industrialization.

Generally, the ancient but rapidly changing social order of Japan seemed to adjust more readily to the entirely new categories required by industrialism than did America's relatively open system. Jefferson's hostility toward industrialism rested in part on his egalitarian vision: he foresaw that manufacturing would generate a boss-worker arrangement inimical to democracy. He of course understood that the Americans had imported ideas of social class from Europe. The American Puritans of the early Tokugawa period ranked parishioners according to religious criteria which separated the saints and the sinners, but also along property lines, from the freeholders to the unpropertied to the indentured. The Revolution and its aftermath revealed rather distinct splits between creditors and debtors. Yet the United States was socially about as open as any nation on earth, for white men only, at the time it had to cope with the new fact of mill owner and mill worker. In Tokugawa Japan, the official hierarchy put the samurai at the top, followed by farmers, artisans, and merchants. The facts by the end of that period already defied the law: many samurai were weak, and many merchants were strong. The relatively easy transferral to the factories of a compliant work force is probably more easily attributable to old habits of cooperation under a leader than to official stratification. For the new industrial order did require a compliant and disciplined work force. The social order which industrialists inherited from the past by no means assured a cadre of such people in either culture, for both were ambivalent on the matter of unquestioning respect for authority.

The Japanese, perhaps, somewhat less so than the American. The Confucian code of the Tokugawa period is about as unequivocal as can be on the matter of obedience of servant to master. For the most part, that code transferred easily to the industrial setting. Yet the samurai tradition condoned and even honored loyal disobedience. That practice was evoked only rarely among the samurai, as "civil disobedience" is evoked only rarely by Americans. But both traditions are alive in factories in both countries today.

Some Christian sects emphasize loyalty to authority more than others. Christian scriptures contain admonitions to servants to obey their masters as surely as the Confucian texts of Tokugawa. Such writings have even been quoted by owners against striking workers in the United States, but surely not for the past half a century. The other side of the American coin is the religious tendency toward antinomianism, as old as the first New England colonies, and the political tradition of civil disobedience in the name of some law higher than man-made law, a tradition stretching from some of the revolutionists through Thoreau to Martin Luther King, Jr. The waning authority of the boss which is presently visible in both Japan and the United States must be seen in the perspective of the general movement on this planet to question authority, centuries old in "modern" countries. No one who looks at that evolution could be much surprised at reports of workingmen's unrest in either country.

But then it is a mistake to speak of the American labor force in such simplistic terms: it has come from all over the world. Japan has always been able to depend upon indigenous workers, with a smattering of Chinese and Koreans at the fringes. Variations in the workingman's culture occur there between the old urban working class and the newer one in the prefectures. In the United States, on the other hand, the workingman's culture is complicated by all the ambiguities of the history of American immigration, perhaps the greatest mass migration in history. The early Yankee or Anglo-American workers were products of rocky New England farms, "hard scrabble" operations. The Irish who left home to escape hunger and English persecution of the 1840s found in America only the grubbiest jobs, digging canals and building beds for the railroads; at the doors of the factories they saw signs saying "No Irish Need Apply." So it has been with subsequent waves of immigrants, first from northern and western Europe, then from southern and eastern Europe. Factory jobs have been thought of as better than what was available to most first-generation immigrants. Americans of African ancestry, however, have been out of phase: one of the oldest groups in America, dating probably since 1619, they didn't enter the industrial force in any numbers until the time of the labor shortages of World War I. The point of all this is that for newcomers, factory jobs looked good, while for those who had moved beyond them, they looked bad. All the complexities of attitudes of various ethnic and national groups toward all the others, all the jealousies and animosities, are distilled in this history. It has been lodged in the whole array of ugly and insulting terms for the many groups: "only a 'Hunky' (or a 'Greaser' or a 'Wop') would do that work." Some Americans are still not fully graduated from those habits of mind. Such attitudes were underscored by anti-Catholic and anti-Jewish religious prejudices, and gained "scientific" sanction in the days of social Darwinism. While the Japanese have been hierarchical, too, in their social thought, no Japanese industrialist could lend to his condescension toward his workers "racial" or religious prejudice. He was always dealing with Japanese, inferior to himself only in social status. The strain of Jeffersonian egalitarianism has never died out in America, but for many white Anglo-Saxon Protestants, people of different ethnic or religious backgrounds were excluded from participation in that vision.

The massive immigration into the United States lasted until early in the 1920s when it became clear, particularly to labor leaders, that the country had accumulated a surplus of workers. Before about the time of World War I, labor shortages had influenced the market, and American workers were consequently paid better than their European counterparts. In Japan, rising birthrates in the nineteenth century, and increased productivity on the farms, released younger sons to the labor market, and periodically, as in the 1920s, there have been more workers than jobs. (Presently, they suffer from a labor shortage—or, perhaps more exactly, underemployment of large numbers of people.)

Related to the chronic labor shortage in the United States until about 1920 was the large fact of the frontier. Theoretically, at least—and political leaders often preached the theory—the frontier acted as a "safety valve" for discontented workers back east. Practically, most farmers near the frontier were farmers from earlier frontiers, plus immigrants from Germany and the Scandinavian countries, but, until the open land was virtually all claimed in the 1890s, the urban worker could tell himself that if his job became intolerable he could always pack up and head west. No such psychological safety valves existed, of course, for the Japanese worker, except for relatively small numbers who emigrated to the United States, Canada, Brazil, and elsewhere. After the United States excluded Orientals from immigration in 1924, one of these valves closed. Popular support in Japan during the 1930s for expansion into Asia is somewhat better understood in the light of this fact.

Also related to the labor shortage and the fact of the frontier was the pressure of the success ethic in America. That ethic in its Western form was introduced into Japan, and the slogan *risshin shusse*, "make something of yourself," gained currency in the Meiji period. Yet the official expectation was that people would improve themselves for the common weal, not the private, and when officials decided that the private was gaining too much favor, they abandoned the slogan. The historical facts of labor shortage and open frontier in America for much of the nineteenth century kept the doors to success there wide open, for white Anglo-Saxon Protestants. If few workingmen actually moved west, not a few saved from their relatively high wages and began their own enterprises. The French visitors Tocqueville and Chevalier were astonished in the 1830s and 1840s by the ease with which Americans could rise from modest beginnings to financial success. But by the end of the century, the amount of savings required for the prosperity of a new business venture began to rule out such easy victories. The demon inside men imploring them to rise in the world, and nagging them with the accusation "failure" if they did not, was not silenced, however, when doors actually began to close. A good many American workers still blame themselves for being "merely" workers.[4] It is my impression that while the success demon has a much more hospitable environment in Japan than in other Asian countries, while Meiji slogans and the postwar examination system in the schools have fed it, and while studies of Japanese workers turn up an occasional expression of self-dissatisfaction, the demon has finally nothing like the same hold on the Japanese bowels that he has on the American.

Then there is the matter of theory, or rather, historically, of theoreticalness. Laissez faire, bolstered by a peculiar reading of Christianity and of such "sciences" as biology and anthropology, gained in the late nineteenth century the status of an orthodoxy. Industrialists were told, and a good many of them were happy enough to believe, that they could not in all conscience become sentimental about the plight of their workers. Their proper duty was to make profits, and in order to make profits labor must be accounted for on the cost side of the ledger. The worker was of necessity an abstraction. These attitudes became, through court decisions, the law of the land. Corporations were officially labeled "persons." The fiction was legally maintained that the person who had just emigrated from Bohemia to work for United States Steel was the equal in the eyes of the law of that "person" United States Steel, but in practice the latter benefited more from the interpretation than the former. The Constitution held that no man could be deprived of life, liberty, or property without due process of law, and strikes were held to be conspiracies which deprived those persons of property. This fiction was not finally and completely eradicated until 1936.

Here the point is that the Japanese entrepreneur might also exploit his workers, even with governmental encouragement, but they were exploited as workers, rather than abstractions, and the excuse was not a fiction but a reality of corporate and national power. Furthermore, the tradition of paternalism has ordinarily been reciprocal: one takes, but one must also give, and the etiquette of this relationship is clearly established. Early in the history of Japanese industrialism, from 1910 on, big firms established the *keiei-kazoku-shugi* policy for industrial relations, patterned after the ideal family business. As in such a business, workers were instructed that they shared the interests of their employers. The system was clearly hierarchical, but those at the top promised lifelong employment, living wages, and various welfare provisions. In those days, American workers, as I have said, were struggling against the legal fiction of equality with their bosses, as well as those bosses' practical power to prevent collective reprisal in the form of strikes, boycotts, and the like. Actual working conditions were often onerous and dangerous in Japan as in the United States. Yet a theory whereby those conditions could be ameliorated in a humane manner won acceptance in the circles of power, at a time when the same could not be said of the United States.

Two comments might be made about the history of the Japanese which could explain a worker's attitude toward his lot in life. For one thing, his work has always been associated with the national destiny and that, for a compact and homogeneous people, is a more visible goal than, ordinarily, for the sprawling and heterogeneous American people. At first, as I have said, workers would help the nation catch up with the West; then they would contribute to the wars with China and Russia, then the Greater East Asian war; more recently, to recovery, then to the economic miracle of fantastic growth. I do not have any information about how much ordinary workers today are moved by the notion of "Japan, Incorporated," but compelling evidence does exist that members of the industrial elite, who have gained permanent employment with solid companies, feel very much a part of those enterprises. Other reasons may exist for that feeling, but it's enough to say that indeed they are a part of the enterprises, for life, with guaranteed promotions. American workers change jobs more often, particularly when they are young, and identify measurably less frequently with the companies for which they work.

The other historical fact which, since the Occupation, might influence the Japanese worker's attitude toward his job is that the educational system gives everybody the theoretical chance to get enough formal schooling to lift him beyond blue-collar work. This theory holds for the United States as well, of course, but its culture places much less emphasis on the system of examinations which are rungs on the ladder up. In fact, social mobility, the incidence of young people getting jobs ordinarily considered preferable to those of their fathers, is about equal in the United States and Japan.

We have noticed the rice farmer's habit of cooperation, the English yeoman's independence. We have also noticed that New England textile mill owners soon abandoned paternalism, unlike their Japanese counterparts. Japanese workers still tend after hours to associate with social groups formed on the job, while Americans tend to think of their jobs as unimportant parts of their lives, not to be carried away at quitting time. The contrast is not quite as sharp as that, however. A study of a team of Americans making steel tubes detailed the careful teamwork required in the job, and reported that all members of the team, from more to less skilled, liked the work. Furthermore, that work group carried over into a social group after quitting time. (United States Steel closed the plant.)[5] That pattern is apparently rather exceptional in the United States, but ordinary in Japan. An American anthropologist working in a Japanese factory was astonished to see his fellows retire at quitting time to play *go* (similar to chess or checkers) together in a game room in the factory. Friends also may leave the factory together, to go to a sake bar or pachinko (a kind of pinball machine) parlor. Historically, workers at a given American factory would live nearby, and might stop off together at a neighborhood saloon, but now their homes are dispersed, and the typical scene at quitting time is of workers hurrying to their individual automobiles, on their way home. The workingman's saloon still exists in the United States, but as social center its importance has diminished with the move of factories to the suburbs. In days when labor union morale was higher than it is today, the American worker derived some social nourishment at the union hall, but I am told that most such places are quite lifeless these days. The importance of their social group to the Japanese people has often been remarked. We have known since the Elton Mayo studies of almost a half century ago that the social context is also very important to the American blue-collar worker. The American culture seems to provide fewer means than the Japanese for satisfying this desire. Is it possible that the highly praised American individuality is a mystique, belief in which leads to unfulfillment?

If the two governments have wished, historically, to encourage workingmen's sense of participation in the national economic enterprise, they have seldom so indicated by their actions. Through most of the political history of the industrial period, they have been extraordinarily generous with entrepreneurs, but careless about ensuring that those men shared their receipts equitably with the workers who helped earn them. Particularly during the first half century or so of the period, owners exploited their workers in ways that seem today merciless: long hours, low pay, miserable and unsafe working conditions. Workers' attempts to win collectively through unions improvements which they were powerless to win singly suffered steady harassment until 1936 in the United States and 1946 in Japan.

The labor movement began in both countries among skilled workers, such as printers and shoemakers, in the early nineteenth century in America, and among ironworkers, ship carpenters, wood sawyers, printers, plasterers, and railroad engineers in Japan in the 1890s. Leadership in union building came mostly from within the working class in the United States, from intellectuals in Japan. Some, such as Takano Fusataro, studied in the United States and learned lessons from the supremely pragmatic Samuel Gompers. Both labor movements have historically remained nontheoretical in their demands, concerning themselves with questions of factory safety, restrictions on child labor, and such. Yet a parallel theme runs through both movements in their early stages: the basic threat to a workingman's humanity posed by the very fact of the factory system. The American Knights of Labor, which flourished after midcentury, suggested in its very name a hope to recoup lost dignity. An early leader, Uriah Stephens, objected to the kind of unionism which had been merely economic, the "trade" union: "It was only because the trade union failed to recognize the rights of man," he said, "and looked only to the rights of the tradesman—i.e., the wage earner—that the Knights of Labor became a possibility."[6] After the Knights' demise in the mid-1880s, no important labor organization in the United States troubled itself with these larger questions of human dignity. Directly, at least. Their attempts to gain more money, decent working conditions, and the legal right to collective bargaining aimed at the same goal through less idealistic methods.

The early Japanese counterpart to Stephens might be the aforementioned Takano. Addressing some workers, he, too, pressed the subject of human dignity, largely conceived: "You workers . . . are people without capital who provide a living for others than yourselves. One of your arms and one of your legs are, so to speak, devoted to the support of society." Reminding them of the disaster that befalls workers and their families when they become old or crippled, he concluded, "You are really as helpless as a candle in the wind."[7]

Today, only about one-third of the workers of the two labor forces are in unions. The craft union tradition in the United States gave way in the 1930s to industrial unionism, organized into the Congress of Industrial Organizations, which now coexists with the old elitist American Federation of Labor. Many local unions in many places are somnolent, except during periodic wage negotiations. Since the war, the Japanese labor movement has become more ideological, and unions such as those of teachers and of workers in certain heavy industries seem seriously so. Yet 90 percent of the unions are "enterprise unions," "left wing in ideology, right wing in action."[8]

The Japanese political parties which would improve the condition and prestige of workingmen, the parliamentary Communists, the Socialists, and the small Social Democratic party, do not get a chance to do so, except in many of the big metropolitan governments. Their collective popular strength nationally rivals that of the conservative Liberal Democratic party, but the kinds of coalitions which have won some city elections have not been effected on a national level. In the United States, the unionized workingman began to gain considerable political power as the New Deal entered its second phase in 1935 and 1936. After a kind of dignification during World War II, when American industry managed its own miracle of production, and a kind of twilight glow during the Truman administration, the American blue-collar worker has generally lapsed again into oblivion. The noble figure of post office murals of the 1930s and war propaganda posters of the 1940s has been displaced by Archie Bunker, the ignorant, bigoted, and harried protagonist of the most popular American TV series of 1971–1972 and subsequent seasons. The naturalistic fiction which celebrates the workingman had a vogue in Japan in the 1920s, in the United States in the 1930s, and in Japan again just after the war. If by chance workers ever took any satisfaction from this sort of literature, they can hardly do so presently, when such writing is clearly out of fashion.

A certain stream of more or less anonymous history in both cultures may influence the manner in which *skilled* laborers view their life. That tradition celebrates the skills, difficulties, and even dangers of certain crafts. For most Americans, white-collar jobs are more prestigious than blue, even though they may pay less and perhaps challenge the intelligence no more. A garage mechanic, for example, who graduates to parts manager, a job involving pieces of paper and a necktie, may guard that distinction jealously. Before the war, the Japanese officially recognized the higher status of white-collar workers *(shokuin)* than blue *(kōin)*. The importance of that distinction is diminishing nowadays, however, so that, for example, many Japanese blue-collar workers wear coat and tie to and from work, and change to working clothes at the plant. Although American law has never officially recognized the superior status of white-collar workers, an open secret is that judges have often de facto done so. A good many workers in both cultures, in any case, scorn the distinction. The same look of bemusement may be seen in the eyes of construction workers in both countries as they watch soft-handed young men with neckties and briefcases gingerly stepping around their powerful equipment: They know who *really* gets the work done. The term *pencil pusher* is one of contempt among American workers. Centuries ago, a Japanese wrote this poem:

> I start work in spring
> Making willow-wood buckets
> With no time for rest.
> Now and then I steal a glance
> At the orange-tree blossoms.

Another old poem:

> The dust of our saw
> Has the fragrance of flowers
> In a mountain breeze.
> The breeze strews our sawdust blooms
> From the sharp teeth of the saw.

And:

> When the spring arrives
> And I sit outside, working,
> I am never bored.
> With a chisel in my hand
> I can raise flowers from stones.[9]

Lore about the crafts in the United States, where a greater premium is placed upon strength and courage than on poetry, is of a more rough-hewn sort. The pile driver's craft is rendered superhuman in the figure of John Henry, the lumberman's becomes bigger than life in Paul Bunyan, the locomotive engineer's becomes daring unto death in Casey Jones. The surefooted ironworkers who tread those beams hundreds of feet above the sidewalks and rivers are among the richest in lore, but miners, sailors, fishermen, steel puddlers, all the craftsmen with skill, daring, strength, or endurance work among yarns that celebrate their calling. People with tough work in Japan and the United States walk with the same confident and somewhat arrogant swagger.

These bits of history, of ambivalent feelings toward industrialism, of social class and attitudes toward authority, of possibilities for mobility, of propensity to identify with the group, and of pride in the craft, lead us easily to the record of present accommodations toward industrialism, the culture of the worker. The lines seem straight enough. To repeat, a man calculates his present condition at the intersection of contemporary standards and what history seems to him to make probable.

As models around which to organize this discussion of the blue-collar-work culture of Japan and the United States nowadays, I wish to use three that have been suggested by a task force of experts who recently prepared a report on work in America for the Department of Health, Education, and Welfare. I believe evidence will indicate not only that they are applicable as well to the Japanese work culture, but also that we can learn something from parts that are not applicable.

The task force experts begin with Abraham Maslow's well-known hierarchy of human needs: (1) physiological requirements (food, habitat, etc.); (2) safety and security; (3) companionship and affection; (4) self-esteem and the esteem of others; and (5) self-actualization (being able to realize one's potential to the full). They make the point that the very success workingmen have had in achieving goals at the bottom of this hierarchy breeds dissatisfaction at its higher reaches. Then they suggest a second model, that of Frederick Herzberg, which sees job satisfaction and dissatisfaction as feelings relating to different aspects of the job rather than to the same continuum. Dissatisfaction comes from low pay or a bad environment—incompetent bosses, dirt, and noise—while satisfaction comes from a sense of "achievement, accomplishment, responsibility, and challenging work." A third model, a survey of over fifteen hundred workers by the University of Michigan corroborates Herzberg's: all the characteristics of a good job, as they saw it, had to do with its intrinsic interest, and the means to get it done well.[10]

Good pay, the first requirement on Maslow's list, is rather low in the Michigan study, perhaps because of relative affluence. This is the issue, however, which most often is the focus of the overt expression of

dissatisfaction—strikes—in both countries. (But in the small enterprises at the lower half of Japan's "split-level" economy—in those tiny
factories or shops, that is, where pay and security are low—more
strikes have been caused by alleged unfair labor practices than by low
pay.) Workers in neither country believe they get a fair share of the
profits their corporations garner. A comparative look at this complaint
may or may not shed some light on the justice of it. American workers
are paid more than any elsewhere in the world. While it is difficult
because of large bonuses and fringe benefits to place Japanese workers
on a scale of wage comparison by country, their pay is clearly not
commensurate with Japan's third rank in the world in GNP. They are
gaining rapidly on workers above them on the wages list, but at present
they are probably somewhere around tenth. Furthermore, the cities of
Japan are desperately short on adequate housing, and the cost of what
is available is disproportionately high. Workers in both countries hold
that overtime is necessary to buy anything beyond the necessities of
life, but American auto workers are presently insisting that overtime
work be optional.

Maslow's model asserts safety to be an almost elemental need. The
Michigan list seems to take it for granted. Yet in 1968, 14,311 American workers died in industrial accidents, and 90,000 suffered permanent impairment from such accidents; in 1969 about 5000 Japanese
were killed and about 297,000 suffered serious injury. Many jobs are
still very simply dangerous.

One point at which a Japanese model might differ from the three
American models above is job security. Japanese workers with good
companies can assume it, under ordinary circumstances. For many
American workers, it is a source of worry, yet in a way it is a worry they
have visited onto themselves. Their long battle to achieve official
recognition of their unions included sanction for their preference to
make job tenure based on seniority a matter for the union to decide,
not management; at the same time their habit of changing jobs rather
often, comparatively, complicated such decisions. Even now, rules
allow employers to fire an American worker when it can be shown that
because of changing technology or production needs the position is no
longer required. In contrast, custom requires a Japanese employer to
find another job for a worker who is automated out. Two very practical
reasons seem to guarantee his following that custom: company loyalty

is higher in Japan than in the United States, and Japanese workers are noticeably less resistant to technological change since they aren't threatened by it. The custom is strong enough so that some Japanese who quit a company feel reluctant to rejoin it if their aspirations elsewhere are disappointed. An interesting variation on this pattern is that over half the workers who choose to work in small enterprises in Tokyo, in spite of many disadvantages including those companies' vulnerability to failure, do so because of their "homelike atmosphere." In the more purely contractual arrangements in the United States, it is not unknown that workers are fired just before they become eligible for pension plans. No wonder insecurity nags American workers, particularly as they grow older.

A different sort of insecurity troubles Japanese workers. American retirement benefits are, on the whole, better. Retirement benefits from the governmental Social Security plan are meager, but sustaining life is possible with them. Members of a number of unions can supplement that with income from other pension plans, though some of them are undependable. Japanese ordinarily must retire at fifty-five, ten years earlier than in the United States, and the governmental pension is wholly inadequate, paying less than a tenth of their ordinary income. Many companies supplement this income with lump-sum allowances to old employees when they retire, but again these are far from adequate to last a person through, say, twenty more years of life. Workers in small industries may have no retirement benefits at all, though a law in 1971 was intended to improve that situation. These facts help account for the enormous rate of personal savings which Japanese accumulate, compared with Americans, or anybody else, for that matter. This is true for companies as well as individuals. Savings even of very small firms were large enough so that the "dollar shock" of 1971 caused many fewer failures than had been anticipated.

The other good or bad qualities of jobs, as attributed to them above, seem to gather themselves into three groups: companionship; pride of workmanship, including the capacity to do work properly and see it finished, which in turn yields "self-esteem and the esteem of others" and, presumably, recognition of it by authority; and "interesting work," which practically seems to mean variety and challenge. All these are the "intrinsic" values of Herzberg's formulation, the values which "raise motivation or productivity." If we hear fewer reports of dissatisfaction among Japanese workers than American, it may be that these matters are handled better, on the whole, in Japan. If Japanese workers are in fact better satisfied, this would also bear out Herzberg's theory, for they make less than half as much as Americans, in base pay, for more work—about 205 hours a month, on the average, compared with about 165.

We have already noticed that Japanese workers within a given company maintain a solidarity that is rare in the United States. Company policy and worker preference reinforce one another. Workers consult one another on the best ways of doing a particular job. Even workers who are antagonistic in matters of politics, for example, or union policy, separate those theoretical differences from friendship on the job. Many kinds of organizations reflecting different personal interests—hobbies and sports, for example—exist within particular factories. Perhaps no necessary connection exists between company loyalty and personal friendships with fellow employees, but that's the way it generally works in Japan. Some American companies offer their employees similar opportunities, but American workers generally say they prefer being left to their own devices once the shift ends.

In the company town of Hitachi, employees of the company proudly wear buttons that identify themselves as such. A survey of white-collar workers at Hitachi indicated that 90 percent of them conducted their lives off the job in ways that would not hamper their work the next day. Blue-collar workers responded similarly. Seventy-nine percent of them said that they chose to work for the big firm on the grounds of suitability to their abilities and character or of interest in the work. Yet the loyalty of Japanese workers to their company can be overstated. Robert Cole found it much stronger in a factory which recruited its workers from rural regions than in a Tokyo factory manned by citified workers. The former, incidentally, mostly lived in company dormitories, so they were rather thoroughly immersed in the company all the time. At the latter plant, Cole heard a worker say, "We work to protect our standard of living and not for the benefit of the company."[11] The other variable is age: younger people, even white-collar workers, identify less with the company than older ones do. Still, the contrast with American workers generally holds. Whitehill and Takezawa found that American workers mostly distrust the kinds of fringe benefits which can be construed as limiting their freedom to "go it alone." They prefer a "highly contractual" relationship with their companies; theirs is generally an "armed truce" with management. Contrarily, Japanese mostly feel "in the same boat" with their employers, willing to share their adversities. "The Japanese worker," concludes a comparative study, "is more highly motivated to work, in the strict sense of equating individual and organizational goals, than the American worker."[12] One can assume that even the younger workers will identify with their companies as they grow older. The system of employment gives them every sane reason for doing so. "Here in Japan," a labor leader has said, "you don't sell your labor to the company, you sell yourself."[13] Very advanced technology in their big factories combined with what the Japanese call the "working bee" ethic equals, understandably, *very* high production.

This "working bee" ethic, this Japanese worker's identification with his work and with his company, apparently seems ominous to American employers, even slightly sinister. As Japanese competition with American products presses harder and harder, articles on this subject appear with increasing frequency in the American press. It threatens to cause as much difficulty in mutual understanding as more obvious matters, so we might pause to look at it with some care. The following excerpt from an internationally syndicated column typifies attitudes which I have observed in several places.

Not long ago an American visitor to Japan on his way downtown early one morning stopped to watch a group of workers assembled in military formation outside a small factory. They were singing lustily.

"What are they singing—the national anthem?" asked the American, turning to his Japanese companion.

"The company song, of course," said the Japanese.

"Well, I'll be damned," said the American, and burst out laughing.

"But they mean it," the Japanese said quietly. Indeed they do, and there isn't anything funny about it.[14]

The attitudes here are complex. The American laughed presumably because company loyalty of this sort is not thought to exist in the United States and perhaps because he thinks it queer that it occurs in Japan. The response of the Japanese assumed that the Japanese indeed did mean it, as the columnist assumes they do. Both Hiroshi

Minami and Kazuko Tsurumi have pointed out (partly, no doubt, in refutation of Ruth Benedict) that while Japanese may act out expected roles, they often have strong reservations about them, and Cole corroborates this as regards blue-collar workers.[15] The columnist's later comment that the singing symbolizes the "awesome disciplined energy" of the Japanese echoes an aspect of the ancient American fear and dread of the Japanese, the subconscious suspicion that they possess some mysterious power which Westerners do not. Nobody, to my knowledge, has made clear why group loyalty is culpable. It is possible to achieve such loyalty in the United States, as students of American labor practices have been pointing out for thirty-odd years. Much recent publicity about Americans missing work, malingering, and committing sabotage has obscured the demonstrable fact that American workers do identify with their companies if they consider their bosses competent and the product good, and that they do value hard work, given the same circumstances, if the work is intelligently and humanely organized. Even young American workers are still strongly committed to hard work, and to the profit system itself, but find that work is ordinarily organized in a way that frustrates them.

We are dealing here with a matter of ordinary human dignity, a worker's feeling that he is competent to make judgments concerning the work he is doing. If the foreman is often unpopular, so is the efficiency expert, who is unlikely to have performed for any length of time the tasks he makes recommendations about. (Frederick Winslow Taylor called his pioneering programs of time-motion study "The American Plan.") If one considers the importance of high morale in motivating people to work hard, perhaps he could conclude that such experts contribute to inefficiency. At any rate, for the Japanese at least, the old *keiei-kazoku-shugi*, family system, is very efficient.

Failure to consult workers about the methods and standards of the work they do is naturally one of the greatest sources of dissatisfaction among them. The 1973 negotiations between the United Auto Workers and the "big three" manufacturers had little to do with money. "Adult treatment" was the main issue. "They can get foremen that stop treating us like two-year-olds," said a UAW committeeman: "We'll work. You can't goof off when the cars or the parts keep coming at you. But you can work a lot better if you don't have somebody on your back all the time."[16] Another auto worker had a similar complaint: he was a relief man, expected to do more kinds of jobs than he could handle. "And then the foreman comes up there and starts nagging you—you tell him you can't keep up with it. You can't keep up with it and he still keeps nagging you and nagging you." The tone here is desperate enough, but things can get worse: two foremen instead of one. "That's not right—it gets confused."[17] Conversely, of some thirty experiments in various factories in the United States and Europe where workers were consulted on the organization of their work, or even planned it entirely, dissatisfaction decreased and production increased. Strangely, while American workers are more jealous than their Japanese counterparts about consultation on technological change—the Americans' job being perhaps at stake—they're more willing to let management decide who gets promoted. Japanese workers are typically given a voice in the appointment of their foremen, and they feel strongly about that right. One result is that they are on comparatively better terms with their foremen. They consult them not only about problems that come up on the job, but also about personal matters. The foremen, in turn, identify themselves with the workers, and will complain to their managers when, for example, they set unrealistic production goals. Generally, the atmosphere, as Cole found it in a Tokyo diecast plant, was "gregarious" and "spontaneous." The only time he witnessed the formality of a bow was when a worker was thanking his boss for time off when his mother-in-law died. The language of the workers was "colorful," poetic, and mostly the language of intimates, free of the distinctions that ordinarily mark differences in status: "if one judged by the language alone, the factory is one of Japan's more democratic institutions." This "streamlining of social relations," he believes, demonstrates that precedence is given to production rather than traditional etiquette; the same workers do in fact attend to social forms outside the factory.[18]

Pride in the manufacture of a good product is the last "intrinsic value" I wish to touch on. Research in both countries verifies that this is important to workers. I recall the cynical pantomime played out by the last man on an American automobile assembly line I once visited. He had a big rubber hammer, and it was his job to whack into position any body parts of automobiles passing before him that appeared to him to be awry. His face, as he played his role before the tour group, said, in effect, "Now you know: this is a shoddy operation." For years after

Japanese imports began to trickle into the United States in the 1950s, Americans recalled their prewar reputation: also shoddy. Now, I believe, even people who might not wish to recognize their high quality have no choice but to do so. Japanese of my acquaintance register shock when they hear my tales, standard in American folk-lore, of "built-in obsolescence." Perhaps their economy, now chiefly geared to consumer goods for Japanese, will come to that, too; but they seem clearly a good distance at present from that form of waste.

Good products help morale, and large companies in Japan maintain three interrelated policies which enhance the intrinsic values of work. These policies apply equally to white- and blue-collar workers. The first, already mentioned, is guaranteed lifetime employment, subject only to such gross infractions of company rules as stealing. Since unions are generally enterprise unions rather than craft unions, they can help management relocate any workers whose jobs are affected by technological change. The second is *nenko*, automatic increases in pay corresponding to the worker's level of education, his age, and his length of service to the company. The third, which makes *nenko* feasible, is job rotation, mobility within the firm itself. This policy also, of course, reduces boredom. Smaller firms attempt to follow these same policies, to the extent that they can. Obviously, they pay off. One need no longer wonder why Japanese workers feel identification with their companies: they *are* identified with them.

An American worker of long service can see a young worker come into the plant and immediately begin earning what the older hand earns, if he is doing the same job. American observers have cus-tomarily scoffed at Japanese personnel policies. Perhaps American skepticism is based again on class snobbery, perhaps a vestige of the old Puritan notion that, if success is a probable sign of virtue, failure is a probable sign of vice. A factory worker, this habit of thought goes, is of the "lower orders," therefore probably lazy, and therefore would loaf if he knew his promotions would be automatic. Perhaps it is true that if one works from assumptions that his fellows are low creatures, they will respond by being low creatures.

The degree of satisfaction or dissatisfaction a worker feels for his condition must of course be measured by that protean barometer, his expectations. Our instruments for weighing such feelings are as unreliable as intuition itself. I made a guess above that the increase in the number of years of a worker's formal schooling might raise expectations. A footnote is necessary here. The examination system in the Japanese schools and the recruitment policies of the corporations and government bureaus are presently such that a young man or woman can predict with some accuracy what his job opportunities are going to be like forever, after he reaches his last hurdle. If at the end of middle school he or the system decides that's the end of his education—and this now applies to few Japanese—the working career that is probable for him is the lower half of the "split-level" economy, service trades, or the most menial of clerical jobs. A high school diploma can net one a position in the industrial elite or a slightly more interesting office job. So far, the situation is tighter but still similar to that of the United States. At the next tier, differences exist. If examination results route a Japanese student to a university with great prestige, a position of great promise is almost automatically assured him. The up escalator from less prestigious American colleges is very much wider than that for graduates of little-known Japanese colleges and universities. Former Prime Minister Tanaka, as almost everybody knows, was the first since the war who was not a graduate of Tokyo University. Beginning with Franklin Delano Roosevelt, the presidents of the United States have come from Harvard, no college, the United States Military Academy, Harvard, North Texas State Teachers College, Whittier, and the University of Michigan. The point is that the tighter system in Japan makes prediction of probabilities, and therefore the adjustment of expectations, easier. Not that anyone would wish the American system to close the crevices through which citizens with less prestigious or limited formal schooling can scramble to success. But the greater breadth of those crevices in the United States creates not only some opportunity for success, but also a larger opportunity for self-recrimination if success isn't reached.

Education changes expectations, but it seems a safe hunch to presume that the mass media influence them more. How many besides saints are philosophical enough to be completely impervious to the glamour promised by the TV commercials in either land? Life, assuming one buys the right products, ought always to be full of handsome and smiling young men and women in idyllic settings. I can supply no facts, but people seem to buy the stuff that is hawked, except on those rare occasions when marketing research goes wholly awry, as with Ford's famous failure so dear to humorists, the Edsel. The following remark by a Detroit auto worker may be more instructive than we wish to recognize. A group of workers at a bar are lamenting their having to work overtime. Their wives and children beg them to stay at home more. But most of them want the extra money. "You get no luxuries on 40 hours a week," says one of them. "If you work extra you can buy the color TV and that washer and dryer. Did you see that show about Germany on TV? It said they close up shop at 6:30. Those people aren't LIVING though. They got no color TV, no car, one suit."[19] The strength of the net of industrial capitalism is suggested in those remarks, and the advertising man's success in generating desires.

I do not expect to spend enough time watching daytime soap operas either in Japan or the United States to validate this point, but it is my impression that in both cases the settings are of upper-middle-class arrangements. That also seems true of most evening family comedies. A norm is suggested, in other words, which encourages the success of the commercials. (I speak of commercial television in both countries, not of public television.) It is impossible to believe that people do not take these norms at least somewhat seriously. The manner in which the Japanese market was prepared for, then supplied with, certain consumer goods such as refrigerators, electric fans, and rice cookers, and the way in which consumers responded, seem proof enough. Yet the question of how far the advertising men can go is a good one. Children who have grown up with television seem particularly canny about its wiles. And perhaps the fine novelist Kobo Abé is accurate when he writes, "It only happened in novels or movies that summer was filled with dazzling sun. What existed in reality were humble, small-town Sundays . . . a man taking his snooze under the political columns of a newspaper . . . canned juices and thermos jugs with magnetized caps . . . boats for hire, fifty cents an hour—queue up here . . . foaming beaches with the leaden scum of dead fish . . . and then, at the end, a jam-packed trolley rickety with fatigue." We are all kidding ourselves, says Abé: we know our market-ed leisure is tedious and sometimes noisome, but we are afraid to openly acknowledge it. So we see "miserable, unshaven fathers, shak-ing their complaining children by the shoulder trying to make them say it has been a pleasant Sunday. . . . people's pathetic jealousy and impatience with others' happiness."[20] A certain wise skepticism guards people who are accustomed to disappointment. The Japanese shrug and say *shikata ga nai,* something like "it can't be helped." A shrewd resignation is also lodged even in the simple American "oh, well . . ." Most men, said Thoreau, when the railroad at Concord was first signaling the industrial revolution, "live lives of quiet desperation." "Men think they ride the railroad, but the railroad rides them."

Quiet lives need not be desperate. Yet another variable may be important in the comparison of expectations—that is, psychological skills in confronting a life which has ordinarily been monotonous, day by day, for most people everywhere, and which still is for most people even in huckster cultures such as Japan and the United States which promise otherwise. Japanese housewives have a somewhat rueful little boast that they can find *chiisana kōfuku,* "small happiness," or "happiness in a hidden corner."[21] When we were comparing the travel books of Bashō and Mark Twain, we might then have noted a sharp variation in what was held to constitute an experience. Bashō had learned to find value in the most fragile event. Mark Twain often denigrated what he called "gaudy effects," but he was drawn to them. What constituted an event for Twain ordinarily had a higher voltage than Bashō required.

I believe something of this difference persists in the two cultures, but skillful people in either place can wring significance and meaning from experiences which seem to gross sensibilities dull and trivial. "I have travelled a good deal in Concord," wrote Thoreau, chaffing his countrymen's fad for world travel. (Concord in those days was a very tiny hamlet.) A recent newspaper interview with a man who had been taking tickets on a Tokyo subway for a dozen years showed how he transformed the work into a study of character. In earlier days, when poor people cheated on their fare, he could understand and forgive, but, nowadays, he asked, how can one explain cheating by people who are obviously prosperous? A resilient man like that might be the one who solves such a riddle. Lucy Jefferson, a black worker in a fashionable Chicago hospital, enjoyed shocking white people out of their stereotypes by displaying the fact that she was an avid reader of difficult books: "I read such things as *The American Dilemma* and I walk around with the book in my hand, see? I defied them in so many ways. I almost terrified 'em." People on the elevator begin to question her:

"What are you reading? What are you reading?" So she made a game of it. "I was having the best old time. I was absolutely terrifying 'em." In the course of her game, she read more and more notoriously difficult books, and unnerved more and more white people. If we can believe the taped interviews by Studs Terkel in *Division Street, America*, those Chicagoans who maintain their equipoise and humanity are not necessarily those with wealth, power, or even much formal education; they are those who have developed such psychic skills.[22] The same can be said of the occasional interviews with "uncommon common men" and women appearing in the Tokyo English-language newspapers.

Yet surely those are unusually resourceful people. I take it that nobody's nervous system has become so blunt that it is satisfied with the routine work which most people are required to do in Japan and the United States. Perhaps some larger perspective than this one is important to this discussion. A sense of the ease of the labor of most Japanese and Americans, and their bounteous rewards, compared with most people in most places most of the time reduces many of their statements of discontent to the level of carping. Yet the local and contemporary standards speak loudest, and discontent is a fact of the lives of many of the people we have been talking about. In both countries, it begins to set in hard after the age of thirty or so among those workers who can see that their careers are unlikely to take any dramatic turns for the better. Given the systems, this is less traumatic for Japanese than Americans, but it exists in both places. A defensive resignation appears among such people as they approach middle age. "Yes, I'd like to work in the die plant," says a thirty-four-year-old semiskilled Japanese press operator, "but there's no chance, and besides who needs it as long as I'm making out O.K. in my pay."[23] "There's no chance to be a foreman," says a thirty-three-year-old machine operator in an American automobile factory. "Advancement is very slow. There are few who get anyplace." Or a forty-five-year-old stock picker in the same plant: "I used to hope that I could get on supervision, but I'm giving up that idea. I'm getting kind of old . . . and they pick younger fellows and put them on now."[24] This resignation is often linked to hope for the children: I'll stick to this job and save my money to send my children to college; then they'll have a better life than I've had. Paradoxically, while this hope for a better life runs through much of the literature about American workingmen, Gans found in Levittown that parents encouraged the sort of high school curriculum which points students toward industry, not college.

Workers in both cultures can adjust to their lives by scaling down their definition of success, to fit their own condition. A Japanese worker says, "It's still possible for a working man to get ahead." His standard, then, is working to own a home, taking care of his family properly, and saving money for retirement. "It's constant striving that makes the difference; it's the difference between the guy who on a hot day squanders his money on beer, while another drinks a glass of milk and saves."[25] Even given the perimeters of the two systems, personal habits and goals make a difference. An American is allowed a grander optimism, less of a scaling down of the dream. "A lot of people think getting ahead means getting to be a millionaire. Not for me, though." He speaks not of "just breaking even," but of adding and adding to "possessions," "personal property." He, too, is worried about money for retirement, and adds that if, then, he had two or three houses such as his own, and $5,000 in the bank, he'd figure he'd "got ahead quite a bit."[26] Many young people in both cultures seem to be rejecting the yardstick of possession which these men have used to measure their own lives without bitterness, and also the habit of patience with which that yardstick is employed.

Some workers in both cultures maintain what probably ought to be called a fantasy, that they will someday buy a farm or a small business, and get out of the factory. "I'd be my own boss and whether I succeeded or not would be my own responsibility," says a Japanese factory worker;[27] and many Americans share the feeling. That an element of wishful thinking is involved in this is evident when we remember that, even if a worker could save enough to begin a business, the record of failure of new small businesses in the United States is 80 percent in the first year and informal inquiries have disclosed that the figure is very high in Japan as well.[28] Such fantasies can lead to the sort of despair which comes from delayed decision and self-blame. A thirty-two-year-old American auto worker says, "It's my own fault. I was going to work here for a year after I graduated from high school and then be a printer's apprentice. But then I bought a car and that was my downfall. I couldn't afford to leave if I was going to have the car. Then I got married—and I certainly couldn't afford to quit."[29] "I always planned to get out of the factory," says a Japanese worker, but "things just dragged out."[30]

Thus, there may be the necessity to blow off steam. The following examples seem to me to show with great clarity behavior that is typical of the two cultures. Professor Cole is talking with two left-wing students at a bar frequented by militants. They sing Vietcong liberation songs there, and waiters dress like Russian peasants. One of the workers says, "We like to sing here on weekends and march in demonstrations because it gives us a release from the tensions built up while working a sixty-hour week. And by doing this we go back and put in a hard day's work on Monday again. . . . We don't need a union at our shoe factory because our boss is a guy we can talk to, and, besides, we will never make it into a big successful company if we have a union."[31] Studs Terkel, in a different work from that cited above, is talking with a steelworker, a husband and father.

You're at the tavern. About an hour or so?
    Yeah. When I was single, I used to go into hillbilly bars, get in a lot of brawls. . . .
Why did you get in those brawls?
    Just to explode. I just wanted to explode. . . .
You play with the kids . . . ?
    . . . When I come home, know what I do for the first 20 minutes? Fake it. I put on a smile. I don't feel like it. I got a kid three-and-a-half years old. Sometimes she says, Daddy, where've you been? And I say, work. I could've told her I'd been in Disneyland. What's work to a three-year-old? I feel bad, I can't take it out on the kid. Kids are born innocent of everything but birth. You don't take it out on the wife either. This is why you go to the tavern. You want to release it there rather than do it at home. What does an actor do when he's got a bad movie? I got a bad movie every day.[32]

Quiet desperation.

Studies as old as Robert Bellah's *Tokugawa Religion* (1957) and as new as George De Vos's *Socialization for Achievement* (1973)—the former relating the drive to succeed among Japanese to the way religion has long reinforced social, political, and economic values of that kind, the latter recounting the way child-raising and other familial patterns work toward the same end—have told us how the

"Oriental Calvinists" value success. Nevertheless, it is my hunch that the achievement demon, statistically speaking, damages fewer psyches there than in the United States. If it is true that Japanese in fact identify themselves more easily and closely with social groups they belong to, perhaps a Japanese of modest achievement can vindicate the modest role he, like most people, must play by applauding the success of the larger drama he participates in. Most egos formed in cultures that urge success need all the help they can get.

American workers more often than Japanese say that they are working only to live, and that life is what happens after working hours. Are the leisure hours in Japan as dreary as Abé has said, in the quotation a few pages back? Is it true, as Paul Goodman says in *Communitas*, that in America leisure does not refresh?

The same communal skills of rice growers which facilitated transition to factory work also transferred well to urban neighborhoods. Neighborhood associations, again under the leadership of the most prominent man around, took care of such common problems as protection, water supply, and waste disposal, and served perhaps more importantly as sources of community. These associations still exist in some places, but now the majority of Tokyoites live in apartments or danchi, where several of the old institutions which create neighborhood fail to exist, notably the public baths and, usually, the little neighborhood specialty shops. (In Tama New Town, outside Tokyo, the old shopkeepers who had served the community have been installed in the new buildings, in little open-fronted shops almost as attractive as the old.) Old Japanese residents of traditional neighborhoods did not greet newcomers in the American fashion, tendering welcome with pies or cakes or homemade bread; rather, it was up to the newcomer to earn his welcome. One wonders how this works when a new danchi is opened, and all the inhabitants are new. We do know that the people in some danchi have organized into purchasing cooperatives, for fish, vegetables, and the like—a healthy sign. The enormously prestigious PTA also assumes some of the old social functions of the neighborhood associations.

Many American neighborhoods grew out of ethnic ghettoes. Recall that immigrants arriving in strange American cities tended to huddle together with fellows of like language, customs, and religion. Many of these communities gained political sanction, with the ward boss system. Even in days of poverty, these neighborhoods often functioned successfully, as informal mutual-aid societies as well as loose but often warm social organizations. Many such neighborhoods were declared to be slums by the housing and road-building projectors following World War II, and their inhabitants were dispersed to lonelier lives in high-rise public or low-cost housing projects. For the open and friendly atmosphere of the spacious American neighborhoods, where newcomers are more or less sincerely welcomed, has notoriously failed to pertain in American apartment buildings. There, Riesman's phrase "the lonely crowd" is particularly apt. A young mother in a Chicago housing project says, "But as far as life in public housing is concerned I don't think it's a very good place to raise children. They can't make noise, they don't have freedom. They can't do like they can in a small town. They can't lay on the grass, they can't climb trees." Turnover of occupants is rapid, and the city breeds suspicion among neighbors. Or, perhaps, they resent the conditions of their lives. So they usually stay to themselves.[33]

Factories in both countries have been for some time moving to the suburbs, but the number of factory workers moving there, too, into family-owned homes, seems larger in the United States: while the percentage of dweller-owned homes is slightly higher in Japan than the United States (64 percent to 62 percent), the Japanese percentage is lower in urban areas (55 percent to 58 percent). A good many Japanese workers in small industries live in with the families they work for. Generally, if one juggles all the statistics about room sizes and population density per room, it appears that Japanese people have somewhat less than half the amount of living space that Americans have.

If, therefore, Japanese workers, white collar and blue collar, delay their steps home after work rather more than American, the cause is surely in large part the kind of physical accommodations they find there. Articles one sees seem to try to suggest that the husband's "stopping off" is some sort of long-honored tradition, but the fragility of that notion becomes apparent when one remembers how recently most Japanese were members of farm families, working together. The image of the Japanese home which some sentimental Americans might still entertain resembles the clean, uncluttered elegance of the aristocrat's classical teahouse. Doubtless many Japanese would prefer that, with the addition of a Western kitchen, at least, and perhaps a living room. In sober fact, most Japanese workingmen must settle for two or three tiny rooms, sadly cluttered, and a share of a bath and toilet. Housing is also still inadequate in the United States for working-class people at the lower registers, but Americans of the industrial elite are likely to have very pleasant five-room houses in the suburbs. That may be small comfort if they have to fake it in front of the kids, like the steelworker quoted above.

How do Americans and Japanese spend their after hours? Napping and watching TV, mostly, by all reports. But that isn't the whole story, of course. What we would really hope to know is whether recreation re-creates the person fragmented by his job, whether during his leisure hours he can find the amenities missing from the factory and office, perhaps even some of the excitement missing from a bland life. In trying to answer such questions, one should probably allow himself subjectivity. Statistics about spending at the race track, or at pachinko or slot machines, or about tour bus mileage, don't seem to answer. A couple of obvious points might be made. To even speak of a "leisure crisis" is certainly bizarre, given the whole toiling history of man. Second, it seems almost equally as strange to an American, accustomed to thinking of the skills which the Japanese have traditionally acquired in the meditative arts, to keep reading reports that managers have difficulty in persuading their employees, particularly those with white collars, to leave work during holidays and vacations, and that some of them have resorted to bounties to encourage a certain amount of loafing. Why did the Japanese borrow the word *leisure* from English and *vacance* from French? One suggestion has been that the Japanese language has no equivalents, since not-working was traditionally frowned upon. After consultation with Japanese friends, I lean to the simpler explanation that the English and French languages enjoy a chic. Certainly the old Japanese poems and stories contain references to plenty of leisure among even ordinary sorts, and plenty of vacations at least among the well-to-do.

Relaxation from the routine of work may take forms that aren't recognized in the usual essays on leisure. The quick, casual laugh on the job may do as much good as institutionally approved coffee breaks. The two-week vacation, saved for and planned for during fifty weeks, and savagely performed, may be of little help in restoring the spirit, while a thoughtful, disciplined, and humane use of spare minutes each day can prevent the psychic drought which makes the vacation so desperately sought after. Casual observation is suspect, but appearances say that a larger number of Japanese know the technique of relaxation. On the subway, or lounging at lunch hour, many bodies go limp, free of the tension one sees in so many American bodies. Or at lunch hour one also sees many people playing catch or volleyball with friends. Japanese companies encourage calisthenics. We are talking about proportions here. Some Americans, of course, know how to relax. The impression one gains from watching, however, is that fewer do.

Conversely, the number of ergs of energy expended on the Japanese job seems higher than the American. Young men and women in the offices often move from task to task at a dogtrot, something almost never seen in the United States. Workers in the small manufacturing shops squint at their work with a kind of concentration reminiscent of the warriors in the old ukiyoe, cross-eyed with intensity. European observers of the American scene such as Chevalier and Tocqueville have commented on the restlessness, the busyness of Americans. That is a somewhat different matter, however. What is pointed to in the American character is a lack of repose, a kind of churning which is not always productive in work or play. George Santayana's "last Puritan" disavowed Puritanism in order to adopt hedonism, but he pursued hedonism with Puritanic intensity. It's as though the Japanese metabolism has more gear speeds including a slower one than Americans have, and a faster, and as though their automatic gearshift senses the appropriate time to slip from one to another.

I have said that the Japanese have less leisure than Americans. Some, such as small shopkeepers, would appear to have none at all. I have also said that the Japanese think of their work as a more important aspect of their life than American workers do. Paradoxically, the Japanese also seem to take their "after hours" more seriously than Americans do. When an American is asked "What do you do?" (A question occurring more frequently in the United States, I am told, than in Japan), he is likely to respond by naming his job, while a Japanese is likely to respond by naming his company *or* his avocation. For many Japanese, perhaps a larger number than Americans, devote themselves to some *shumi*, some hobby, perhaps for a lifetime: flower arranging, classical Western music, tea ceremony, history, calligraphy, and a long list of other possibilities. These arts are by no means limited to women, although competence in one or more of them is thought to be a prerequisite to proper wifehood, among people with any social pretension at all. Nor are they limited to the upper classes, although lessons in some of them are very expensive. Many American working people have a contempt for what is thought to be "high" culture, as an affectation of the leisurely rich, and one seldom sees, for example, working-class Americans in an art gallery. People of all strata are seen in a Japanese gallery; in fact, department stores devote their top floors to gallery space—and people from all walks of life show up.

Most leisure activities for most people, presumably, are spontaneous and informal: conversation, television-watching, puttering in the garden, window-shopping, playing with the kids. Japanese husbands and older children do more of these things away from their crowded homes than Americans do. Coffee houses and inexpensive sake or beer bars thrive in enormous numbers in Japan. The young can sit for hours in a coffee shop enjoying the kind of recorded music which is the specialty of the house—jazz, classical, chanson, or whatever, over one cup of coffee or tea. Their fathers stop off more often than their American counterparts at little bars—not the expensive kind which are mainly for businessmen on lavish expense accounts. American youngsters at their coke-and-milkshake spots listen to top pops on the jukebox, make more noise, and stay for shorter periods. They mostly get there by automobile. The workingman's neighborhood saloons of their fathers still exist, and serve similar functions to the Japanese sake bars, but as middle- and lower-middle-class people move to the suburbs and take their money with them, the old neighborhood sweet shops and drugstores and saloons begin to disappear.

Conversation among the young of both countries seems to flourish best away from their elders, but in the United States, with bigger homes, this can sometimes occur naturally enough in some corner of the house. Americans have also sponsored centers especially designed for talk, music, dancing, and perhaps Ping-Pong or pool among the young; such establishments are fairly rare in Japan, and those that exist are usually set up by charitable institutions or local governments in the hopes of encouraging a "wholesome" environment in which young people do what they would do anyway.

Wives talk less with their husbands in Japan, to all appearances, since the latter are home less; the American style of social life in which couples who are friends of either the husband or wife or both come to visit in the home is quite rare in Japan, again in part because of cramped quarters. This custom, incidentally, is less frequent among American blue-collar people than among their white-collar contemporaries, a subcultural difference not easily attributable to the size of the home. Wives in Japan do much of their conversing along the little shopping streets—Japanese have a more distinct choice between shopping in their neighborhoods in little specialty shops, or going to some urban nucleus to the big stores. Or they may chat in the public baths, marvelous social centers where a person sheds his rank with his clothes before entering. Such baths don't exist in the new, high-rise danchi, unfortunately, so that outlet is disappearing as fast as the workingman's saloon in the United States. Or, if they live in old, established neighborhoods, the wives chat with neighbors. American wives, in a land where walls do not separate houses as they do in the older Japanese neighborhoods, chat easily in their backyards, or in their kitchens with neighbors at the mid-morning coffee klatches, or at the neighborhood or housing-project laundromats. It seems safe to say that generally the Japanese housewife's life is more private, more closely concentrated on the home and family than the American's, although again the American blue-collar habits approximate the Japanese more nearly than those of their white-collar fellows do. The American propensity for joining clubs is by no means confined to the middle class—American Legion Auxiliaries, bowling clubs, Eastern Star lodges, card-playing groups, and such have a considerable lower-middle-class clientele. Japanese generally are less clubby than Americans. When they associate after hours, they do so mainly with friends from work. Professor Tsurumi has studied "circles" among women who work in textile mills, associations which serve the splendid purposes of friendship and group therapy. In the villages, the wives may join tour clubs. All in all, urban wives seem to have a less companionable time of it in Japan than small-town housewives, but that as we have noticed is also true of American housewives in big housing developments. But again, easy and casual neighborliness is less characteristic of the crowded Japanese than of the spacious Americans. In densely populated areas of the United States, the cautious habits more closely approximate the Japanese. Perhaps such cultural habits derive from the simple geographical fact of tight proximity. Those products of that other tight little island, Britain, behave in a reserved way that resembles the Japanese much more closely than, let's say, that of the inhabitants of a smallish prairie city such as Des Moines or Fort Wayne.

The reserve in the big American housing developments in the cities, however, also stems from distrust rather than the ancient respect for privacy among crowded people. Mostly, these developments are built in the place where old slums have been torn down, but the urban renewal men can't tear down old fears, old hatreds, old frustrations. Those linger in the neighborhoods like ghosts. The irony, of course, is that the modernity which forces people's bodies more closely together holds their spirits more and more apart.

If conversation, on or off the job, is likely to be the most important form of recreation in each culture, television—at its worst, something close to anti-conversation—comes a close second. To speak first of educational television, American public television begins to catch up with Japan's NHK and Britain's BBC, but it's an uphill go. NHK has one channel which is specifically and strictly educational, with classes that can be taken for credit, and no-nonsense lessons in languages, cooking, etiquette, history, and such matters. A standing remark in Japan is that if the housewife stays home and watches the appropriate television fare, she can become better educated than her husband. The other NHK channel carries more entertainment, even pop music and Mama-shows (soap operas, to Americans) which are meant merely for entertainment, but the general level of their broadcasts is very high. On Sunday nights, for example, for some years, NHK has shown one or another historical drama, widely followed, quite accurate, beautifully produced, and movingly acted. Educational television in the United States has its share of triumphs as well, but is less well supported. Commercial television in Japan seems to manage as few triumphs and as many cultural insults to its viewers as American commercial television. To quote a student of mine, "Any culture is capable of mediocrity."

Japanese use rather more of their spare time in reading than Americans do. The average Japanese family reads a newspaper a day, and ten weekly journals each month. The circulation per thousand people of daily newspapers is 492 in Japan, 309 in the United States. (Japanese newspapers carry much less advertising than American, so the consumption of newsprint there is a little more than one-third America's.) The per capita production of books is about the same: with half of America's population, the Japanese produce about 30,000 books a year, as opposed to about 60,000 in the United States.

At the head of the list of ten best sellers in Japan in June 1972 was the fifth volume of a monumental historical novel about the war between Russia and Japan. The second book was by Kakuei Tanaka, soon to become prime minister, in which he described his plans for Japan's future. The third was the *Introduction to the Sermon of Wisdom*, by a Buddhist teacher, the fourth another historical novel intended to correct the Fuji clan's history of Prince Shotoku, the fifth a psychological study of old people, the sixth a translation of *Only One World*. On the rest of the list were two books that probably ought not to be taken seriously, and two that ought. The level of seriousness, in other words, seems considerably higher than that of the list for July 1972 in the United States. (The lists in both countries change slowly.) The American fiction list then was headed by a quickly written fantasy called *Jonathan Livingston Seagull*, followed by works by two authors famous for grinding out best sellers, Herman Wouk and Irving Wallace. The only really serious work of fiction, Eudora Welty's *The Optimist's Daughter*, ranked tenth. It must be reported, however, that in late 1973, a translation of *Seagull* was at the top of Japan's list.

No numbers are available with which to talk about participation in sports in the two countries. Both people are earnest sportsmen. An American tendency of a few years ago to let passive interest overtake active interest at a fairly young age has been somewhat checked by a renewal of concern over physical fitness, so new joggers, cyclists, tennis players, and serious walkers presently combat the heart ailments which Japanese worry less about and the obesity that they need worry about hardly at all. Company bowling teams and baseball or softball teams thrive in both cultures, but bowling is less fashionable in the United States. Both cultures have their fishermen; hunting is comparatively rare in Japan. Skiing may be less expensive in Japan because of the proximity of slopes, but swimming, while in a great many places in the United States still limited to the well-to-do because of the expense of artificial facilities, is still more general there than in Japan, which has fewer pools per capita (where are those great Japanese Olympic swimming teams of the 1930s?). Basketball and American football in Japan remain the province of young men at the fashionable private universities with Western ancestry. Mountaineering exists in the United States but many fewer people climb, surely because of geography. Motorized camping is enormously popular in the United States, if that's a sport. Volleyball and Ping-Pong are taken more seriously in Japan than in the United States. The Japanese have some possibilities open to few Americans: judo, kendo, aikido. Soccer has long been popular in Japan, and is becoming more so in the United States, but mainly among college boys and immigrants. For want of any hard facts, let me hazard this guess: a decidedly greater shortage of space in Japan and somewhat less available leisure take their toll on people who would otherwise be active, but a longer acquaintance with affluence and passive leisure take their toll on a number of Americans who feel that they would rather like to be more active physically than they actually are.

It's possible to be somewhat less vague about spectator sports. Baseball is the most popular in Japan, sumo second. Both are very ceremonial sports, both require of the competent spectator very minute and careful observation of the quick move made after rather long pauses for ritual and for mental preparation by the athletes. The stock phrase by American newspapermen is that baseball is "a game of inches." The same can be said of sumo. The huge men are incredibly quick, and their slightest shift of hold on the belt can make all the difference. What is interesting here is that baseball is the American spectator sport with the most lore going for it, a mythology which some of the best novelists—Bernard Malamud and Mark Harris, for example—have codified. Attendance figures are slippery to handle, but it appears that baseball has fallen into third place, behind basketball and football, in popularity. The general complaint among the anti-baseball faction is that it is too slow: we learn something about the rhythm which is comfortable to Americans from this. Basketball has the advantage of being the sport that almost every male has participated in, at least in some alley. Just as British kids kick a soccer ball around almost as second nature, Americans in most sections of the country have their fathers mount a net on the garage door and grow up shooting baskets. Football fifty years ago was a sport for wealthy college boys, so the immense recent popularity of professional football takes some explaining. The Freudians interested in the American male's uncertain sense of his own masculinity and those who speak of Americans' love of violence have both made their explanations, but the game also appeals to those skilled in watching closely. It is as complex as sumo, and as violent; even its ritual qualities begin to accrue, particularly as it is performed for television.

Behind these sports, the list is long. Horse racing in both countries claims the attention of millions, but a fair share of these may never watch a race: betting amounts to billions of yen, and millions of dollars. Automobile racing in the United States takes many forms, from the drag car through various forms of the stock to the "Indianapolis" car; Japanese also watch the cars, probably less often; but they probably watch the bicycles and the motorcycles more often. Soccer is more popular in Japan than the United States, and so is boxing. A bizarre newcomer to the American scene is the roller derby, supposedly designed for lower-middle-class spectators, interesting in that its staple is violence, and violence among women. One would probably be fairly safe in predicting that it will never become popular in Japan. But not really safe.

Commercial leisure. The eye for the dollar or the yen is equally acute. American businessmen sell boats and campers at a dazzling rate. Japanese put up four-story buildings which a friend has called "leisure department stores," including bars, restaurants, bowling alleys, perhaps a cabaret, perhaps a pachinko parlor. Pornographic movies and bookstores, sauna bath houses, massage parlors, and of course prostitution, technically illegal in Japan, and in 49/50ths of the United States, all make money.

When Americans and Japanese have a considerable chunk of leisure time to look forward to, they more often than not plot a trip. In both cultures, until very recently, and among all but the wealthy, the plan was for a domestic tour. The standard American vacation of two weeks in the summer looks more relaxed than the traditional Japanese clusters of four or five days at New Year's and during "Golden Week" in early May, but of course a great deal more distance is involved. The Japanese have every kind of natural beauty that one would wish for and many artifacts as well, in relatively small compass. They also have good train and bus service that moves regularly into the remote corners of the land. Americans depend on the automobile for vacations, except for a few who fly or take a bus. Sharp rises in gasoline prices, and threatened shortages, have not yet changed the picture dramatically. A whole recent folklore has developed about the painfulness of the American family trip, by car, during that hectic two-week vacation. The tourist attractions in Japan during the days when tourists are most numerous can also be pretty hectic. The grouping of people is different. Americans travel as families, Japanese as groups of school children, company employees, or rural wives who have joined a tourist club. The picture, then, is of American nuclear groups, as opposed to more homogeneous sets of middle-aged women, or children, or middle-aged male white-collar workers.

Overseas travel was impossible for most Americans and most Japanese until fairly recently (soldiers excepted). Charter flights and the possibility of accumulating savings changed this. Two and a half million Japanese and the same number of Americans traveled abroad in 1972, again often in tour groups, but not necessarily. Japanese secretaries have been known to save for years to make a tour to Guam, or Hawaii, or perhaps the continental United States or Switzerland or France or Sweden. More and more Americans have availed themselves of the old patrician's habit of traveling to Europe—seldom anyplace else. Again, group flight fares brought such a trip within the range of many more Americans than could think of it a few years earlier. The recessive-inflated economy of the mid-1970s led to some decline in foreign travel for Americans.

With their short history, Americans enjoy many fewer richly traditional holidays than the Japanese. A few religious holidays such as Christmas for Christians and Yom Kippur for Jews are full of meaning for them. A few holidays, such as St. Patrick's Day and Columbus Day, nourish the pride of particular ethnic groups. New Orleans has its gay Mardi Gras, Philadelphia its Mummers. The civic holidays such as Independence Day, Memorial Day, and Labor Day seem for most people to be empty of import except insofar as they yield three-day weekends. Probably few "advanced" civilizations are as arid in this respect as the American; the Japanese, on the other hand, are as rich as Italians. To their own list of holidays which cluster around New Year's Day and "Golden Week," they add, by appropriation, what pleases them, such as Christmas and some Buddhist days. Then each community has its ancient Shinto festival, rich in lore. In the early 1970s when an anthropologist from the city visited a three-day village festival, she lamented in the *Japan Interpreter* that urban Japanese are "folk without festivals." Her phrase is only hyperbole defining the intensity of the experience, for the Tokyo neighborhoods have their own, and the people one sees at them seem happy to be there. If "salary men" in their dark suits seem less exuberant in the parks at cherry blossom time than do country people, they are nevertheless there, and presumably not entirely drained of feeling. The Japanese, too, have their civic holidays such as Constitution Day, which appear to affect pulse rates only minutely. Yet, on the whole, Japanese have many more special occasions which succeed in raising communal and personal spirits than do Americans. It would be a mistake, however, to underestimate the pleasure millions of Americans, especially in rural areas, obtain from county fairs and state fairs, week-long descendants of harvest festivals.

We return, then, to a larger perspective. If the lives of "average" Japanese and "average" Americans fall short of the *akarui seikatsu* or the "good life" promised by politicians and advertising men of the two countries, if their jobs are often boring, even subhuman, and if their leisure often seems passive and without the capacity for refreshment, they nevertheless are more free from hunger, exposure to the elements, and endless drudgery than almost any people in all of past history, and are pampered by more instruments of human pleasure. American slang declares, "a lot you got to holler," meaning, roughly, "what on earth do *you* have to complain about?" Well, pollution, crowding, and an unwelcome American military presence for the Japanese, war, racism, pockets of poverty, *and* pollution for the Americans. No harm will be done by asking the tired question once more: Dare one suppose that a *somewhat* bright new life is possible without these burdens? Are Japanese and American leaders so profoundly lacking in ingenuity that they will be unable to devise means whereby Disraeli's "two civilizers of men"—increased wealth and increased leisure—are less an unmixed blessing?

CHAPTER 6

Fiction and the Popular Imagination

By glancing here and there at Japan's and America's traditions in fiction, we might discover some interesting matters deep at the marrow of the two imaginations. Occasionally, perhaps, we might learn something about more overt social attitudes. I can imagine no work of art which is not in some way a social gesture; at the same time, I know of many critics who interpret too simplemindedly the social import of a work of art. The fact that the Japanese have a tradition of fiction about well-to-do ne'er-do-wells does not of course say that Japan is a culture of well-to-do ne'er-do-wells. Nor does the American fiction which celebrates the outcast wanderer reflect a society full of outcast wanderers. We cannot even say with confidence that those models are particularly compelling to some secret inner man in Japan or the United States. But the persistence of forms in which those images are cast might tell us something.

Long fiction seems to be the literary form which is presently predominant in both places. Fiction, we assume, both captures the imagination of a people and helps shape it. Novels, whether political in any way or not in subject, have an effect which may be thought to be political in that they comment on earlier novels, and either conserve their forms or try to demolish them. Some comment on earlier culture, in other words, is lodged in later cultural artifacts. A Japanese writer is wealthier than the ordinary American, since he has the whole world's literature available to him, besides his own long and rich tradition. Which does he choose to emulate, which to reject? If, for example, he chooses a subject Western novelists have been working with, and handles it in a manner similar to that of earlier Japanese novelists, Japanese culture through that act has been reinforced at the same time that it has become slightly broadened. American writers have mainly reacted to Western models only. (Earl Miner's *The Japanese Tradition and American Literature* concentrates on Hearn, Aiken, Stevens, and Pound among the Americans. Apparently fiction has accepted the Japanese imprint less readily than poetry.)

The novels we will focus on are serious ones being read by serious people. Mainly, we will look at novels from the twentieth century, but we must look at them in two perspectives, in order to place their traditions. The first is ancient history, the beginnings; the second is the mid-nineteenth century, when Japan was bending to the wave of Western influences, and when American literature was beginning clearly to differentiate itself from English literature.

American prose fiction still echoes in many ways the Homeric epics of the eighth century before Christ, and the great drama of fifth-century Athens. The narratives of the Old Testament, some of which are roughly contemporaneous with Homer, seem to have made less impact on prose fiction, even though until recently all Americans knew them well. They do, of course, reinforce the instinct for storytelling, and particularly storytelling linked to moral and religious imperatives. Most educated Americans until a generation or two ago knew the classics in both these traditional streams. They would have been less familiar with such later ancestors of the modern novel as the fourteenth-century Italian Boccaccio or the sixteenth-century Spaniard Cervantes, though those men found their way into the American imagination by way of English writers even before they began to be read directly, in the early nineteenth century. Seventeenth- and eighteenth-century Americans could read the Greek, Latin, and Hebrew classics without censure, as they were considered morally and intellectually "uplifting." A reader of English and American novels in those days, however, would be thought by his neighbors a spendthrift of time and probably a wastrel of morals.

Written Japanese fiction was born of Japanese court ladies of the Heian period, the tenth and eleventh Christian centuries. Japanese had had their oral tales of the gods, not unlike Homer's. And scholars had been for centuries bringing back analects and other writings from China. The Chinese are said not to have valued narrative much, yet these writings ought not to be overlooked any more than the Hebrew scriptures. Akutagawa Ryūnosuke, whose finest work was published in the 1920s, spoke of practically memorizing as a child old Chinese tales.[1] While the learned Heian gentlemen were composing poems in Chinese, their ladies were writing their *monogatari*, diaries, and pillow books in the Japanese idiom, more amenable than the Chinese to "evoking direct feelings, for picturing the world as they actually saw it."[2] The most famous of these works, of course, is Lady Murasaki's *The Tale of Genji*. Roughly similar in perception are *The Tale of the Lady Ochikubo* and Sei Shonagon's *The Pillow Book*. *Genji* seems the work most fruitful for comparison with Homer, and it is the work which is most clearly an influence on the Japanese imagination today. Jun-ichiro Tanizaki, for example, spent many of his last years in translating it into modern Japanese.

Some differences that occur in these earliest works of the two literatures are still apparent. First of all, what is celebrated in *Genji, The Iliad*, and *The Odyssey*? Achilles is a warrior, full of pride, restless, preoccupied with the question of honor. Odysseus is a crafty wanderer, eager to experience the world yet longing to return home, in order to set his land in order, finally a shrewd politician. Prince Genji is a wanderer, too, but not a warrior, not a politician. He is instead "the radiant one," talented, full of love and devotion to elegance. All three are honorable men, but Achilles and Odysseus maintain their honor in large part by gaining vengeance through force of arms, while Genji's honor comes, generally speaking, from his accomplished discriminations among feelings and kinds of beauty, and more specifically in almost unerringly meeting his human obligations. That was no small chore, incidentally: he incurred a very large number of them.

The images that stick in the mind are illuminating. Achilles, sulking in his tent, nursing the tender pride that Agamemnon had wounded, or dragging the dead body of Hector behind his chariot. Odysseus, outwitting the uncivilized Cyclopes, then bragging about it, or tired, and hungry, sweet-talking the Princess Nausicaa into taking him to her father's palace; or cannily testing the loyalty of his workers, his wife, even his father. Genji, daubing his nose red to amuse the child

Lady Murasaki, or dancing so beautifully the emperor wept, or aging, finding new beauty to love in his mistress's child, persuading his wife to take the child as her own. The Japanese of course have their warrior heroes, widely celebrated in the popular arts, but the interesting fact is that they haven't much found their way into the usual canon of serious fiction. Perhaps geography alone explains the presence throughout the Western tradition of warrior heroes; the peoples of Europe hadn't the security of the turbulent Japan Sea to protect them from outsiders, so their Aeneas, their Beowulf, their Roland, their Henry V are dear to them. Here we encounter an interesting similarity between Japanese literature and American. Heirs to the tradition of the epic warrior, but also (if this is important) protected by the Atlantic from potential enemies, the Americans have never made the warrior a hero of *their* serious literature. The heroes of American fiction are never as high-born as Prince Genji—Genji, however, was illegitimate—but they often contain the same qualities. Leatherstocking, Huck Finn, Ishmael, Ike McCaslin can see beauty and can feel love, though in rather different terms. Women, for example, play small roles in their adventures; not so with Genji.

Another striking difference between the Homeric epics and *The Tale of Genji* is found at the point of conjunction between subject and form. Homer's work is tightly plotted and teleological, Murasaki's is episodic and loosely cyclical. Plotting is an imposition of rational plan on what William James called the "wild, buzzing confusion" of experience, a search for order. The Western imagination has found pleasure in geometric symmetry and in movement toward resolution. The Japanese have preferred, as Donald Keene has concluded, irregularity, suggestion of things unspoken, an unfinished look.[3] The resolution of the two Homeric epics is toward some rough tally with justice, though Homer's gods provided mortals with justice in a ragged enough form. An individual character in *Genji* might feel wronged, and return to haunt him. Yet justice doesn't seem to be the point. Rather, perhaps, it is the celebration of *mono no aware*, the bittersweet feeling which accompanies a sense of the transience of love, life, and beauty.

In form and subject, then, the two literatures differed widely in their origins. Each literature, as I have said, took a decisive turn in the middle of the nineteenth century, a turn definitive of the modern culture of each people. Those were the years when a new Japan and a new United States were taking shape, but there were also reasons intrinsic to the discipline of literature itself for serious writers to feel the need for a new literature. At the same time, in both cultures, strong pressures resisted change. In Japan, change was to occur when writers read Western literature, but the Meiji oligarchy was preaching—as noted earlier—"Western techniques, Japanese spirit." Their hope was that Japan could build a strong enough economy and military to resist Western power without sacrificing traditional esthetic and moral forms. In the United States, the opposition to change came from readers, so that what was at stake was the American writer's livelihood. Most Americans in the 1830s or so preferred English books for serious reading, such as Sir Walter Scott's tales of the marvelous adventures of medieval heroes; or else, opportunistic American authors, catering to sentimental women of leisure, poured forth maudlin novels about troubled courtship and suffering in the name of Love. Serious American writers who tried to forge a national literature were largely unread.

The Tokugawa literature upon which the new influence was to be superimposed had centered around the haunts of pleasure, the elegant and refined women of the water trades, the wealthy middle-class heirs of Prince Genji who courted them, and the delicate and ephemeral pathos of their lives. Manners, subtlety of perception, above all an awareness of the transience of pleasure, these were the values the Tokugawa writers treasured. By the end of the period, however, "Japanese literature had dropped to one of its lowest levels. The popular authors of the time specialized in books of formless, almost meaningless gossip."[4] When Japanese began going to the West, during the Meiji period, they didn't expect to find literatures worth their attention, but of course they learned differently. Poor Fukuzawa Yukichi, who had taken advantage of the Dutch trading post at Nagasaki assiduously to teach himself Dutch, found when he reached Europe that, alas, he had "learned the wrong language."[5] The literature that attracted them was not the worst in Victorian Europe: Zola, Turgenev, Dumas, Bulwer-Lytton. Two of the greatest writers to emerge from this mix of Japanese and Western were Sōseki Natsume, who lived for a while in England, and Mori Ōgai, who spent four years in Germany. French literature, however, over the long haul, has appealed most to the Japanese. Of the Americans, only Poe found much favor in Meiji Japan. What is interesting here is that the best of the results were by no means antithetical to the Japanese tradition. Mori Ōgai, for example, called his *The Dancing Girl* an *Ich-Roman*, but the form of the fictionalized diary had ancient roots in Japanese literature. Sōseki's themes of loneliness and ephemerality, again, are familiar ones to the Japanese, and still appeal to young readers today. Of Sōseki, more later.

The early American writers of fiction who were trying to be "American" frequently took European models and set them in America. Irving, for example, took German folktales, among other things, and transported them to a Hudson River setting, Charles Brockden Brown imported the popular Gothic mode, and James Fenimore Cooper used Scott as a model upon which to set Leatherstocking in action on the American frontier. The cultural nationalists of the late 1830s, as we have seen, cried out against such imitation: "We have listened too long to the courtly muses of Europe," Emerson preached; already the American is "suspected to be timid, imitative, tame." What emerged from a group of writers over the next half century, working almost in solitude and often in poverty, was indeed a literature clearly distinguishable from the English. First, the language was different. The masked and ironic New England language of Thoreau, the sailor's voice of Melville, the Mississippi River dialects of Twain cannot be confused with British English. The romantics among them adapted a symbolic eye for things from their Puritan ancestors: the palpable facts and events of the mundane world shadow forth deeper and more permanent truths in the mind of God. (The Puritans, however, were considerably less vague than their descendants about the meaning of the word *God*.) The American imagination, publicly cheerful and optimistic, proved itself to be very dark and introspective, not so different from that of its Puritan ancestors, in the lugubrious tales of Poe and Hawthorne, the brooding cosmic pessimism of Melville, the misanthropic cynicism of the late Twain. Poe, Hawthorne, Henry James, and sometimes even Twain were tight formalists, but the grandest creations of the American imagination turned out to be sprawling, and impatient with form: Melville's *Moby Dick*, Whitman's *Leaves of Grass*, and Twain's *Huckleberry Finn* (all modern American literature, said Hemingway, began with that book). Finally, as Richard

Chase has pointed out, the American novel pits the lonely hero, often an outcast, against social codes which are hostile to his decent fulfillment; the English novel, typically more realistic, takes the social code seriously, and satirizes the protagonist who can't manage to fit into it.

This impatience with closely knit construction, this formal impudence of Melville, Whitman, and Twain, is important. American literature contains many works whose beginning, middle, and end comport with Aristotelian tradition: Hawthorne and James, for example, work in this tradition. But beginning with *Moby Dick* and *Huckleberry Finn*, a convention develops of open-ended novels, novels that do not snap shut in the final pages, but rather present the protagonist still in process. He is even actually on the run in a good many recent novels, on a dead run. What is important here is that this convention moves American literature closer to the Japanese than to its European antecedents. The Japanese novel, like the Japanese garden we noticed earlier, suggests process, and typically remains unresolved. Even the formalist Henry James had to face complaints that his *Portrait of a Lady* seemed unresolved, to readers who expected resolution. Events "group themselves," he answered, and the novel may conform to that assessment of experience. That seems to describe many Japanese novels: events "group themselves."

Now it is time to focus on two extremely influential novelists from our middle perspective, around the turn into the twentieth century. Henry James and Sōseki Natsume are still widely read and respected by their countrymen. Both were extraordinarily cosmopolitan and extraordinarily versatile. James and his notable brother William were schooled in their home and through travel with their philosopher father, who sought out the most interesting minds of Europe and North America, for his own edification and that of his two sons. James lived in New York, in Geneva, Paris, and England, among other places, finally becoming an English citizen. Although his journals don't explicitly testify to much direct Oriental influence, he would have been certain to have received some at second or third hand—if from nowhere else, from the New Englanders more or less of the transcendentalist persuasion who came to dinner from time to time when he was young. At least one passage in his novels seems to me to show this very clearly.

Christopher (Columbus?) Newman (New Man?), the protagonist of a rather early novel, *The American* (1877) is a seeker not unrelated to an archetypical American hero of which I will say more later, but his particular mode of seeking is to give up business, and go to France to find culture and a perfect wife. He manages very little of the former, but he almost snags the latter. Finally, the subtle Europeans outsmart him, and he loses her, in a manner particularly painful to his protestant soul, to a convent. His first impulse is to work vengeance; then he broods. Then he stands outside the wall of the strict nunnery to which she has committed herself:

The place looked dumb, deaf, inanimate. The pale, dead, discolored wall stretched beneath it, far down the empty side street. . . . Newman stood there a long time. . . . It was a strange satisfaction, and yet it was a satisfaction; the barren stillness of the place seemed to be his own *release from ineffectual longing.* [Italics added.]

Then he goes to sit a while in the cathedral—the Protestant meditates in the cathedral.

He said no prayers; he had no prayers to say. . . . Newman sat in his place, because while he was there he was out of this world. The most unpleasant thing that had ever happened to him had reached its formal conclusion, as it were. . . . He leaned his head for a long time on the chair in front of him; when he took it up he felt that he was himself again. Somewhere in his mind, *a tight knot seemed to have loosened.* [Italics added.]

The peculiar form of his release seems to me to be clearly Eastern; no prototype exists for it in the Western tradition except in some rather obscure forms of mystic Christianity and perhaps in hard-core New England transcendentalism. One other link to the East—extremely tenuous—can be demonstrated in Henry James. David Dilworth has compared the doctrine of "pure experience" in Henry's neurologist-psychologist-philosopher brother, William, to that of an important modern Japanese philosopher, Nishida Kitaro.[6] William, like his brother, must be thought of among the most imaginative and thoughtful minds in America's history, but the only other excuse for bootlegging him into this discussion is that his brother also built his brilliant fiction out of pure experience in a way that is unusual in the canon of American literature, at least before his time. In a typically

American manner, however, that experience is heavily freighted with moralistic import.

Sōseki Natsume became accomplished in three literatures, Japanese, Chinese, and English. He always felt uncomfortable working with English literature, but for a number of years it was his profession, first as a student, then as a high school teacher, then again as a student in England sponsored by his government, and finally as the successor to Lafcadio Hearn at Tokyo University. (Sōseki and James would have been in London at the same time in 1900 to 1902.) His own study went well beyond literature, however—there were periods in his life when he positively disliked it—and he read in philosophy, psychology, all the disciplines which he felt would help him understand mankind. Among the English writers he particularly favored Meredith, Swift, Sterne, and Addison and Steele. Few men are able to develop good taste quickly in arts so different from those of their own culture: Sōseki's preferences indicate that he was exceptional even in this. Furthermore, he could write respectable Chinese poetry. Finally, he devoted himself to his own literature. Like James, his literary digestive tract was remarkable, and his capacity to create fiction which was both reminiscent of his tradition and quite original as well as permanently important must put him alongside James in the ranks of people who make the existence of humankind a fact worth celebrating.

Unlike James, he had to earn money from early in his life. Furthermore, he took on the burdens of wife and family, also unlike James. The volume of his important works is smaller than James's. Both men, however, lived lives devoted to their several crafts, diligent, earnest, psychically troubled but outwardly rather pacific. It is a rare thing for a novelist of the first rank to be also of the first rank as a theorist of literature and as a literary critic as well, but both men were. Sōseki wrote creditable work in Chinese and also good haiku; James wrote for the theater and also did social commentary of high quality. Both, in other words, were thoroughgoing men of letters. Each is of course finally known as a writer of prose fiction.

Needless to say, neither was immediately a finished artist, though early works of both of them have a freshness and spirit which can still hold readers. *I Am a Cat* (1906), Sōseki's earliest novel, was at first a success, and still remains one, partly because of the Hoffman-like formal conceit which makes the cat the observer of humanity, but in addition because of the interest the cat arouses in the duel between a wealthy family in all its power and an intellectual family in all its intelligent powerlessness. James's *The Bostonians* (1886), also an early work, is likewise characterized by a youthful flair for satire, in this case also of intellectuals, but more acidly, of reformers of the Bostonian persuasion.

We might better dwell on two mature works, written toward the close of long, arduous careers, lives spent thinking about and practicing the craft of the novel: Sōseki's *Kokoro* (1914) and James's *The Ambassadors* (1902). *Kokoro* is a three-part novel about a student who becomes a friend of an unproductive and aging scholar, and of his wife.[7] That relationship reflects on the young man's relationship to his dying father, in part two. Part three, the latter half of the novel, is Sensei's (the "master's") long suicide note to the student, explaining his life and the error in it which has led to years of sorrow and a sense of guilt. In *The Ambassadors*, a middle-aged man of letters is sent by his benefactress in New England to fetch home a scion who is thought to be lost in depravity in Paris. He goes, only to be caught up himself in the charm of Paris, its esthetic mode as opposed to the code of business and morality at home. Somewhat mistakenly, somewhat correctly, he decides that the young man's way of life is superior to that of his New England home, but he himself, given his character, is incapable of relaxing into such a life, and so he returns home.

Those are the externals, but even there we find important comparisons and contrasts. James's material, what he considers an event worth writing about, is far quieter than what most American writers work with. Strangely, most Japanese novels contain less strident materials than most American novels, yet *Kokoro* has the bloody suicide of a friend of Sensei's, more lurid than anything in *The Ambassadors*. The movement of *The Ambassadors*'s plot, however, is typically *toward* something; it moves in the direction of Strether's small epiphany, his discovery that the young expatriate's life, full of beauty, is marred not only by adultery, which Strether in spite of his attempts to be "worldly" is unable to take lightly, but worse by young Chad's essential crassness beneath his elegant surface. The student in *Kokoro* learns something, too, the answer to the enigma of Sensei's character and the meaning of some odd remarks he has dropped in the first section of the book about good and evil—the almost accidental nature of evil, the moral equality of men to whom such an accident has not happened. But Sōseki's narrative eye never shows this *process* of learning. Sensei's testament is all we get, in a novel which seems essentially to belong to the student. What he learns, how he makes use of Sensei's testament, is in the *yohaku*, the "remaining white," the part of the canvas that isn't painted in. Nor are we told how the student relates in his mind the complicated message more or less successfully imparted by Sensei and the experience of running out on his dying father, an act akin to Sensei's in that it involves a breach of feeling for a fellow human being.

All literature, I take it, has its *yohaku*, all literature is selective. Yet long prose fiction in the West tends toward what Erich Auerbach calls "plenitude." It fills in the *necessary* spaces, as when Homer, to use Auerbach's example, flashes back at a climactic moment in old Odysseus's life to tell us how he was initiated into manhood, how he got his name, what the critical details of his heritage had been. Or, as James said, a scene must be "rendered." The difference between James and Sōseki in these works is in what they take to be necessary information about their characters. James among American novelists is uncommonly elliptical at some points in his narrative. Westerners following Aristotle insist that a work be self-enclosed, as I have said; the Japanese typically allow for much more of the work to be performed in the viewer's imagination.

This parsimony extends to the number of characters admitted into the usual Japanese novel—a change from the old *monogatari*. *Kokoro* has only five characters of more than passing significance. James likes to help himself in delineation of character by placing at angles around his central character, like refracting mirrors, lesser characters with attributes that are comparable to those of his main characters. That in part accounts for the high density of population in his novels; but the Western novel generally, either of the picaresque variety, with its series of episodes, or of tighter construction with plots and subplots, is busier with character and event than the typical Japanese novel. Let me pause here to mention again a point which I discussed in connection with Bashō. The Japanese idea of what *constitutes* an event is ordinarily much more modest than the American. Some of this was apparent in the travel books by Bashō and Mark Twain. A kind of psychic economy operates in Bashō and the later novelists who resemble him in many ways; that kind of sensibility gets a lot of mileage out of the most fragile occurrence. As James put it in his "Art of Fiction," "It is an incident for a woman to stand up with her hand resting on a table and look at you in a certain way." It seems to me that most Japanese authors would agree, but that most American authors would ask for gamier fare. That contemporary of James, James McNeill Whistler, influenced like others painting in Europe at the time by the Japanese print, also liked a bold, clean canvas. Yet even James and Whistler, and certainly most American novelists and painters, are ordinarily more given to plenitude, and less to *yohaku*, than Sōseki or his contemporary, the printmaker Yamamoto Kanae; and the latter achieve cleaner and more striking design.

We are talking about a short novel, then, and a very long one—*Kokoro* comes to about 85,000 words, *The Ambassadors* to about twice that many. The materials are much the same: filial piety, the reprehensible deeds men do for love, fidelity to friendship, the practical consequences of our actions on the lives of others, even the "generation gap" of about 1910. *The Ambassadors* is one of James's many "international novels" which deal with the contrast between American and European culture; *Kokoro* contrasts, briefly but importantly, the manners of Tokyo and those of the provinces. Both writers deal with the psychology of guilt, though in different ways. Sōseki is interested in the consequences of guilt: Sensei has been burdened for years by the knowledge that, in competing with his good friend for the love of the woman who would marry Sensei, he may have contributed to his rival's suicide. His own decision to commit suicide is as much a result of knowing that guilt would cloud his and his wife's lives together as it is of guilt itself. James, too, is interested in the practical consequences of guilt, its importance as it affects relationships between person and person. Particularly, he is interested in the New England habit of mind which, without evidence, attributes innocence to oneself and guilt to another, especially if that other is European. Then James also dramatizes the way in which the same mind is inhibited in its capacity to enjoy beauty by the subconscious fear that such enjoyment is somehow morally tainted.

The materials of the novels are similar in many respects. The moral arithmetic we apply to them includes no absolute numbers, as many American novels do. We are entirely within the realm of friend and friend, lover and lover, family and family, and in both novels the numbers are relative. The traditional Japanese vocabulary for handling the kinds of human problems which arise in *Kokoro* are *giri* and *ninjo*. *Giri* refers to duties one owes one's superiors and elders, and one's family. "Won't you be a good son?" the student's mother implores, and Edwin McClellan, the translator, notes, "The word in the Japanese text is *oya-koko*, which means 'filial piety.' " *Ninjo*, then, are those human affections that come naturally, in friendship or love. The conflict between *giri* and *ninjo* is the axis on which many Japanese stories turn. The student *tries* to be a "good son." As his father nears death, day after day, yet lingers on, he postpones his trip to Tokyo, to see Sensei, the friend with whom he feels most compatible. When he receives word of Sensei's impending suicide, however, he can wait no longer, and dashes off, though deeply troubled about leaving his dying father. One of the beauties of the novel is that we see the student no more after that. We know he carries in his pocket Sensei's long letter explaining his guilt and his decision to die. How the student will relate that testament, which ends by saying that it is intended as "an example for others," lies in the *yohaku*.

James's international novels examine, among other things, the conflicts between two vocabularies, the moralistic one of the presumed innocents from America, and that embodying the taste and beauty of the Europeans. Neither party is wholly able to understand the other, and neither has a vocabulary wholly adequate to understand experience in its totality. Chad's friend assures Strether that Chad's relationships with the excellent Mme. de Vionnet are "innocent." We aren't sure what Chad's friend means by that, though perhaps it refers in some large sense to the incapacity of Mme. de Vionnet to harbor any evil intentions. Strether, intelligent as he is, assumes the sexual meaning, in the old New England way. Mme. de Vionnet comes closest to understanding all. Near the end of the book, after Chad has announced his decision in the grossest possible terms to leave her and go home to the family business, this colloquy between her and Strether occurs. Strether wishes not to abandon her, would like to comfort her, but she refuses easy sentimentality.

"You don't care what I think of you; but I happen to care what you think of me. And what you *might*," she added. "What you perhaps even did."

He gained time. "What I did—?"

"Did think before. Before this. *Didn't* you think—?"

But he had already stopped her. "I didn't think anything. I never think a step further than I'm obliged to."

"That's perfectly false, I believe," she returned—"except that you may, no doubt, often pull up when things become *too* ugly. . . ."

In purely human terms, we are disappointed in Strether's evasiveness, his incapacity to be candid with the sad and splendid woman. His knowledge of the standards of the French culture is finally merely intellectual. He has come very far in his awareness of how cramped his New England psyche really is, and how much more of life than he has ever known is open to people; yet he cannot act on this knowledge even far enough to comfort Mme. de Vionnet's desolation.

The manner in which we are enclosed in ourselves is also at the heart of *Kokoro* (no pun is intended: *kokoro* is translatable as "heart," but probably more accurately "the heart of the matter," or perhaps something like "soul," without its theological implications). Sensei cannot give love fully to the wife he loves; she cannot reach him. The student cannot speak frankly with his dying father, or penetrate Sensei's cloud of guilt. All those people who want to love, and cannot, fill the novel. Part I of *Kokoro* ends as follows. In a rare burst of pique, Sensei's wife scolds her husband.

"How many more times are you going to say, 'When I die, when I die'? For heaven's sake, please don't say 'when I die' again! It's unlucky to talk like that. When you die, I shall do as you wish. There, let that be the end of it."

Sensei turned towards the garden and laughed. But to please her, he dropped the subject. It was getting late, and so I stood up to go. Sensei and his wife came to the front hall with me.

"Take good care of your father," she said.

"Till September, then," he said.

I said goodbye and stepped out of the house. Between the house and the outer gate, there was a bushy osmanthus tree. It spread its branches into the night as if to block my way. I looked at the dark outline of the leaves and thought of the fragrant flowers that would be out in the autumn. I said to myself, I have come to know this tree well, and it has become, in my mind, an inseparable part of Sensei's house. As I stood in front of the house, thinking of the coming autumn when I would be walking up the path once more, the porch light suddenly went out. Sensei and his wife had apparently gone into their bedroom. I stepped out alone into the dark street.

I did not return to my lodgings immediately.

Somewhat later, thinking of all of Sensei's talk of death, and of his father's impending death, he says, "As I am sitting here now, helpless, though I know that my father is waiting to die. . . . I felt then the helplessness of man, and the vanity of his life."

Both novels, of course, evoke "felt thought." If one compares the passage above with the earlier one quoted from *The Ambassadors*, I believe it will be evident that James calls on our intellectual skills rather more than our emotional to fill in the interstices, and Sōseki on our emotional rather more than our intellectual. The image of the tree, with its promise of autumn, then of the lights going out, separating the student from a husband and wife already separated a bit by their spat, then the lonely young man contemplating death, all of that evokes an adjective describing feeling: "lonely." The James passage is emotionally potent, too, for we sympathize with the equally lonely Mme. de Vionnet. Yet James keeps us busy thinking: why is Strether holding back? how is it that she understands something more about guilt than even a New Englander? James keeps us at finishing sentences, deciphering what is meant from what is said.

That slight difference in emphasis on the part of the reader's imagination to be exercised seems generally to hold in the two literatures. James surely resembles his Japanese contemporary more closely than most of his American contemporaries do. Partly because of the enormous weight of James's art on his successors, and partly because of the influence of Western literature in Japan, catalyzed by Sōseki, that difference grew slighter as history wore on.

Now I wish to change my mode of discussion to a topical one, and concentrate on the two literatures in two later periods: writers we associate with the period between the two world wars—the "modern classics"; and then some good post–World War II writers. In this arbitrary manner, I believe I can make some comparisons and contrasts in a short space. Before we go any farther at all, however, we should notice that some examples from the literatures are hardly comparable at all. This is particularly true of what Philip Rahv calls the "redskin" tradition in American literature, "uncooked," impudent in form, and energetic. It is in what he calls the "paleface" tradition—quieter, formally tighter, well "cooked"—that we find closer similarities to the Japanese literature of the central tradition. Edward Seidensticker, the fine translator of Japanese literature, has written an essay comparing Kawabata with James and Hemingway, and I would certainly agree with that choice. Yet for all of James's psychological subtlety, and all of Hemingway's economy, neither has created an image quite like the following, on page 4 of Kawabata's *Snow Country* (1935, 1947).[8] The protagonist, Shimamura, is on a train heading north to revisit his lover, a snow country geisha, Komako. He has been watching another young woman who is seated nearby, Yoko. Shimamura notices that only the forefinger of his left hand remembers Komako: "Taken with the strangeness of it, he brought the hand to his face, then quickly drew a line across the misted-over window. A woman's eye floated up before him. He almost called out in his astonishment. But he had been dreaming." He wakes up to the fact that it is the reflection of one of Yoko's eyes. Because it is growing dark outside, the lights have been turned on in the train, making a mirror of the part of the window he had wiped the mist from. Thus he can watch her. She is single-mindedly attentive of an ailing older man. "Shimamura could see from the way her strength was gathered in her shoulders that the suggestion of fierceness in her eyes was but a sign of an intentness that did not permit her to blink." The man is ill, but somehow the scene carried nothing of "the pain that the sight of something truly sad can bring," for "it was all completely natural, as if the two of them, quite insensitive to space, meant to go on forever, farther and farther into the distance." But Shimamura's "strange mirror" plays further tricks.

In the depths of the mirror the evening landscape moved by, the mirror and the reflected figures like motion pictures superimposed one on the other. The figures and the background were unrelated, and yet the figures, transparent and intangible, and the background, dim in the gathering darkness, melted together into a sort of symbolic world not of this world. Particularly when a light out in the mountains shone in the center of the girl's face, Shimamura felt his chest rise at the inexpressible beauty of it.

I think nothing in American literature manages this same tight unity of carefully calculated ways of seeing, the impact of Yoko's image, and the fusion of all of this into light, time, movement, landscape, and generalized space, all converging in a psychological state with physiological effect. Eyesight of a peculiar kind, emotion, motion, light, and landscape become metaphysical, without losing physicality. The cold light of Yoko's eyes and the light from the mountain merge in the imagination into some transcending glow, but Shimamura's chest rises all the same. Kawabata can catch a glimpse of synapses one did not know the nervous system capable of, then transform them into a pattern which is harmonious with that of nature itself.

The closest American approximation that I know of to this delicate and complex handling of a flow of sensations and emotions is a passage from Jean Toomer's *Cane* (1923). The protagonist is an educated northern black who has returned to the Georgia of his forefathers. He walks toward the woods with Fern, a beautiful woman who holds strange spiritual powers over men. Once somewhat promiscuous, she "became a virgin again"; now men somehow wish strongly to do kindnesses for her. She is angry at the gossipy people who are watching them. "Under a sweet-gum tree, and where reddish leaves had dammed the creek a little, we sat down. Dusk, suggesting the almost imperceptible procession of giant trees, settled with a purple haze about the cane. I felt strange, as I always do in Georgia, particularly at dusk. I felt that things unseen to men were tangibly immediate." People have visions in Georgia, the protagonist tells us; he wouldn't be surprised now if he should have one himself. "A black woman once saw the mother of Christ and drew her in charcoal on the courthouse wall."

Without knowing why and "without . . . noticing it himself," he takes Fern in his arms. Then he focuses on her. "Her eyes, unusually weird and open, held me. Held God. He flowed in as I've seen the countryside flow in. Seen men." Fern runs away from the "confusion of . . . emotions," then "fell to her knees, and began swaying, swaying. Her body was tortured with something it could not let out. Like boiling sap it flooded arms and fingers till she shook them as if they burned her. It found her throat, and spattered inarticulately in plaintive, convulsive sounds, mingled with calls to Christ Jesus."

To illustrate writing which I consider uniquely American, here are some passages from William Faulkner's *The Hamlet* (1940). (An earlier version of them appeared in 1931 as the story "Spotted Horses.")

The crafty, conscienceless, and unfalteringly successful swindler Flem Snopes—a hyperbolic personification of the compleat capitalist, in Faulkner's scheme—has brought from Texas a load of terrifically wild horses to sell to his fellow citizens of Frenchman's Bend. Sure enough, the people are duped, almost hypnotized, into spending money they absolutely cannot spare for the fierce and treacherous beasts. Before anyone can rope his own purchase, however, the horses break out of their pen:

Then an indescribable sound, a movement desperate and despairing, arose among them; for an instant of static horror men and animals faced one another, then the men whirled and ran before a gaudy vomit of long wild faces and splotched chests which overtook and scattered them and flung them sprawling aside and completely obliterated from sight Henry and the little boy, neither of whom had moved though Henry had flung up both arms, still holding his coiled rope, the herd sweeping on across the lot, to crash through the gate which the last man through it had neglected to close, leaving it slightly ajar, carrying all of the gate save upright to which the hinges were nailed with them, and so among the teams and wagons which choked the lane, the teams springing and lunging too, snapping hitchreins and tongues.

One of them, belonging to Eck Snopes and his son, runs into Mrs. Littlejohn's boardinghouse where the traveling salesman Ratliff is staying.

They saw the horse fill the long hallway like a pinwheel, gaudy, furious and thunderous. A little further down the hall there was a varnished yellow melodeon. The horse crashed into it; it produced a single note, almost a chord, in bass, resonant and grave, of deep and sober astonishment.

The horse moves on into Ratliff's bedroom; he is in his underwear, leaning out the window.

For an instant he and the horse glared at one another. Then he sprang through the window as the horse backed out of the room and into the hall again and whirled and saw Eck and the little boy just entering the front door, Eck still carrying his rope. It whirled again and rushed on down the hall and onto the back porch just as Mrs Littlejohn, carrying an armful of clothes from the line and the washboard, mounted the steps.
"Get out of here, you son of a bitch," she said. She struck with the washboard; it divided neatly on the long mad face and the horse whirled and rushed back up the hall, where Eck and the boy now stood.

The horse moves on. "It galloped to the end of the veranda and took the railing and soared outward, hobgoblin and floating, in the moon."

Later, Ratliff, one of Faulkner's favorite characters, retells the story to a group of townsmen who loaf around the village store. " 'Maybe there wasn't but one of them things in Mrs Littlejohn's house that night, like Eck says. But it was the biggest drove of just one horse I ever seen.' " As Ratliff talks, Eck and his son, purchasers of a horse, sit expressionless, squatting against a wall, eating cheese and crackers, "save for the difference in size, identical." " ' I wonder what that horse thought Ratliff was,' one [of the listeners] said. He held a spray of peach bloom between his teeth. It bore four blossoms like miniature ballet skirts of pink tulle. 'Jumping out windows and running indoors in his shirt-tail? I wonder how many Ratliffs that horse thought he saw.' " Slowly and carefully, Ratliff moves toward the nub. Eck, like many of the townsmen, had been swindled by his own kinsman, Flem Snopes. "The laughter stopped."

Several qualities in these passages strike me as peculiarly American. The events themselves are outrageous: violent, brutal, and broadly comical at once. (Some stage comics in Japan work this kind of material.) Everything is exaggerated and unlikely: the craftiness of Flem, the gullibility of the other townsfolk, the ferocity of the horses, the courage of Mrs. Littlejohn and Eck's son. The experience being imitated is larger than life. One recalls that the tall tale is a characteristic form of American folklore.

The traditional manner of *telling* a tall tale is reserved to Ratliff. Faulkner's own mode is typically exuberant, his long sentences splashing over one another like restless waves, his imagery almost violent in surprise and impact. Ratliff's deadpan style is the one recommended by Mark Twain, in "How to Tell a Story," often exaggerated, too, in its understatement, its illusion of cool objectivity concerning outlandish events, and its selection of details which are incongruous, such as the horse's crash into the yellow melodeon, or the man's peach spray, "like miniature ballet skirts of pink tulle," or the pinwheel image, or the word *vomit* to describe the breaking of the pack of horses. The brutal and the funny are juxtaposed. Faulkner reveals the social situation here deftly. Quietly, humorously, apparently speaking of other matters, Ratliff makes his point. Beneath the rather formalistic style of narrative and banter and the ritualistic whittling lies a good deal of tension, as they move toward recognition of the truth (Flem had used a man from Texas as his cover, pretending only to be his aid).

Faulkner can work in modes other than these, but in these I believe him to be most recognizably American and furthest removed from the Japanese tradition.

If certain quintessential skills of the two national literatures reveal traditional differences, other qualities of the literatures remind us that storytelling is a universal human activity, and that modern authors separated by half a globe have similar concerns. Looking further at Kawabata and Faulkner, we find some similarities—and, again, differences. First, let's look at their method of building symbols within a work to charge the suggestiveness of the work as a whole.

Kawabata, though immersed in his youth in European literatures, later consciously dedicated himself to the Japanese tradition, to making fiction in some way do the work of haiku. Faulkner, after a short experience abroad as a soldier, spent most of his life in his native southern village. An heir to Hawthorne in some respects, to Mark Twain in others, he developed a personal range of skills which were all unmistakably southern. Both writers, focusing intently on their own traditions, manage thereby to make the kind of widely felt statement that is recognized by the Nobel committee for literature.

Another look at *Snow Country*. Shimamura goes to the snow country, the mountains, because in Tokyo he "tends to lose his honesty with himself." Komako, his lover, is clean, honest, straightforward, but already at twenty, a part-time geisha, showing signs of her mortality. His last trip to see her is blessed with all the beauties of autumn, and they are imaged brightly. That season is dear to Japanese sensibilities precisely because it precedes winter. But mortality as well:

Each day, as the autumn grew colder, insects died on the floor of his room. Stiff-winged insects fell on their backs and were unable to get to their feet again. A bee walked a little and collapsed, walked a little and collapsed. It was a quiet death that came with the change of seasons. Looking closely, however, Shimamura could see that the legs and feelers were trembling in the struggle to live. For such a tiny death, the empty eight-mat room seemed enormous.

As he throws one dead insect out, he thinks of his children at home! Then, picking up a dead moth, he wonders "how to account for such beauty." Then it snows. The novel, very quietly, has moved toward a feeling of finality. During the course of an amiable conversation, Shimamura half-consciously insults Komako. She is barely recovering from this wound to her spirit when they hear a fire alarm, and run toward it. At this moment, Shimamura becomes aware of the unusual clarity of the Milky Way.

She raised her left hand a little and ran off. Her retreating figure was drawn up into the mountain. The Milky Way spread its skirts to be broken by the waves of the mountain, and fanning out again in all its brilliant vastness higher in the sky, it left the mountains in a deeper darkness.

Then, suddenly, they see Yoko's body falling from the fire. The last line of the book reads, "As he caught his footing, his head fell back, and the Milky Way flowed down inside him with a roar."

This ending seems a resolution which denies my earlier assertion that Japanese fiction is not teleological in the Western fashion. Yet I believe it does not. In the Aristotelian scheme, reiterated by such Americans as Mark Twain and Henry James, the germ of every event ought to reside in preceding events, and a law of probability must govern the climax. But Yoko's apparent death is as gratuitous as a motor accident. Shimamura may perceive something new of transcendent permanence in his experience of the Milky Way, but that, too, happens with no preparation whatever, other than the general awareness that seasons follow one another, and that one can regain honesty with himself in the snow country. Enlightenment just happens, given proper circumstances.

Now let me turn to Faulkner's *Light in August* (1932). Faulkner uses circles and arcs to suggest something like the cyclical nature of things Kawabata was interested in. Although he claimed once that the word *light* in his title simply referred to the fierce sunlight of a Mississippi August, evidence within the novel indicates that the southern country term for birthing—*lightening*—might also work, for many burdens are released in the novel, at the end. The novel is a tryptich, the panels of which merge at the climax. For Lena Grove, a character who epitomizes wifehood and motherhood, the arc begins in search of the father of her baby; when she finds him, he rejects her, just at the time of the birth of her baby; but she wanders on, always able to find men to help her. Presumably, some babies later, and never out of harmony with her role, she will come full cycle. For Hightower, the defrocked minister, the circle is the past in which he is trapped, as in a triple-tiered fence: the past of the South's lost war, and his grandfather's inglorious part in it, of his own absurd preoccupation with that past which causes such bizarre behavior at home and in the pulpit that he loses his wife and job, and finally of his self-enforced immobility since being afflicted by those losses. For Joe Christmas, the circle is the long trip from his home north and west and then back home again, in search of freedom and identity. In the South his personal identity is closely tied to his "race"; he doesn't really know whether he's black or white. "The street" he follows in his search runs through much of the continent, through work in oil fields and wheat fields, through "fierce yellow days of labor and hard sleep in haystacks beneath the cold mad moon of September, and brittle stars"; it was "fifteen years long." Finally, the street runs full cycle back to his old land, Mississippi.

Faulkner's symbolism is abstract, geometric. Suggestions about the world inside the novel don't radiate naturally and inevitably from those arcs and circles; meaning must be lent to them. They therefore have a cerebral quality to them that differs from Kawabata's symbols. Kawabata's mountains and insects are not empty of idea, but idea seems less a separable or necessary part of what they signify.

Methods of characterization in the two novels differ in some of the same ways. Faulkner's characters are constructs; they aren't intended to be "realistic" in any literal sense of the word, but rather representations of types in a manner not far removed from medieval morality plays. They are embodiments of analyses of southern types, human types. Noh masks, of course, enforce on that drama an abstraction of human character, too, but the typing is of actual human types, such as the beautiful young woman and the wise old man rather than embodiments of abstracted human qualities such as, let's say, "fertility" or "catatonic historicism." Types of Noh are from a demographic chart; in the Western morality play, they are from a sort of moral valence chart. Faulkner's still have that quality; Kawabata has moved farther toward realism.

Kawabata and Faulkner apparently are interested in human character from somewhat different perspectives. Since these perspectives seem typical of the cultures, let's look further. The difference comports with the two cosmologies, at least obliquely. Faulkner wants to know the beginning, middle, and end of his characters. Kawabata wants to know the practical consequences of his characters' qualities, at given times, when they touch others.

Poe and Hawthorne, notably among Faulkner's predecessors, had explored what became called in Freudian days "depth psychology." They worked with the dark recesses of the human psyche—guilt, the death wish, bizarre passions, images of enclosure, isolation, decay. And they examined possible sources for these spooks of the nervous system. By Faulkner's time, all these preoccupations had the further sanction of scientific psychology. Perhaps from such precedents, perhaps from Homer's old model of plenitude, he tries to give us everything, the character of the parents, the quality of the upbringing, the trauma of adolescence, everything. Kawabata provides us with very little of that information. Rather, he concentrates on the most minute emotional details of the *telling* exchanges between people. We might say that the Japanese author's interest in psychology is *practical*, as well as esthetic, the American's *metaphysical*, as well as esthetic. We know nothing of Shimamura's or Komako's origins or of their parents' skill in child-raising. We do know that their love grows after an episode in which he decides with Komako's knowledge against accepting the services of an awkward young prostitute, climbs a mountain instead, and runs down full of joy to encounter Komako. We know also that their love diminishes, late in the novel, after the following conversation. Shimamura says,

"You're a good girl."
"Why? Why am I good? What's good about me?"
"You're a good girl."
"Don't tease me. It's wrong of you." She looked aside, and she spoke in broken phrases, like little blows, as she rocked him back and forth. "I'm not good at all. It's not easy having you here. You'd best go home. Each time I come to see you I want to put on a new kimono, and now I have none left. This one I borrowed. So you see I'm not really good at all."
Shimamura did not answer.
"And what do you find good in me?" Her voice was a little husky.

The conversation goes on, Komako clearly fishing for a reinforcement to the compliment that Shimamura has so stingily made. Then,

They were silent for some moments. Komako seemed to be looking back on herself, and the awareness of a woman's being alive came to Shimamura in her warmth.

"You're a good woman."

"How am I good?"

"A good woman . . ."

"A good woman—what do you mean by that? What do you mean? . . ."

She stared at him, scarlet with anger.

I am told, incidentally, that the translation comports very well with the American English "good girl" and "good woman." Thus the hurt to Komako's spirit turns on a word, perhaps heedlessly said, perhaps obstinately.

Another way of putting this is that the psychology of a good many American novels puts the emphasis on the *cause* of certain human interchanges, while the Japanese novel typically works on the practical human effect of the exchange between certain human beings.

When we turn from Faulkner to Hemingway, we find a greater compatibility with Kawabata's method.

In *Snow Country*, just before the final episode, the fire, Shimamura visits the nearby villages in which Chijimi linen has historically been woven. That was a linen particularly noted for its whiteness and its coolness. It was woven by agile-fingered young people, working intensely in competition with one another, during the snow season. Now the villages seem run down. Weaving the old linen became infeasible economically, and the people of Chijimi have turned to other weaving, not the kind that brought pride and intensity to their lives.

All this reflects on the events of the novel, but only obliquely. Komako's clean, light skin in his memory is akin to the pure, snow-bleached linen. The linen is cool to the skin beause of some interplay of hot and cold, again suggestive of the volatile Komako. Is Shimamura, who wears an old Chijimi garment, worthy to be clad in such fine stuff, lovingly and painstakingly woven by the earnest young people? The transience of love contrasts with the durability of the linen, which even graces permanent art as the costume for actors on the Noh Stage; but then it's temporary, too, as is even the village culture which centered on its production. The short Chijimi episode shines little reflections all over the novel, like one of those revolving globes made of small mirrors which one sees in ballrooms. This method is more oblique than the sort of symbolism which opens out from some one-to-one equation, such as "insect" suggests "fleeting life," and "circle" suggests "search and return." Let's call it "refraction" as opposed to "reflection."

Late in his career, Hemingway could use the reflective method in the old American way, in *The Old Man and the Sea* (1952). In *The Sun Also Rises* (1926), however, he uses refraction in a way that's very similar to the Chijimi episode. The world-weary and sterile little coterie of expatriates who people that novel decide to quit their bored carousing in Paris, and visit a festival in Spain. Brett is attracted to Romero, the dedicated young bullfighter. Jealousies that ensue, aggravated by hangovers and gross sensibilities, threaten to mar Romero's career, the festival, and the bullfight which is the climax of the festival. In the midst of this, Hemingway tells us about how steers are employed in controlling the bulls. "A gate opened and two steers came in, swaying their heads and trotting, their lean flanks swinging. They stood together at the far end, their heads toward the gate where the bull would enter. 'They don't look happy,' Brett said." Then the bull "explodes" into the ring, "his head up, the great hump of muscle on his neck swollen tight, his body muscles quivering as he looked up at the crowd on the stone walls. The two steers backed away against the wall, their heads sunken, their eyes watching the bull. . . .'My God, isn't he beautiful?' Brett said. We were looking right down on him." Then a second bull is released, and heads for the steers. "The two steers turned sideways to take the shock, and the bull drove into one of the steers." The bull moves toward the second steer, but hooks him only lightly. "The steer came up to him and made as though to nose at him and the bull hooked perfunctorily. The next time he nosed at the steer and then the two of them trotted over to the other bull." The steer that had been gored, then, is ignored by the others.

Hemingway's use of the steers is oblique. They shed light on the characters, and their social grouping, but only indirectly. Jake is literally a steer, having been emasculated in the war, and he is no match for the bullfighter Romero in bull-like virility. Yet he is an aficionado, his life has a bit of the discipline of Romero's, his mentality is not that of the steer. Cohn, like the gored steer, has been rejected by the little fraternity which includes Jake, Mike, and Brett, and whose rules forbid the kind of sentimental behavior that Cohn is guilty of; on the other hand, Cohn is a skillful boxer. Only the bulls and Romero are wholly beautiful, in this scheme. Hemingway's method here is not, it seems to me, much dissimilar to Kawabata's.

Both Junichiro Tanizaki's *Some Prefer Nettles* (1928) and F. Scott Fitzgerald's *The Great Gatsby* (1925) turn on a conflict between old and new values. Neither is merely sentimentally nostalgic: the old values show signs of corrosion, the new at least some surface glamour. Characteristically, old values for Tanizaki are lodged in bunraku, the old puppet theater. Both Tanizaki and Kawabata use traditional art forms, and appreciation of their paraphernalia—Noh masks, the cups for the tea ceremony, the samisen—as representatives of old Japanese sensibilities. Interestingly, Fitzgerald's narrator Nick holds to old *moral* values, quite abstractly conceived, and he admires Gatsby, a scion of old economic heroes such as Ben Franklin and James J. Hill. The decadent present of the 1920s is represented in a number of ways, but in important ways it is embodied in two lukewarm and indecisively adulterous women, Misako, the wife of the protagonist Kaname, and Daisy Buchanan, Gatsby's lover who can be faithful neither to her husband nor to Gatsby. The status of the institution of marriage is one yardstick of what time does to culture. Misako's hankering after modernity takes the form of avowing a lover whom she says she plans to marry; yet she can't quite shake the habits of a Japanese wife. She lays out her husband's clothing and defers to him publicly. Nor can she finally decide to divorce him. Daisy, perhaps in part reacting against her husband's own tawdry affairs, flirts openly enough with Gatsby until her husband's temper explodes; then she retreats to the safety of old money (Gatsby's is new) and the old, boring marriage. Neither novel is moralistic about the institution of marriage in any copybook manner. Gatsby's almost absurdly earnest courtship of Daisy has about it something almost heroic. Tanizaki casts no moral judgment on Misako, and certainly not on her father and his very traditional young mistress O-hisa. Rather, the institution is used as an example of the incapacity of the spoiled bourgeoisie of the two cultures to function decisively and fruitfully, suspended as they are between two sets of values.

If marriage is a yardstick, symbolic geography is a map of time, in both novels. For Fitzgerald, it moves from east to west according to the scheme of "the contrast" described in an earlier chapter, "East Egg" on Long Island suggesting old and decadent wealth and culture, phasing out to middle western hope and innocence. Tanizaki's geography isn't so neat on the compass, but phases from the small and ancient puppet-stage town of Awaji, through old Osaka to newer and grosser Tokyo, Shanghai, Europe. The manner in which the two authors use this geography is what is interesting to us here. In Tanizaki, the attributes of those places as ordinarily perceived are all that he requires. In little towns like Awaji the arts taken so solemnly by the learned men in the cities really do thrive among "the folk" in something like their original condition; but poor O-hisa, with all her delicacies, had trouble finding a place to relieve herself there. Tanizaki's Osaka is simply Osaka, Tokyo, Tokyo. Fitzgerald, perhaps as inheritor of the symbolic eye of the old romantics, perhaps as author in an unstoried civilization, feels compelled to construct significances for his places. Sometimes he moves to surrealism. West Egg, says Nick of the new-rich Long Island town, is a "night scene by El Greco." "In the foreground four solemn men in dress suits are walking along the sidewalk with a stretcher on which lies a drunken woman in a white evening dress. Her hand, which dangles over the side, sparkles cold with jewels. Gravely the men turn in at a house—the wrong house. But no one knows the woman's name, and no one cares."

I do not wish to imply that Fitzgerald's method here is inappropriate to his ends. On the contrary. His book is what Hawthorne called a "romance," as opposed to a novel, for he wished to distinguish a narrative which mixes the "actual" with the "marvelous" from realism in the English tradition. What is to be noticed here is that important authors of American fiction, with the exception of Howells and a few others, have never felt at home with the realistic mode the Japanese authors ordinarily work in. Again, *Gatsby* is resolved in the end: Gatsby is killed and the decent narrator, Nick, moves back to the Middle West where he belongs. Typically, *Nettles* is unresolved, though faint signs indicate that Kaname is leaning toward the old values embodied in O-hisa.

Now, a switch from Tanizaki and Fitzgerald to Tanizaki and Hemingway. *The Sun Also Rises*, like *Some Prefer Nettles*, concerns characters who are in a limbo of time. "You are all a lost generation," Gertrude

Stein told them, and Hemingway used that line as the epigraph of his book, along with a passage from scripture which speaks to the cyclical rhythms of nature. The war-riddled expatriates, as we saw, visit a Spanish fiesta, and see peasants for whom those cycles of death and regeneration are not remote scripture, but are rather the experienced conditions of life. A man attains his dignity in his span between birth and death through skill and work and ritual, which sometimes requires the renunciation, in Buddhist fashion, of unworthy desire.

Tanizaki dramatizes the little pains of indecision which inflict men and women wavering between old ways of being and new: "Every worm to his taste; some prefer nettles." The tone of the novel consistently carries out the suggestion of the title. Kaname is not literally emasculated as is Hemingway's protagonist Jake; his relationships with his wife, however, are restricted to those gestures which are necessary to keep up appearances before the world and before their son. That difference may suggest the comparatively slight difference in the way the novels are managed. Jake puts up a bold public front, and masks the pain of his sexual loneliness, but the pain is demonstrated as more profound than what nettles inflict. Tanizaki works with a spectrum of attitudes, carefully graded. Hemingway counterposes two rather sharply defined sets of attitudes, the ennui and sterility—physical or psychic—of the Paris group, and the vitality of the Spanish group, in art, love, and death as represented in the bullfight. Hemingway is one of the finest grained writers in America since James, yet the texture of his novel is somewhat rougher than Tanizaki's. As artifacts, however, they are strikingly similar: carefully wrought works of art about how carefully wrought works of art (that is the way Romero's and the puppeteers' crafts are handled) are men's principal stay against confusion when the times are out of joint.

One peculiarity of some American "modern classics" which differentiates them, I believe, from all serious Japanese literature of the period is suggested by *The Great Gatsby*, but is most clearly exemplified by Faulkner's "The Bear" and Hemingway's *The Old Man and the Sea*: the mythic and heroic. If Gatsby is the heir of folk yarns about "captains of industry," the other two protagonists are heirs of an old heritage of superhuman hunters and fishermen. Those works have evolved from the honorable old folk genre, the tall tale. We are asked to believe that the boy Ike McCaslin, anointed by destiny and learned beyond his years, stood unarmed and face to face with Old Ben, the ancient, fierce bear, and that old Santiago, farther out at sea than he had ever been, caught an eighteen-foot marlin. The lone hunters, in contest with nature at its most powerful, and winning. Faulkner is not merely nostalgic. His myth-laden novella, only a more grandly imagined and finely worked version of yarns one still hears in country-town barber shops, proclaims that such feats are a thing of the past, for the wilderness died with the bear. Hemingway's language and method proclaim that his narrative, too, belongs in some realm beyond realistic fiction, in the tradition of *Moby Dick*. I intend no denigration of these admirable works when I say that the stuff they are made of occurs in Japan only in the popular arts. The protagonists of serious Japanese fiction of this century do not operate at the outer limits of human possibility; they remain very much within them. Their writers didn't have to borrow from the international celebration of the antihero. Their tradition, as we have seen, was already full of scapegraces. Later we will see that Dazai Osamu comes close to pushing *that* sort of protagonist toward the edges of human possibility.

If myth is a dimension of literature which contemporary Japanese novelists do not appear to be interested in, Americans do not seem to have the knack of erotic themes in the way Japanese do. As we have seen, the erotic tradition runs from *Genji* to the late Tokugawa novels about the Yoshiwara "floating world." Kawabata and Tanizaki, then, could write their masterpieces with strong conventions behind them. Most American authors until about World War I skipped sex as subject entirely or handled it gingerly through veiled hints. During the 1920s, Henry Miller, working in Europe, dealt with sex, but did so in the manner of an adolescent who had just discovered the subject. Recently, of course, many American writers consider sexuality to be a subject for literature, but I can think of none who completely escape prurience. Often sexuality is treated in the manner of the dirty joke of folklore, ranging from funny, as in Barth's *Giles, Goat Boy,* through less than funny, as in Roth's *Portnoy's Complaint*, to disgusting, as in Burrough's *Naked Lunch*. Kawabata and Tanizaki can write about sexuality as a truth. Sometimes it is a strange truth, as when Tanizaki in *Diary of a Mad Old Man* considers foot fetiches. Even then, the manner is that of a scientist who is objective in his study but not without feeling for its object. Tanizaki in that novel and in *The Key* and Kawabata in

The House of the Sleeping Beauties and slightly in *The Sound of the Mountain* anatomize the dying eroticism of old men, a subject which Western writers can see in no other light than comic, if they see it at all (*Diary*, too, is far from serious, but not quite in the sense of the smutty joke). Americans, said the sage Henry Adams early in this century, considered their triumph over sex one of their greatest achievements. Having thought better of it later, they seem unable to assimilate the idea in their deepest imaginations.

If we can speak of an "international style" in architecture after 1945, we can do so in literature as well. The methods and motifs aren't quite as monolithic as the tall building in the early style of Le Corbusier seen all over the world; but certain of them seem to run through all the industrial cultures: loneliness, alienation, and the search for identity, sometimes turning on the hyperbole of insanity; the threat of some social structure called "the establishment" or the "power elite"; the animal imagery for discussing mankind, alternating with the robot or puppet; the mood of the absurd, the method of irony; the antihero as protagonist. Donald Keene quarrels with a parochial attitude among some Westerners who assume literature of this description is appropriate for Westerners but who complain that Japanese writers depart from their traditional forms to write such. Certainly no grounds exist for disagreeing with him. At the same time, continuity always accompanies change, and we would want to be suspicious of any prediction that what has been unique in Japanese and in American literature would be dissipated into the international wind entirely so soon. After only a quarter century of rebuilding, Japanese architects have evolved forms that are identifiable as the *Japanese* International Style. We will look into that in the next chapter. Can the eye perceive anything peculiarly Japanese in Dazai, Mishima, Abé, or Oë? or peculiarly American in Bellow, Malamud, Updike, or Pynchon?

The justification for putting Yukio Mishima and Saul Bellow under the same glass is no better than doing the same with Kawabata and Faulkner. In this short perspective they seem possibly the two most important writers of the quarter century following the war. Comparing them also helps us see differences that make a difference. I choose for comparison the two novels which I suppose to be best known, *After the Banquet* (1960) and *The Adventures of Augie March* (1953).

The material of *After the Banquet*[9] is the unlikely courtship and marriage of Kazu, a beautiful and vital middle-aged owner of a famous restaurant, and Noguchi, an aged politician of high principle; and also an election campaign he is persuaded to undertake, Kazu's active and somewhat unseemly participation in that campaign, and the aftermath of Noguchi's defeat. On the face of it, that seems more teleological than is traditionally Japanese. Many of the events of the novel have the quality of substantiality which we might identify as Western. Yet not quite. Noguchi, with his high "Chinese" principles, discovers that Kazu tried a number of gambits during the campaign which he considered bad form; she had done so without consulting him. Furthermore, he plans retirement after his defeat in a backwash clearly incompatible with her vitality and sociability. She secretly borrows money to reopen her garden restaurant, he discovers the fact, beats her, strikes her name from the family record, and sends her packing. This would seem to be a resolution in the Western manner, but the last pages describe the beginning of a new cycle. The last chapter is entitled "Before the Banquet." The texture of the last chapter seems "Japanese," as well. Kazu is overseeing the refurbishing of her old restaurant and garden. Her old gardener has volunteered his services: "Kazu, watching the garden take on day by day more of its former beauty, could not feel that the image gradually emerging like a thermotype was the same garden she had known." Kazu had treasured the old garden "like a precisely drawn map that she had memorized and cupped in the palms of her hands." She had once believed that she understood human nature completely, a faith shattered by her recent experiences. Yet, there are new beginnings. "The garden, once folded up so small, had swelled like a paper flower in water and had become a vast park filled with riddles and mysteries. In it plants and birds pursued their quiet occupations unmolested. The garden was full of things Kazu knew nothing of; each day she brought back one from the garden, little by little making it her own. The garden's hoard of fresh, unknown ingredients was limitless, and would probably enrich Kazu's fingers inexhaustibly." Finally, to top it off, Mishima gives us sure signs that Kazu has netted a new man. Another strong and vital woman, befitting the long Japanese tradition of such women. Permanence is posed against transience, as in a haiku. Nature is internalized in the sensibilities.

The form of *The Adventures of Augie March* is very traditional:

picaresque, but with the special American requirement that the picaro is a seeker after some important truth, perhaps some final truth. Like *The Adventures of Huckleberry Finn*, the book is comic in method, but serious in intent. Not quite as lowly in caste as Huck, Augie nevertheless has to scramble to survive in the Chicago Jewish ghetto of his boyhood. Like Huck, he tries in various ways to fit into the more or less respectable society around him, but his temperament is too honest, impulsive, and full of compassion to enable him to do so. Each event seems to move him toward a goal which he seems never to reach. Augie never resolves his hankering; he remains in process; but resolution is felt as the goal of the novel, like the carrot dangling on a stick before the mule. The last base he is on, a love affair with a warm and passionate woman, may promise permanence, but we can't be sure. (In fact, *Herzog*, published about ten years later, takes up in some ways where *Augie* leaves off.) Again, most of the episodes have a loud thump about them that traditional Japanese literature would avoid. Augie is, in American slang, "rambunctious," unruly, energetic, hungry. Toward the end of the novel a friend asks him about his "campaign after a worth-while fate." Says Augie, "Alas, why should he kid me so! I was only trying to do right, and I had broken my dome, lost teeth, got burned in my progress, a mightly slipshod campaigner. Lord, what a runner after good things, servant of love, embarker on schemes, recruit of sublime ideas, and good-time Charlie! Why, it was a crying matter, no fooling, to anyone who might know which side was up, that here was I trying to refuse to lead a disappointed life." Augie sees the joke on himself, and therefore looks "desolated." His friend laughs. "You know why I struck people funny? I think it was because of the division of labor. . . . I didn't know spot-welding, I didn't know traffic management, I couldn't remove an appendix, or anything like that."

Some of the old differences, then, exist in these books: a finer grained Japanese texture in contrast to the more bombastic American idea of what constitutes an event, the Japanese pattern of cycle and the American of process, and the woman at the vital center in Japan, the man in the United States.

Other novels in the tradition of the seeker continue to help define the American imagination in the postwar period. Perhaps the finest of these is Ralph Ellison's *Invisible Man* (1947), though it is more carefully patterned than most. Although his protagonist is specifically a black man in search of freedom and identity, Ellison does not rule out the possibility that he is speaking for all Americans. Other versions of the novel of the seeker have been written by Bellow, Bernard Malamud, John Updike, Thomas Pynchon, and others.

American literature in this period in fact seems more self-consciously American in form than Japanese literature seems self-consciously Japanese. The old hungering for myth persists. All of Faulkner's works hung together in this way, making of his Yoknapatawpha County the setting of a whole culture, rendered bigger than life, overhung with a brooding sense of destiny and the land. Bernard Malamud brought to bear a whole array of Western mythologies, and particularly the fisher king mythology used by T. S. Eliot in *The Waste Land*, on his baseball novel *The Natural*. John Updike, beginning with *The Centaur*, is doing likewise with his little community in eastern Pennsylvania.

Mishima possibly excepted, as I say, most Japanese writers of the period seem for the most part mainly *modern* writers. Dazai Osamu's protagonists in *No Longer Human* and *The Setting Sun* are only in degree more thoroughly isolated from the rest of humankind than Malamud's in *The Assistant* or than several characters in Katherine Anne Porter's *Ship of Fools*; and his method of dramatizing the fact, aside from the Japanese propensity for using diaries, seems standard enough. Kobo Abé's *The Face of Another*, a novel about identity, may have been suggested by the Japanese fascination with masks as manifested in Dazai and Mishima. Some other Japanese and American novels from this period pair themselves, inviting the kind of comparison which could disclose national and international characteristics.

Kenzaboro Oë's *A Personal Matter* (1964)[10] and John Updike's *Rabbit, Run* (1960) are two of them. Both protagonists, young married men, find their responsibilities too grave for them. The burdens their marriages impose are far from light. Rabbit's wife is an alcoholic, perhaps in part because of his own childish ways; in a stupor, she lets their baby drown in the bathtub. Bird, Oë's protagonist, is an unsuccessful teacher in a cram school; when his baby is born, doctors inform Bird that it is probably a monster. Throughout much of the novel he must decide whether or not to take hints from the doctors that it be allowed to die. Rabbit and Bird have dreams of flight. Rabbit in fact early in the novel simply takes off in his automobile, heading south, but just as capriciously, then, heads back home. Bird's hopes are better crystallized. He wants to go to Africa, and he spends hours poring over maps. Both are harried by in-laws who disapprove of them. Both men, in their restlessness, take on lovers. Bird, in an ending which seems not wholly earned by what has come before, learns that his baby isn't as abnormal as he had been led to suppose, and chooses to accept his domestic burdens and live with them. Rabbit, having made Ruth, his very decent lover, pregnant "runs—ah, runs," at the end.

As I read Updike, he is turning the traditional novel of the seeker back on itself. A naive minister, Eccles, believes that Rabbit is, in effect, cut on that old model, so he pampers his whims on those grounds: there is something fine in Rabbit which society inhibits, he believes. Supposing, Updike seems to be asking, these heroes are merely shallow people, lacking in the stamina which any social endeavor requires. When Rabbit runs out on Ruth, there seems to be little doubt that he's a rat. Updike's novel appeared first. I do not know that Oë had read it before he wrote *A Personal Matter*. The parallels, however, except for the endings, are striking. (There are even similar scenes early in the novels of the two men testing their own boyhood skills, Rabbit playing basketball with some little fellows, Bird testing his strength on one of those machines built for the purpose.) Could Oë have been building from a type of character out of *his* literary tradition, the somewhat intellectual ne'er-do-well, in order to shape him to a Tokyo version of an international modern man? Rabbit's restlessness is in part personal: his fame as a high school basketball star could never be recaptured thereafter in the pedestrian life he was more or less sentenced to by his limitations of character and intellect. Bird's malaise seems to be more universally urban and modern. Africa is a more clear-cut opposite to Tokyo than some vague sunny South to Rabbit's little Pennsylvania city. The birth defect of Bird's baby, a catastrophe heaped onto alienation that was already severe, seems rather a special case; given the environment in which big city babies are born, however, an argument could probably be made for the appropriateness of this element of the novel.

At any rate, if the "convergence theory" falls short as it applies to industrial organization, as studies that were mentioned in the last chapter indicate, if it falls short where one would expect it to apply most readily, it certainly seems to be exemplified in these two novels. Neither of them violates its own tradition badly, each resembles the other from a very different tradition.

I hope it is not too great a stretch of the imagination to say that Kobo Abé's *Woman of the Dunes* (1960)[11] and Thomas Pynchon's *The Crying of Lot 49* (1966) share a modern theme as well, the theme of entropy. Both authors demonstrate in all their work an astonishing knowledge of science. Abé's central image of entropy is natural: sand. Pynchon concentrates on communication devices (dozens of them). These images are at the center of severe critiques of the modern culture of Japan and the United States.

Abé's protagonist, a teacher, had been interested in sand before he became so completely immersed in it. Because of his interest in a kind of beetle that inhabited the sand, he began to study sand.

Sand . . . didn't even have a form of its own—other than the mean ⅛-mm. diameter. Yet not a single thing could stand against this shapeless, destructive power. . . . The cities of antiquity, whose immobility no one doubted. . . . Yet, after all, they too were unable to resist the law of the flowing ⅛-mm. sands.
Sand . . .
Things with form were empty when placed beside sand. The only certain factor was its movement; sand was the antithesis of all form.

Abé doesn't use the word *entropy* in the novel, yet this man of science surely knew that his controlling image, as he handles it, was definitionally entropic.

Niki, the protagonist, out on an insect-collecting expedition, finds himself pressed into service by the elders of a village that is virtually inundated by sand. "Love Your Home" is the motto of this desolate place, so out of love certain people are kept prisoners, virtually, at the bottom of deep pits, shoveling sand. Niki is placed with a thirty-year-old widow, the strong, vital, and warmhearted woman we are familiar with in Japanese fiction. In spite of himself, he grows fond of her, yet he never relaxes in his attempts to escape. At the very end, two things happen. A scientific experiment he is trying, in order to get fresh water for their pit, begins to yield success. As Abé handles this, the potential practical benefits of the experiment are much less important to Niki than his sheer scientific delight in it. Then, the woman is taken off to the city hospital with an extrauterine pregnancy. The villagers leave the rope ladder in the pit: he could escape; he chooses not to.

The cultural dimensions of entropy are managed with a double-edged blade. Certainly the villagers' mode of survival against entropic sand is human culture in the least elevated form conceivable—yet it *is* survival, and that, given the circumstances, assumes some nobility. On the other hand, Niki's recollections of life in Tokyo suggest a culture without vitality. His conversations about sex with his Tokyo lover are dessicated by cleverness and intellectuality. "Rather than losing their passion, they had frozen it by over-idealizing it." Nothing like this with his woman of the dunes! Niki identifies a friend, presumably a fellow teacher, only as the "Mobius strip": "a Mobius strip is a length of paper, twisted once, the two ends of which are pasted together, thus forming a surface that has neither front nor back." Occasionally, Niki is allowed to see a newspaper from the city, and he discovers that there isn't "a single item of importance." His own scientific interests seem merely sterile until he hits on his experiment at the end, an experiment he calls "Hope." The love he finally feels for the woman proves one kind of new humanity, his exhilaration about his experiment, another. Humanity of these kinds are finally man's stay against entropy.

Thomas Pynchon wrote a sketch called "Entropy" before his first novel, *V*, was published. *The Crying of Lot 49* turns on the question of whether the American culture is beset by some mammoth conspiracy of evil, or whether it is only entropic. Along the way, it acts out some comments on *The Human Use of Human Beings*, the book by the great scientist Norbert Wiener which made popular some ideas about entropy as they apply to communications theory and culture. Oedipa Maas, the protagonist, is made executor of the estate of a former lover, whose financial adventures, as she begins to untangle them, weave in and out of every conceivable kind of illegal, immoral, unwholesome, and disgusting enterprise. As seeker (perhaps the first female in this old tradition), she is constantly frustrated by conversations in which nothing is revealed and instruments of communications which don't communicate anything worthy of being communicated: Muzak, radio, television, computers, movies, electrified rock groups, signboards, graffiti, a mad psychiatrist, a child actor turned lawyer, an Elizabethan revenge tragedy, and on and on. One demented acquaintance has even invented a Maxwell's demon machine, which he insists will do work if someone who is sensitive enough concentrates on it. At somewhere near this point, communication itself verges off into the mysterious, as does Abé's sand, and we begin to encounter discussion of extrasensory perception, miracles, divine revelations; a ballroom full of deaf people perform all kinds of dances without once colliding. Is the mad and repulsive culture Oedipa begins to discover in southern California a horrendous plot or is it an absence of meaning, maximum entropy? She is poised, at the end, for a further clue. But the reader is given to understand that the only comfort that Pynchon can offer us is Oedipa's earnest and increasingly urgent search itself. Like Niki, she is deepened by ordeal; she becomes more fully human. Such full humanity, I repeat, is a stay against entropy.

One quality which differentiates *Lot 49* from *Dunes* is that it is very funny. As it approaches its final pages, the humor disappears, as does Joseph Heller's in *Catch-22* and Ken Kesey's in *One Flew Over the Cuckoo's Nest*. All three of these books are intensely serious in their denunciation of the American culture. So was Twain's *Huckleberry Finn*, and so were parts of Faulkner's *The Sound and the Fury* and *Light in August*. The central strategy of this tradition is overstatement and understatement, to achieve new perspective. Oedipa, for example, learns that people who wish to protest against the governmental system have set up an elaborate underground postal system; then she sees what kind of letters the system yields: "Dear Mike, how are you? Just thought I'd drop you a note. How's your book coming? Guess that's all for now. See you at The Scope." The incongruity between the ambition of the scheme and its paltry product is of course humorous, but the essential emptiness of the lives of the people who find the gesture important is pitiful. The existence of the huge Yoyodyne industry which apparently sells nothing underlines the wastefulness of large sectors of the economy (the American taxpayer does subsidize aircraft factories) and its capitalist's cruel opportunism is perhaps exaggerated only slightly by Pynchon's conceit of a cigarette-filter enterprise which uses charred bones from a graveyard of soldiers. Pynchon is probably not the greatest contemporary humorist in America, but he's good, and he's working in an honorable tradition. Americans, whose history is one of grand promises, and whose boasts of having fulfilled them are so often illusory, require the antidote of honest perspective.

Lot 49 is an intensely American novel, set in California where all the extravagances of the American culture are amplified; it could hardly be produced by another culture. Abé's work is perhaps in one respect like some architecture I will mention in the next chapter. Visionaries of some future benign international culture understand that it will almost necessarily be homogeneous in many ways, but they hope its parts will maintain their cultural integrity. The pervading image of sand is a universal one, with symbolic suggestions of a concern which is generally modern. Yet *Woman of the Dunes* strikes me as a Japanese novel in a way that *A Personal Matter* does not. The following passage has not quite the psychological complexity of the one quoted earlier from the opening chapter of *Snow Country*, but it comes close. Having failed in an attempt to escape from his pit, Niki is discouraged and irritable. "One day, as he stood urinating and gazing at the grayish moon, posed on the edge of the hole as if it wanted to be held in his arms, he was suddenly seized with a terrible chill." The chill is unlike any he has experienced. It is at "the marrow of his bone . . . like ripples of water . . . spreading out from the center. . . . It was as if a rusty tin can, clattering along in the wind, had gone through his body." Violent images occur to him: "the moon was like a grainy, powder-covered scar," which then becomes a "white skull." Finally, with his heart jumping irregularly, "like a broken ping-pong ball," and with the October wind's "reedy voice sounding through empty, seed-less husks," he decides that the cause of this state of mind and body is "jealousy of all things that presented a form outside the hole": "streets, trolley cars, traffic signals at intersections, advertisements on telephone poles, the corpse of a cat, the drugstore where they sold cigarettes." The fusion of psychic state, physical state, and the natural environment, the delicacy of the insight into that fusion, and the bold and original imagery with which it is rendered seem not far removed from that scene in *Snow Country*.

I find that no close parallel suggests itself to Dazai Osamu's *No Longer Human* (1948),[12] or, as its translator Donald Keene has sometimes more literally rendered the title, "Disqualified as a Human Being." Keene points out, I think accurately, that its kinship is most obviously to the work of Poe and Beaudelaire. Of the important postwar American works, Bernard Malamud's *The Assistant* (1957) comes most readily to mind. Both protagonists have been warped by their beginnings and their past actions into a psychic shape that almost completely disqualifies them from ordinary social intercourse. Malamud's promises to reenter society at the end, aided by the trust of a woman and a determination to learn the teachings of the Jewish faith. As Dazai's Yozo moves from alcoholism to addiction to morphine, his lungs deteriorate, and we are given to understand that there is no possible escape for him from his condition. We do not see the total significance of the novel, all but the final few pages of which is in the form of three journals Yozo has kept, until we read its last word. The journals had been a record of his growing self-hatred. But the proprietress of a bar, one of many women he has exploited, has the final word: "he was a good boy, an angel."

Dazai has not left us unprepared for this verdict. Even Yozo is aware that part of his fear of other men (not women) comes from a deeply felt conviction based upon observation that they are selfish and hypocritical. He himself became an accomplished clown in order to mask his true feelings toward them, his fear and often his contempt. Society, as in the traditional American novel, is an enemy he habitually shuns except when he's drunk. But then what is "society?" he asks himself. We must attend to his answer later.

First, to repeat, the book is mostly more "modern" than traditionally Japanese. Although not closely plotted in the Aristotelian manner, it is teleological. Yozo becomes very abstract and theoretical about the nature of God, of evil, of the individual in society. The book, further, is intensely egocentric in the manner of modern neo-romanticism.

Yet it feels different from *The Assistant* in ways that still seem typical of the cultures. It is limned differently. Although Malamud is rather elliptical about the background of his protagonist, he uses many brush marks to characterize him once he arrives on the scene of the destitute New York grocery where he chooses to stay. Dazai is not without the paraphernalia of modern depth psychology. Yozo's stern and stoic—but by no means cruel—father "never left . . . his heart for a split second." But why didn't Yozo's brothers and sisters react similarly? We are not told, and can only guess some Poe-like hypersensitivity in Yozo. Nor can one say with precision that he is particularly sparse in the number of details he gives us about his debauches and the shame that accompanies them—though the novel is short. Yet there is a single-mindedness in their selection which still puts one in mind of line drawings. Nothing that is not absolutely essential to the delineation of what Yozo believes to be elemental in his character reaches the pages. Malamud cannot be accused of being wasteful. But the standards that he is working with require that his elements of plot, character, setting, and so on work appropriately with one another. The result, at any rate, is the old impression of American plenitude as opposed to the Japanese habit of severely withholding from the canvas whatever might deflect our eye from its bold lines. Below the level of its art, as Keene tells us,[13] Dazai's book is in part autobiographical. In elevating it to art, it seems to me, he stylized its lines in a very traditional manner.

That, then, brings me again to Dazai's concern with the individual and society. At this point, further reference to *Some Prefer Nettles* is useful. In that book Tanizaki does something that I think would never enter an American's mind to do. All the way through, he represents the *surfaces* of things—the patina of old puppets, cosmetics on Misako and the Polish prostitute Louise, the discoloration of O-hisa's teeth and her shiny coiffure, the black robes of the puppeteers, and so on. American writers, of course, have worked with the masks people wear. Of one of Katherine Anne Porter's characters in *Ship of Fools*, for example, a critic writes, "When Miss Porter describes Frey- tag . . . as . . . 'quite untroubled and good-looking,' she is out- reaching the novelist's narrative description. She is showing Freytag's mask, the mask of a man not really untroubled, but in the worst trouble the world has ever known."[14] Tanizaki goes further: people's surfaces are analogous to those of objects, even of cities. Osaka's culture, as opposed to Tokyo's, is described with this kind of imagery: "There was in it something too of the quiet, mysterious gloom of a temple, something of the dark radiance that a Buddha's halo sends out from the depth of its niche. . . . It was a low, burnished radiance, easy to miss, pulsing out from beneath the overlays of the centuries." Tanizaki has but a short step to go, then, to consider the appearances people put on their actions, the decorum of the relationship between Misako's father and his doll-like O-hisa and the attempt to "keep up appearances" in the Kaname-Misako marriage, especially in front of their son. Tanizaki provides himself a transition even for this step: the illusion of the puppet stage, the masks of the puppets—"The lady puppet in Osaka in fact is unable to use her eyes at all." Form in art then becomes, by association and implication rather than explication, associated with form in life. The old man is speaking: "To conform to a type, to be the captive of a form, means the decadence of an art, it is sometimes said. But what of folk arts like this puppet theater—have they not become what they are with the help of hard, fixed standards? The heavy-toned old country plays, in a sense, have in them the work of the race." Because of these prescribed forms, amateurs can do creditable work on the stage, generation after generation. "A few hands and a little equipment, and a puppet theater could be put together to wander lightly over the country. It must have been a deep comfort to the farmers, this theater—one cannot know what a comfort and a diversion." O-hisa's life is a work of art wrought by the old man; she must follow all the forms, as he does. Sly Tanizaki makes it clear only at the very end that she envies Misako's freedom to sing in the Tokyo style and to read women's magazines. Yet Misako's "modern" freedom has left her incapable of decision or action. If Kaname's clear preference at the end is for O-hisa as a *form*, a *type*, even perhaps for a doll *like* O-hisa, the reader understands, knowing the emptiness of such alternatives as Louise and Misako represent, that this is no bad choice for either Kaname *or* O-hisa. The formation of character, the polish one gives it, is a form of art, in Tanizaki's scheme.

What I hope to suggest here is an attitude toward masks, surfaces, the appearances of things that is different among Japanese and American writers. When we speak of American writers' use of "the mask" we have in mind something different from this, a matter of method, and I'll speak of that later. The Japanese have a tradition of the mask as subject, which I believe is important not only to literature but perhaps also to culture more broadly understood.

The face of the beautiful woman of the court as far back as the Heian period was something of a mask, eyebrows shaved and then repainted as disks on the forehead, teeth blackened. The geisha of Tokugawa, as depicted in ukiyoe, is also masked in her white powder and her fixed expression. Noh actors of course are literally masked, Kabuki masked as a matter of makeup and acting style. Several contemporary woodblock printers reproduce masks, from those of the ancient haniwa forward.

Donald Keene discusses the differences between Yozo's use of the comic mask in *No Longer Human* and Mishima's protagonist's in *Confessions of a Mask*. The former is always uncomfortable with his, "a

means of subduing . . . sensitivity, timidity, and self-pity." With
Mishima, "the mask enables the novelist to be whatever man he
chooses to be." His protagonist's "greatest desire is to make the mask
his real face . . . a living part of his flesh."[15] Kind, unfulfilled,
self-deprecatory old Shingo in *The Sound of the Mountain*,[16] joking
around with the daughter-in-law of whom he is so fond, puts an
antique Noh mask to his face:

> As he brought his face toward it from above, the skin, smooth and
> lustrous as that of a girl, softened in his aging eyes, and the mask came
> to life, warm and smiling.
> He caught his breath. Three or four inches before his eyes, a live girl
> was smiling at him, cleanly, beautifully. . . .
> Shingo had felt a pulsing as of heaven's own perverse love.

These excerpts do an injustice to enigmatic complexities in the passage, yet they give some clue to the sense of masks in living faces and
living faces, in some sense, in masks, which this tradition imagines.
Kobo Abé's *The Face of Another* carries this to an ultimate extreme,
when the protagonist through plastic surgery actually tries to assume
an identity different from the one he has wearied of.

Such a theme is in one sense literary convention, the sort of stuff
which literary historians have in mind when they speak of "traditions,"
a type of inheritance like an old suit through which writers show their
worth by adding to, refurbishing, trimming and resewing, or satiriz-
ing. Yet different cultures choose which of their hand-me-downs seem
important enough to them to avowedly reject or accept—or simply
ignore. The mask motif, like the seeker motif in America, is apparently not to be ignored.

Dazai's Yozo adopts his clown's mask to allay his fears of society.
What, he asks, late in the novel, is society? Individuals who adopt that
cloak to give their own views more power, he concludes. That comports very well with the conclusions of Harry Stack Sullivan, mentioned in the first chapter: all our behavior is a result of our assessment
of the reaction of some *one* looking over our shoulder, either in reality
or in fancy. Ronald Dore in his *City Life in Japan* adduces something
like such a notion in his attempt to handle Ruth Benedict's conclusion
that Japan is not a "guilt culture," but only a "shame culture." Probably, in fact, he says, it is little different from English culture (or I would
add, American). We all are likely to behave according to how we

believe some *particular* other people whom we fear, love, or respect will react. Japanese people since Meiji have been troubling themselves about the notion of individuality, which many of their leaders insist is a sine qua non of democracy. Tocqueville, in the nineteenth-century work I have quoted so often, reminds us that in English the word *individualism* still smacked at that time of connotations of selfishness. I'm told that the various Japanese attempts to find equivalents still do so today.

A fiction of momentous importance may be clouding both cultures. The mask which has preoccupied thoughtful Japanese may be more than an amenity of a crowded people; it may be a human necessity. American romantics replaced what Christians called the immortal soul with a secular notion of a precious, immutable, and mysterious entity called "self." That tradition has followed down to such existential psychologists as Rollo May, Carl Rogers, and Abraham Maslow. If we can locate our essential self, and if we can learn to be true to it, so it is said, we are saved.

A rather obscure American psychologist named Kenneth J. Gergen is meanwhile exploring the question, What if true health resides in a skillful use of masks, choosing this one or that one as the occasion demands or suggests?[17] That seems to me to be what many ordinary Japanese do as a matter of course, although certain of their writers, imbued with Western values, scold them for it. To many sensitive Americans, such a suggestion implies insincerity, hypocrisy, a violation of the sacred self. I believe that the idea implies no necessary subversion of basic moral principles; but short of that, why not respect the social dimensions which human beings may not ignore if they are to remain members in good standing of our pack, humanity?

I believe the contradiction between official American attitudes and what is possible in human behavior can be discovered among some of the country's best writers. Mark Twain tells us all about it in his essay "How to Tell a Story." The masked or "deadpan" mode of storytelling in the United States that was mentioned earlier has been useful beyond its effectiveness in narration. Skillful practitioners of it such as Franklin, Thoreau, Twain, and Faulkner have used this mask to reveal another mask they detect, a decorum which hides human frailty, or worse. Folk wisdom and folk art in the United States have been more widely separated than they have in Japan from what is applauded as wisdom or art by licensed pundits, but folk wits in America have always understood some things that the learned have glossed over. While the public, genteel New England poets of the mid-nineteenth century were promulgating a creed of sweetness and light, writers with such pen names as Sut Luvingood and Petroleum V. Nasby were creating an image of America full of gross hypocrisy, raw sexuality, cruelty of the crudest kind, and brutal violence. The conventional wisdom of official America has always held that all proper men are sincere and untainted by vice, and that the affairs of the world ought to be managed on that assumption. Henry James in *Daisy Miller* dramatizes the inevitability with which an innocent young girl who acts on that principle in Europe meets with a tragic death. Woodrow Wilson promised all the world "open covenants openly arrived at." The very wide disparity between what the Spanish-American philosopher George Santayana called "the genteel tradition," and the more mundane perspective on life which folk cynics apply to it has in some instances forced the application of a mask. "Everything deep," said Nietzsche, "requires a mask," and many American writers out of the folk tradition have employed one. I take it that no culture has a monopoly on depth or shallowness. Many Japanese, over the years, have made of their masks subjects of particular study. Americans generally find masks contemptible, except as techniques of narration—observable, incidentally, daily, among ordinary citizens when they become storytellers. All of this might mean that the American has faced with less clarity and subtlety than the Japanese the relationship between the individual self and the society which helps him define himself.

I do not assume that a good novel need prove its social relevance. It is valuable in and of itself, of course. Let me make some further suggestions, however, about literature as social phenomenon, aside from its esthetic value. It is demonstrable that the influences of long fiction as a serious literary form trickle down into mass culture. We cannot be certain how strong are the influences on most people, whether directly or through popular derivatives, though individuals have testified to having been moved by particular authors who have refined certain sensibilities or suggested interpretations of experience, or models for character, or patterns of expectations. If American literature might have encouraged unrealistic expectations either of order and epiphany in life, or of what jewels inside the spirit or out there in space might be discovered by the ardent seeker, it has also in its robust humor discovered new proportions and perspectives. If Japanese literature has often confined itself to anatomizing the ineffectual dabbler in life, it has also captured astonishing patterns of relationships within the human spirit and in society, and between men and nature. These same capacities are observable among people at large in the United States and Japan. Japanese, like anybody else, are capable of producing artifacts that are crude and raw, but their finely textured novels seem to reflect qualities that are *peculiarly* Japanese. Fine-grained Americans are not uncommon, but the rougher-hewn humor of Twain, Faulkner, and Bellow seems *distinctively* American. These qualities in turn corroborate a general American tendency toward the exaggeration, the boast, the inflated vision, in comparison to the general Japanese tendency toward reduction, understatement, affection for the miniature. Tangential, further, are Americans' metaphysical world view and Japanese practicality and realism.

The old clichés about the American emphasis on intellect and the Japanese on feeling come down to matters of degree only: fiction for both is "felt thought." The Japanese capacity to see unity among man's body and spirit and the landscape outside him is comparatively undeveloped among Americans; paradoxically, the American reach after the unity that myth brings seems unimportant to Japanese. For Americans life is still represented as search; for Japanese, its existential quality is what is often celebrated—its *is*-ness still seems the point. Americans appear to be more fully enclosed in a tradition that is national; Japanese have jumped at the international.

Yet we have noticed convergence. And even when the literatures were farthest apart, in Homer and Murasaki, storytelling was similarly a means of understanding the mysteries of love and death, those opposite sides of the same coin of universal circulation.

If those of us who have been charmed by the older Japanese forms cannot hide our disappointment that Oë is no Kawabata, neither is Pynchon Henry James. Nor for that matter is Abé Mark Twain or Bellow Tanizaki. Fortunately, Japanese literature is increasingly available to Americans (though in nothing like the supply in the other direction, either in English or translation), and some American now in diapers may some day capture the beautiful loneliness of *Kokoro*. If the rhythms of almost all modern literature seem a bit frenetic to suit some of us, literature lasts, and we can always return to the leisurely rhythms of the last century, or the eleventh. American literature may be too parochial, Japanese too quick to pick up the "modern." The international culture of the future will be shaped in part by men in Tokyo and Washington who read no novels; but it will also be shaped by earnest young writers from Kamakura and Kokomo, who will brook no advice from me here.

CHAPTER 7

Shelter and Symbol

Shelter, for our homelife, our work, our worship, and all our other communal activities: it is scarcely ever left as bare as sheer necessity dictates. The environment we build around us is a message to those others out there. It tells about our attitudes toward the natural landscape we settle in, and toward the materials we derive from it. How skillful are we in their use, how much pride have we in our crafts? May a temple be built of aluminum? Do we cherish our inherited forms, or wish to act out our emancipation from them? What of our neighbors? Should we show our superiority in wealth to them? Should we cast their dwelling in shadow? Should we blend into their ordinary usages or dare we shock them with shapes never before seen?

The attitudes of the American and Japanese peoples toward their buildings might be expected to correlate in some ways with their attitudes toward nature. Perhaps also with the material of the last chapter: the needs for shelter and for storytelling are very different, but taste in what constitutes a pleasing artifact might very well splash over from mode to mode—resolution, plenitude, symmetry versus process, ellipsis. What is particularly interesting about architecture is that its most important recent practitioners in the two cultures agree quite thoroughly in their theories of good building yet, working from their respective traditions, come up with structures that are rather different. Transcultural teaching has been unusually effective in this discipline even though there is clear national influence in practice.

Between recent agreement in principle and similar ancient origins in pits and burrows, however, lies wide divergence. Consider first the extreme poles, in structures which speak in concrete terms of deep-seated religious beliefs. Shinto shrines are places where worshippers can commune with the *kami* in nature. Originally, they may have been merely designated places, without buildings, but at any rate intrusion of structure between worshippers and nature must be minimal. The holiest of all holy shrines in Japan, the sanctuaries at Ise, are adaptations in untainted natural materials of prehistoric structures. The extreme simplicity of their forms is illusory, but simple they seem. On the other hand, the medieval European cathedral, or the American adaptation of it, closes out nature, and creates an entirely artificial esthetic experience within its heavy walls and stained-glass windows. That contrast is important but at the same time somewhat misleading, since the essentially Protestant culture of the United States reacted violently from the very beginning against the satanic titillation of the senses which occurs in such gorgeous structures. The Puritans countered with a "plain style," an esthetic simplicity which has influenced many American buildings ever since.

Again, we run into counterpoint. Just as the "paleface" tradition in literature has complemented the "redskin," and just as the tradition of lawfulness has opposed antinomianism, the plain style has competed with modes which are more exuberant, showier, more highly ornamented. Similarly, Kenzo Tange describes the Yayoi culture, often thought the more "Japanese," as "a definite, formal aesthetic, quiet, well-balanced . . . dominated by subjective, lyrical frame of mind"; the Jōmon principle, on the other hand, is "the primitive life force of the Japanese, an irrepressible vitality that invariably threatens to destroy formal aesthetics."[1] The ornate Nijō Castle in Kyoto, a feudal stronghold, is a product of the early seventeenth century as surely as the serene and restrained Katsura Detached Palace. (Nor does it do to say that the former shows Chinese influence: such forms were obviously appealing to the Japanese.)

We cannot then rest easy with the stereotypes. Yet Japanese architecture traditionally blends with nature, American (like Western generally) is imposed upon it. The architectural historian Vincent Scully, considering Thomas Jefferson's Monticello *in its setting*, writes, "It is about a man owning the earth. The house caps the conical hill, controls it, like a hero's tomb. That was what the [nineteenth] century to come was to be about: how to control nature: how to own it." Scully recognizes the romantic tradition of love for nature—"perhaps real love for it"—but insists that the "clearly directive instinct" during the nineteenth century was for ownership of the single family home.²

It was almost three hundred years before an American architecture, influenced by the Japanese, related itself to nature in any clear harmony. In the abstract and theoretical Western manner, however, the building of the colonial and early national period which pretended to "architecture" was thought to be natural in that it obeyed natural "law": it was symmetrical, proportioned in "naturally" beautiful ways that had been discovered by the ancients. Christopher Wren, one of a number of great English architects who influenced the early Americans, wrote, "There are natural Causes of Beauty. Beauty is a Harmony of Objects, begetting Pleasure by the Eye. There are two Causes of Beauty, natural and customary. Natural is from Geometry, consisting in Uniformity . . . and Proportion."³

The simple wooden structures of the seventeenth-century colonists made no such claims. As soon as the transplanted Englishmen could emerge from their makeshift huts and burrows, they built framed timber houses out of memory of the rural English homes they had known. These New World homes were organized around fireplaces, either one in the center in modest homes, or two at either end in the more affluent. Vestiges of their medieval ancestry remained in the curious overhang of the second story and in some ornamental brackets. Glass was expensive, so fenestration was skimpy. The simple style is important, since air-conditioned replicas of it still appear in upper-middle-class suburbs in the United States: seventeenth-century English farmhouses for advertising executives in the suburbs of Chicago.

By the eighteenth century, and before the Revolution, a few Americans were wealthy enough to aspire to buildings of the sort that were prestigious in England. The builders mainly used the same books their English counterparts used. Such books disseminated styles based on Palladio, whose vogue was established in England by Inigo Jones, and whose general vocabulary remains with many later architects and builders. These carpenter's manuals were similar enough in their directions about proportions and "proper" methods of embellishing such elements as windows, pediments, and cornices so that a distinctive style marked the landscape, the "colonial," which, again, is still being built. The symmetrical rectangular forms were rather bookish, but the total effect was refined and dignified. This is true of individual estates of wealthy planters in Virginia and South Carolina. Perhaps more importantly, the *collective* effect in some New England towns was pleasing. The town of Shirley Center, settled in 1750, seems to two critics like this: "Nearby along the roads, trim houses stand foursquare beneath arching elms, facing the green or the roads. . . . The common character of the village is asserted by double-pitched roofs, red-brick chimneys, white clapboards, modulated windows, dark trim. . . . The plans and scale . . . speak of orderly societies whose enormously independent builders contrived to produce individual houses that did not contradict the whole."[4]

Immediately after the Revolution, and for some sixty years following, England seemed an inappropriate model, and Americans turned to continental Europe instead, though particularly to Greece and Rome and such monuments as the Greeks and Romans had left on the Continent. Palladio had looked to classical precedents himself, but the reading of those precedents which the Americans now preferred stressed simplicity, sturdiness, substantiality. The rotunda was added to the cube; more and more in monumental buildings masonry replaced wood and brick. The debate about which model was most appropriate became heated. One of the favorite conceits of the revolutionaries was that they were like the sturdy Romans of their republican days. Thomas Jefferson was of this Roman persuasion. Of the Maison Carrée at Nîmes, he wrote, "Here I am . . . gazing whole hours at the Maison quarrée, like a lover at his mistress"; and his design for the Virginia State Capitol proves the sincerity of that love affair.[5] Jefferson's friend the French immigrant Benjamin Latrobe opted for the bulkier and simpler Greek mode, though he varied from it in the columns he designed for the United States Capitol by replacing the sacred acanthus with tobacco leaves and corncobs. Many subsequent public buildings were designed in the Greek manner by Latrobe and his students. (The symbol of Greek democracy was particularly handy to southerners, who did not hesitate to point out that that precedent depended for its labor upon slaves.) Bankers, too, wanted Greek models, symbolizing, apparently, their solidity.

The buildings of the later colonial and early republican periods varied in their symbolism, and in other important ways. But all shared certain attributes. A geometric quality, first of all, particularly a geometry of right angles, so the structures often appear as blocks set down on the landscape. External symmetry, too, even sometimes at the cost of forcing internal space to conform to such external requirements, or, further, falsifying the exterior when uses of the spaces within did not conform to that aesthetic demand. They shared a more or less academic obedience to received wisdom about proportion, rhythm of line, and harmony among parts; to this fact can be attributed the beauty and dignity of the best of them. Finally, they were thoroughly artifact: wood was painted (unlike the earlier Puritan shingles, or clapboard, or board and batten), pilasters were frankly without any but ornamental function, capitals were faithful to ancient "orders," and so on.

These external characteristics almost dictated certain internal conditions. The sense of space within given rooms was necessarily confined: one sat in a cube within a cube. The experience of a room was static, like the Newtonian laws which in those days were held to govern nature and human relationships. Functions of these closed-in spaces were carefully delineated: sleep here, cook here, converse there.

Some buildings, increasingly so as the nineteenth century moved on, shared one other attribute: when individuals, educational institutions, governments, or church congregations could afford it, they tended to build in a rather self-consciously monumental fashion. We hardly wonder at this when it occurs in churches, government buildings, even colleges. The medieval spires thrusting heavenward which churches added, when they could afford to, made a statement that was important to the worshippers. The pillars, the domes, and the allegorically figured friezes and pediments of government buildings spoke to their power, their respectability, their solid roots in ancient tradition. Thomas Jefferson made the University of Virginia an anthology of various classical forms, climaxed by a building featuring a rotunda inspired by the Roman Pantheon; that tells us something about *his* ideas on education. Later designers preferred the Gothic, which tells us about *their* ideas on education. (As late as the Great Depression of the 1930s, Yale University spent tens of millions of dollars on residential colleges, a library, and, of all things, a gymnasium with steel skeletons but Gothic masonry skin; "Girder Gothic," dismayed students called it, and "fourteenth-century Hotel Statler," as they squinted in the recesses of the dimly lit library.)

When, however, the language of ancient temples and palaces enters the vocabulary of family dwellings, one asks what it is that is being said. Probably nothing much different from what the new-rich merchants of the Italian Renaissance were saying, or wealthy English tradesmen of the eighteenth century. But rather incongruously the language was unchanged in the new setting. The well-to-do New Englanders or Virginians of the colonial period and later with their Palladian Georgian homes were saying, We are essentially English gentlemen, honoring the eighteenth-century values of harmony, balance, and modulation of expression; our tastes are refined and elegant without excess. Families that built Greek or Roman projections of themselves were saying in a private way what governments were saying publicly: We are the natural aristocrats which the republican form of government makes possible, even encourages, and precedent exists for us; we are not without historical roots and time-honored legitimacy. For the very rich, such as the Vanderbilt who commissioned a Tudor Gothic mansion (the annual maintenance cost of which equaled the annual budget of the United States Department of Agriculture in the late nineteenth century), what was being said was: I am as rich and powerful as a feudal lord, and can command as much talent as a cardinal. The fashionable architect, Richard Morris Hunt, who designed "Biltmore" for George Vanderbilt among the mountains of North Carolina wrote, "The mountains are in scale with the house." Vincent Scully described Nicholas Biddle's early-nineteenth-century mansion on the Greek style this way: "One recalls the House of Augustus on the Palatine; it was voted a gable by the Senate, which intended by this gesture a delicate allusion to the semi-divinity of its most distinguished colleague. At 'Andalusia,' a nineteenth-century banker gives himself the works, pediment, columns, and all."[6] In other words when an American purchased ornate European exteriors and interiors, perhaps he was making a public announcement of enough affluence to buy more than minimal needs dictated, and a "cultured" more at that: "conspicuous consumption" in Veblen's words, and "conspicuous" waste. Or, afflicted with the attitude that has been mentioned before, Americans' lack of confidence in esthetic matters, their anxiety lest they be found crude or incorrect or unfashionable by European standards, he may have been groping for the sanctions of historical continuity. A romantic and expansive exuberance is detectable too: the man with his new jigsaw may well have enjoyed carving out his "carpenter's Gothic" cornices as much as his client enjoyed his doing so. And it wasn't the wealthy alone who clothed themselves in exotic hand-me-downs: those in more modest circumstances could hire carpenters who were acquainted with manuals enabling them to execute smaller wooden versions of what the rich were buying. The poet James Russell Lowell satirized an elderly gentleman's Gothic rural cottage, where "clothes could be dried in a donjon and pigs kept in a porter's lodge."[7]

A dazzlingly eclectic mélange of styles was available; the professional architects who began to emerge in the nineteenth century almost invariably studied in Europe, then returned home with a wide array of "styles." One of the most influential of the authors of home-building manuals boasted in 1867 that his repertory of plans included "American Log Cabin, Farm House, English Cottage, Collegiate Gothic, Manor House, French Suburban, Swiss Cottage, Lombard Italian, Tuscan from Pliny's villa at Ostia, Ancient Etruscan, Suburban Greek, Oriental, Moorish, and Castellated"[8]—America the melting pot. And at the same time millions of Americans, including most of the new immigrants, lived in crowded, dark, and dirty tenements. If the United States in the late nineteenth century was a moral, political, and economic chaos, it was in its urban places a visual one as well.

Fortunately, earnest architects were at work to set matters aright in their field, paralleling the efforts of the Progressives of the late nineteenth century in politics, economics, and social work. Contributing to their concepts in building was a vernacular tradition which was getting houses built that were quite innocent of academic "styles" or interior stylishness.

It was in Chicago in 1883 that one Augustine Deodat Taylor apparently first framed a building, not of heavy timbers mortised together, but of light two-by-fours joined by nails—a feat just then made possible by the invention of cheap, mass-produced nails. Such buildings required much less labor, hence were cheaper. And they could be erected in a hurry, a great boon to the rapidly growing population of the West. Trained architects sneered at them, and called them "balloon frame" because of their supposed unsubstantiality. Homely many of them undoubtedly were: "bare, bald white cubes," they were called by American architect and critic Calver Vaux, who recommended instead "Moorish arcades and verandas and Chinese balconies and trellises."[9] Nevertheless, most housing for most Americans since then has been balloon-frame constructed, and it is not necessarily unattractive from the outside. And from the inside, the houses may be very serviceable, spacious, light—and comfortable. That's generally what these homes symbolize: middle-class, respectable comfort. Siegfried Giedion has told us, in *Mechanization Takes Command,* how their furnishings tended, through the nineteenth century, more and more toward the overstuffed. In the old architectural debate between beauty and use, Vaux seems at first glance to be on the former side, the vernacular builders and furniture factories on the latter. Then we take a second look: they must have been dreadfully difficult to keep clean, compared with the bare and uncluttered interior of a traditional Japanese home. Then a third look: Giedion also tells us about the mechanization of the housewives' work, begun in the early nineteenth century as a resourceful tack in the woman's liberation movement of that time (it freed the servant girl as well as the housewife), and reaching a climax in the 1920s.[10] The old American faith that technology can cure the problems caused by technology was at work.

One further word about the interiors of the balloon-frame houses. In the nineteenth century, they were cut up more than today into small rooms. Let us put aside the question of the trade-off between privacy for the individual and the interpenetration of space; we return to the image of a person sitting inside a cube which is inside a cube. But was the cube in practice all that constraining? While trained architects brought to America some of Europe's faults, vernacular builders were freeing floor plans, and space itself. I quote again from Giedion, this time from *Space, Time, and Architecture*: "When Wilhelm Bode visited the Chicago World's Fair of 1893 he remarked that 'in contrast to Germany, the modern American house is built entirely from the inside out. It not only corresponds to particular individual demands but

above all to the peculiarities, customs, and needs of the Americans.' "
Bode therefore preferred American domestic architecture to German. He liked the way that the sliding doors between rooms were
almost always left open, to the extent of half the wall space, in contrast
to houses he was accustomed to at home, "with their ridiculously high
ceilings, dark and overcrowded rooms, and luxuriant wall-cover-
ings."[11] American ceilings were generally lower, walls lighter in color.
If one finds cause for humor in contemplating boxlike American
interiors, he must keep in mind the situation elsewhere in the West.
Americans were already moving toward the traditional Japanese
interior, and toward Frank Lloyd Wright.

Not very far yet. In the late nineteenth century, the very rich, to
repeat, very often lived in pretentious and imported boasts of buildings, and very large numbers of the poor were living in dangerous
firetraps.

Japan, too, in the late nineteenth century, erected some buildings
which were bizarre enough. In their haste to house new industrial,
social, and governmental enterprises which they had never before
undertaken, the Japanese imported European builders. Architecture
was hardly experiencing a golden age in Europe at the time: the
Japanese eye thus had to suffer imported ugliness.

The ferment of the Meiji period could not of course erase the past
entirely, and, as everyone knows, the centuries had provided the
Japanese with architectural traditions of supreme beauty (one would
say "supremely functional" as well, were it not for the extreme
vulnerability of traditional structures to fire and earthquake). Once
they recovered from the indigestion brought on by that glut of bad
Western fare, they put their minds to concocting more palatable stuff.
More palatable not only because the Western imports were themselves pompous and gross, but because their own ancient traditions
contained much to tell them about how the new industrial and
commercial functions could be performed in a more gracious environment. The principles of modern international architecture were already anciently embedded in that tradition, as Wright and Tange
discovered, although of course the materials weren't there.

Kenzo Tange believes the sacred shrines at Ise to be the prototype of
all Japanese architecture. "The use of natural materials in a natural
way, the sensitivity to structural proportion, the feeling for space

Hiroshige Ando and George Caleb Bingham, quintessential products of their mid-nineteenth-century cultures, respect reality fully, yet, with their mists, suggest its mysteries. Hiroshige's woodblock above is from *53 Stages of the Tokaido*; below is Bingham's *Fur Traders Descending the Missouri*.

Courtesy the Metropolitan Museum of Art, Morris K. Jessup Fund, 1933

A 1905 house near Hirosaki, in the provincial north of Japan, half teahouse style, half Victorian; a bold meeting of East and West but possibly an imprudent one. Courtesy Asahi Shinbun Publishing Company, publishers of *This Is Japan*, in which this photo appears

The main shrine and treasure house, Ise Grand Shrine. Compare these buildings with such American counterparts in Washington, D.C., as the obelisk memorializing "the Father of His Country" and the imperial Roman housing for the fine sculpture of the brooding Lincoln. Courtesy Norman F. Carver, Jr., photographer, in whose book *Form and Space of Japanese Architecture* this photo appears

The Shokintei Teahouse at the Katsura Detached Palace (Kyoto).
Courtesy Norman F. Carver, Jr., photographer, in whose book *Form
and Space of Japanese Architecture* this photo appears

Falling Water, Frank Lloyd Wright, architect. Courtesy Bill Hedrick, Hedrick-Blessing

Kenzo Tange's Yamanski Communications Building. Copyright The Japan Architect, Shinkenchiku-sha Co., Ltd., Masao Arai, photographer

Frank Lloyd Wright's Price Tower, Bartlesville, Oklahoma. Courtesy
H. C. Price Co.

The unity of nature and artifact: the garden in front of Shokintei at the Katsura Detached Palace (Kyoto). Courtesy Norman F. Carver, Jr., photographer, in whose book *Form and Space of Japanese Architecture* this photo appears

arrangement, especially the tradition of harmony between architecture and nature, all originate here."[12] The form of the shrines at Ise is that of a raised-floor dwelling or a storehouse for grain, which ancient Japanese developed as an alternative to pit dwellings. Their post and beam structure is that of all traditional Japanese buildings. The symmetrically arranged round pillars are immaculately smooth but unpainted. The thatched gable roofs, again, are neat and elegant; but it *is* thatch. Plain boards between the pillars are the walls. The nearby setting is an expanse of white pebbles; the larger setting is an extensive forest of ancient cryptomeria, which finally dwarfs the square enclosures. The shrines are unutterably beautiful.

The effect might be described as artful artlessness. Ornament is present: some gable ends are protected by gold or copper plates; some of the wooden members are vestigial and ceremonial, and clearly set them apart from commoners' dwellings. The simplicity which first impresses one is itself misleading: it is studied and highly refined simplicity. And so is the natural quality of this space sanctified by natural forces; artifacts they clearly are, yet in perfect harmony with the forests, rocks, and streams around them, and the ocean nearby. Every twenty years, they are razed and rebuilt in the same form. Nothing at Ise should decay, or sag, or lose its fresh scent. The ancient forms are eternally renewed.

The shrines, to repeat, are highly refined versions of buildings familiar to every Japanese, just as Noh, Kyogen, and Kabuki are appropriations from peasant folk drama. They were not, in other words, designed to create an esthetic experience different *in kind* from what ordinary Japanese already know. A medieval cathedral and many contemporary American churches and temples are intentionally removed, esthetically, from day-to-day life (like those gaudy movie "palaces" of the 1920s). Not so even the holiest of Shinto shrines. This holds true for other shrine styles as well. But, again, the same could be said for the plain style of the typical Quaker meeting house.

A rather well-known publication of 1936, Harada Jirō's *The Lesson of Japanese Architecture*, tries to summarize that tradition.[13] Harada mentions first standardization, the modular dimensions based on the tatami, the straw floor mats, next "variety in unity," by which I take him to mean something like the visual surprise one experiences in moving one's eyes across a Japanese room, as opposed to the static quality of some traditional Western rooms; or perhaps he means the great differences slight alterations in form make when that form has become conventional. Then come "conformity to a mode of living" and "connection with nature." These attributes appear to be related: not only do domestic dwellings with a long history evolve to suit the needs and wishes of their occupants (and, presumably, the needs and wishes of the occupants bend to the architectural tradition), but the needs and wishes of the Japanese, as we have seen, include easy familiarity with nature. Traditional design allows that: the houses are in fact roofs supported by posts; with the sliding doors open onto the garden, the sense of "inside" as opposed to "outside" all but disappears. The rustic upright post inside, the flower arrangement in the tokonoma, phase gradually into the garden, which is laid out to create the illusion of continuing movement beyond itself. Edward S. Morse was charmed to report when he wrote and illustrated his thorough and detailed description of Japanese homes in the 1880s that while adults in a Japanese home had their household shrine to worship at, the children very often had a swallow's nest in the eaves.[14] (Morse, by the way, joined Ernest Fenellosa and William Sturgis Bigelow to form a trio of remarkable Japanologists from Salem, Massachusetts, working from the 1870s past the turn of the century.) Finally, Harada mentions "simplicity." As applied to certain traditions, that of course is accurate. *Shibui* is the word out of the Japanese esthetic vocabulary which describes the effect these traditions desire: "quiet, delicate and refined . . . austerity in art without severity."[15] It is an architecture, Tange says, "of vistas, of continuity, of perspective."[16]

On the level of technique rather than esthetic principle, Harada says that Japanese buildings are made of wood—without exception, apparently, until modern times, even though evidence exists proving that the Japanese anciently knew how to work stone—that they are dominated by the roof, which has deep eaves, and that the wood is usually left unpainted. It is an architecture designed for summer, for shelter from its heavy rains with breezes relieving its heat. Recognizing this, one then notices that the reverse seems to be true in the United States: its buildings seem designed to shut out the winter. Poor people's houses in the southern states have adapted themselves to heat with their open "dog-runs," but more pretentious dwellings seldom do.

While what has been said above about Japanese buildings is certainly true of some traditions, it is not true of all. Harada and the others refer to the styles most Westerners think of as "Japanese": the styles of Ise and the seventeenth-century Katsura Detached Palace in Kyoto, of the refined and simple teahouses of that century and after, and especially of the shoin and sukiyu styles of domestic architecture. Certainly what has been said does not apply to the ornate, colorful, and pretentious Nikko, beloved by many Japanese and, a short distance from Tokyo, the first stop on the tour of Japan by many Westerners. Nikko is the mausoleum for the great war lord Tokugawa Ieyasu; to Tange, it "seems an almost perfect embodiment of a true autocrat's aesthetic outlook."[17] (A defender of the building, however, says it "is not claptrap architecture built to display the power of a despot lord, it is the continuation of the monumental feast of the arts of the Momoyama period," an embodiment of "dormant undirected passions, magical attachments, and a poetry of nihilism.")[18] The ornamental and monumental Chinese style which one sees much of in Japan is almost entirely confined to Buddhist temples, but it is there.

Another caveat: what has been said of openness to nature is not true of Japanese farmhouses. Tange says that open styles are possible for aristocrats who can afford to take a romantic view of nature, but that farmers, necessarily realistic about her rigors, close her out. In fact, the houses in the various regions of Japan show local adaptations to particular climatic conditions; in the typhoon belt of Shikoku and Kyushu, for example, tile-and-plaster walls are fitted with many drainways and heavy stone walls are built to protect against high winds, while on the windy coast of the Sea of Japan, people lift heavy stones onto their tile roofs. A fine park has been recently opened just outside Tokyo in which domestic building types from all over Japan have been reconstructed. Here one can see the various adaptations, and indeed, they suggest more about hard work and difficult living than they do about harmony with nature.

We must return to look more fully at the shoin and sukiyu styles, outlined by Harada, since they are the archetype of domestic architecture, conventionally. The now-extinct shinden style, with its square central building connected symmetrically by verandas to lesser buildings, a style favored by aristocrats in the Heian period, had clear Chinese prototypes. Edward Morse, in writing of the interiors of homes in the 1880s, described no other types than shoin and sukiyu, though he took note of the exteriors of many simpler peasants' and fishermen's cottages. Foreigners today who manage to seek out and can afford a "traditional" *ryokan,* or inn, find quarters with many of the same characteristics. The shoin style is not used in many dwellings today, but if one can believe settings for movie and television shows in Japan, it seems to remain a beloved memory. Sometimes one also sees films set against the old shinden style buildings.

The shoin style evolved, as Tange describes the process, as a result of the confluence of a number of historical currents. First, before the seventeenth century, some peasants were moving into the warrior and merchant classes, and they carried their memories of their old homes with them. Second, Zen priests, enjoying high prestige at the time, preached the simple life, the principle of *wabi,* which connotes "loneliness, rusticity, and frugality"; third, the shogun in power, parvenue warlords, were nostalgic about the older Japan and set about making their power respectable by adapting forms reminiscent of the old Heian court. The shoin style, Tange tells us, is the old shinden style, with two modifications. The shinden building had few partitions. Symbolically, people of higher orders were ensconced on raised floors. This gesture was dropped in shoin buildings, except for the raised desk alcove, suggesting the honorific function of study, and the somewhat lower floor of the narrow tokonoma alcove, perhaps suggesting honor to the painting and/or flower arrangement displayed there (etiquette requires that a guest admire this display, periodically changed, when he first enters the room). In the shoin style, partitions of sliding, paper-paneled screens appeared, and space was differentiated not to indicate rank, but to indicate the functions which the various spaces were to serve.[19]

The other characteristics of this style are probably familiar to most Westerners: its uncluttered simplicity; its refusal of symmetry, so that one's eye is always refreshed by movement in space and time; its openness to nature, when the inhabitants so desire; its quiet refinement of ornamentation, such as the patterning of bamboo in the screens; the unobtrusive but loving craftsmanship; the insistence upon natural materials in almost all places. (When the tatami mats are relatively new, they exude a wonderfully fresh aroma; the next best thing to a new wife, a standard joke has it, is a new tatami.) Morse contrasted the experiences of sitting in a Japanese room and in one in Boston. His impressions are so sensitive, so far in advance of what most Americans were able to feel at the time, and occasionally so properly Victorian, that I wish to cite him at some length.[20]

First, he emphasizes economy. Japanese houses are inexpensive, and few furnishings are required. "No false display leads them into criminal debt. The monstrous bills for carpets, curtains, furniture, silver, dishes, etc., often entailed by young house-keepers at home . . . —the premonition even of such bills often preventing marriage,—are social miseries the Japanese happily know but little about." Such simplicity does not diminish comfort, he says, then hedges a bit: "their wants are few, and their tastes are simple and refined." Nor is variety in room arrangement wanting; perhaps he has sensed here something we will look at later, the ordering of space in a way that suggests to the eye that more space lies beyond.

Morse ponders how a person would feel if he were suddenly transported from an American home to a Japanese. Spareness would be the first quality he would notice; "then gradually the perfect harmony of the tinted walls with the wood finish would be observed. The orderly adjusted screens, with their curious free-hand ink-drawings . . . the clean and comfortable mats everywhere smoothly covering the floor; the natural woods composing the ceilings and the structural finishing of the room everywhere apparent." And so on. Then he notes the "peculiarly agreeable odor of the wood," which returns his mind home, "to think of the rooms I had seen in America encumbered with chairs, bureaus, tables, bedsteads, washstands, etc., and of the dusty carpets and suffocating wall-paper, hot with some frantic design." "This labyrinth of varnished furniture," he recalls, requires an inordinate amount of tending, besides being, in contrast to the light and air of a Japanese home, "stifling."

Now Morse moves from esthetics to morals. Such simplicity prevents "certain painful feelings that incongruities always produce"; but it also avoids "a table with carved cherubs beneath, against whose absurd contours one knocks his legs . . . and . . . carpets which have depicted upon them winged angels, lions, or tigers,—or, worse still, a simpering and reddened maiden being made love to by an equally ruddy shepherd." "One may take a certain grim delight in wiping his soiled boots" upon such carpets, but they otherwise symbolize—and here we return to the first moral—"the waste and aimlessness of our American luxury."

In explaining the evolution of the variant called the sukiyu, or teahouse, style, Tange stresses cultural forces, the critic Noboru Kawazoe, social. The cult of tea was another appropriation by Zen priests from farmers, of course much refined and conventionalized. *Suki* may originally have meant something like "taste"; but the esthetic sense here should be understood narrowly: the point was to induce a way of life in which one abandoned everything distasteful, and lived "supported by the wind and the moon." The proper setting for such activity would be rustic and simple in the extreme; the farmhouse became the model, again much refined, but retaining its *wabi* feeling. So goes Tange's explanation.[21]

Kawazoe points to the influence of the new merchant class of the seventeenth century—the same who supported Kabuki—with aspirations after culture which had been hitherto denied them. In the shoin style tatami—old symbols of rank—had to be cut to fit. If tatami could be standardized they would become more readily accessible. This occurred: the sukiyu style was governed by demands in the interior and became a freer form.[22]

Thus the middle class in each culture nudged architecture toward freer form, based on how they wished to arrange their lives *inside* their dwellings.

Such, roughly and briefly, was the state of architecture among the two peoples before the "moderns" began their ascent to power. Some of what occurs here corroborates what I have suggested before. Status anxiety among the Americans, as registered particularly in domestic architecture, seems greater, or was more openly expressed, although Nikko is certainly a flamboyant expression of glory in power. At least from a statistical point of view, however, dependence upon impressive façade has been much heavier in America—in fact, the wall surrounding the traditional Japanese house presented no façade at all, or a blank one. Further, the cultural elite of Japan has demonstrated a much greater readiness than its American counterpart to compliment "common" people by borrowing their arts and crafts. The same occasional lack of esthetic confidence we have noticed before which shows in many Americans' almost craven dependence upon "approved" European forms appears in the periodic preference many

Japanese have for things Chinese; but ordinary folk in both places evolved modes of building which seem to contemporary tastes far superior. In fact, the adaptation of Japanese farmers and fishermen to their environment and the American invention of the balloon frame showed great art, or at least artfulness. When the Japanese borrowed from the Chinese or the Americans from the Europeans, the resulting structures were rather stiltedly and bookishly symmetrical, implying a certitude or finality. Both peoples, however, moved away from that, the Japanese of course centuries earlier. The rejection of geometrically regular external forms coincided with freeing of internal space. Americans hadn't yet matched the Japanese skill in merging internal space with external—nature—but by 1900 Americans had pretty well tamed their landscape, and would soon be able to think about living on more amiable terms with it; recall Tange's reminder that Japanese farmers built tight houses. Americans had not yet approached the Japanese respect for natural materials, nor could the level of devoted skill among the artisans of that rapidly expanding society match the Japanese: evidence of this lies in every detail of many buildings. Americans, particularly in the last six decades of the nineteenth century, were vulnerable to faddishness—but the fads were often echoes of earlier convention, sometimes fantastically distorted. Generally, with exceptions as noted, the American hankering was for plenitude, the Japanese for elimination, as in literature.

One further analogy to literature suggests itself. Like their writing compatriots, American architects have labored very self-consciously with symbols. From the nation's beginnings architects kept the Greek, Roman, and Gothic symbols before Americans, very visibly, not only in government buildings, banks, churches, colleges, but even in domestic architecture, as we have seen. In addition to the personal or corporate statements of power, affluence, insecurity, or exuberance these transplanted temples, cathedrals, and palaces might have reflected, something else may also have been at work in the young culture, a rather desperate longing for *some* permanent form in sticks and stones (to borrow from Lewis Mumford) in which to lodge their sense of themselves as a nation. This longing was articulated in the 1830s by one Thomas Hope, in an architectural version of the "melting pot vision." Americans, he said, should borrow from "every style of architecture" whatever in it is "useful or ornamental . . . scientific or tasteful," then add "whatever conveniences or elegances not yet possessed." Improving on the old models, and thus adding to the variety of forms available, Americans could develop "an architecture which, born in our country, grown on our soil, and in harmony with our climate, institutions, and habits, at once elegant, appropriate and original, should truly deserve the appellation of 'Our Own.' "[23] Perhaps few other conceptual sources for a unique national sense of identity were then available to architects.

National culture as it is proclaimed in physical structure cannot of course be evolved overnight. Americans, by the late nineteenth century, were making a beginning. More or less isolated, the Japanese had had many centuries in which to accomplish this, and they did so magnificently. The language of their best buildings bespoke the same subtle and fragile symbolism as the language of their best fiction. In architecture, the symbolism had to do with space.

Anciently, Shinto revered space, and Zen Buddhism reinforced that feeling. Of the ancients, Tange writes, "Instead of thinking in terms of images of the deities, man thought in terms of an image of the space in which the deities moved, and proceeded in various ways to symbolize this space." Thus the form of the Ise shrines, the form that remains as the buildings are continuously razed and reconstructed, symbolizes such space: "When the Japanese people try to glimpse the divine, this form becomes its symbol."[24] Of Zen, Norman Carver, an American expert on Japanese architecture, writes that space plays a "dominant role" generally in Japanese art, and that two concepts from Zen reinforce its importance: "Zen affirmed the reality of immediate experience and yet declared its indivisibility from a present defined as 'the moving infinity'—its oneness with life in eternal flux." Space was permanent, essential, and ultimate; life changes; space and time were relative. "Architecture defined the individual's relationship to this spatial-temporal continuity by its rhythmic extension from the near and definite to the distant and indefinable." The asymmetry of Japanese architecture is explainable in this way, then, as it gives "the feeling of infinite extendability." It breaks from the "structural cage" into a series of "patterns and planes of reference" in continuous space.[25]

This analysis of Japanese thought and feeling about space comports to an astonishing degree with Siegfried Giedion's brilliant reading of Western evolution toward modern architecture, in *Space, Time, and*

Architecture. Here, however, both space and time are pivotal. Mathematics and painting, he says, pointed the way. "The three-dimensional space of the Renaissance is the space of Euclidean geometry." Then, around 1830, a geometry of more than three dimensions developed. Artists also broke out of the limitations of Renaissance perspective. "The essence of space as it is conceived today is its many-sidedness, the infinite potentiality for relations within it. Exhaustive description of an area from one point of reference is, accordingly, impossible; its character changes with the point from which it is viewed. In order to grasp the true nature of space the observer must project himself through it." Post-Newtonian physicists see space as "relative to a moving point of reference"; cubist painters break with stasis in the same way. "The cubists did not seek to reproduce the appearance of objects from one vantage point; they went around them, tried to lay hold of their internal constitution. They sought to extend the scale of feeling. . . . [Cubism] views objects relatively: that is, from several points of view, no one of which has exclusive authority. And in so dissecting objects it sees them simultaneously from all sides—from above and below, from inside and outside."[26] One can imagine an ancient Japanese worshipper, at some moment, at the shrine of eternal space, the internal harmonizing, temporarily, with the external.

Tange goes even further. He is speaking of some of the most profound of the Zen gardens: "They are full of that creative energy which the priests of the Five Mountains sought within themselves. . . . This energy engenders a symbolism with great internal tension." Such energy is well expressed in "dry landscapes," he says, where a single boulder may represent "the infinite cosmos." The famous rock garden at Ryoanji is the ultimate development of this art. Here is the perfect esthetic expression of the Zen concept of void: "five stark rock patterns on a pure white ground of sand, all contained within a small rectangular space. Nothing save this; but the inner tension of the symbols—symbolizing nothing—makes this space seem infinite in its expanse."[27] I don't believe that symbols can "symbolize nothing," though they can symbolize "nothingness." What I believe Tange is saying, however—and I agree with the feeling he attributes to experiencing Ryoanji—is that some symbols can emanate suggestions too fragile to be handled by discursive language. Such was the suggestion about symbols, too, when we looked at Japanese literature.

The symbolism of Japanese buildings, then, inhered in them; Americans were, early on, forced to plaster their symbols on the outside so to speak.

At the very time in the 1870s and 1880s when American architecture—as well as American culture generally—reached a nadir of monstrosity, benign forces were at work. ("Benign," perhaps one should say, according to contemporary lights.) Prestigious firms such as McKim, Mead, and White began to announce that their repertory included "Colonial" styles, and, perhaps nostalgically in the wake of the 1876 centennial, interest was reawakened in the clean and simple forms of colonial architecture, particularly out of the seventeenth century. The so-called shingle style, reminiscent of plain-style Puritan dwellings, was one of several to enjoy some vogue. This was not unrelated to a growing influence of Japanese architecture, and the Japanese influence was not unrelated to a somewhat later development changing American thought about space, Giedion's analysis of which we have just looked at. Then there was the personal impact on architecture of Henry H. Richardson, and the collective impact of the so-called Chicago School.

Richardson's chief influence on more recognizably "modern" architects stemmed perhaps from his honest and straightforward use of materials. His forms were mainly borrowed. He worked much in romanesque, and that gave him the opportunity to build massive stone buildings of great integrity and dignity, asserting their close relationship to the landscape they seemed rooted in. Similarly, the Chicago School, especially from 1883 to 1893, began to build skyscrapers, their steel skeletons rising higher and higher, and becoming more and more frankly what they were, while at the same time the "Chicago window" grew wider and wider, capturing as much light as possible in Chicago's narrow streets. The Chicago architects, confronted with new problems in their rapidly expanding city, and equipped with new materials, put a premium on engineering.

These attitudes, in large part in the person of Dankmar Adler, contributed to the work of America's first authentic genius in architecture, Louis Sullivan; the influence of Chicago on Sullivan and Sullivan on Chicago was reciprocal. No merely technical solution was ever enough for Sullivan, however. When later functionalists tried to derive sanction by quoting his dictum "form follows function," they misunderstood his faith that no merely pragmatic function will satisfy a visionary human spirit such as his own or that of his star pupil, Frank Lloyd Wright. Not that either of them could ever achieve the clarity in words that they achieved in structure. Essentially mystics, they wrote like lyric poets. "For the *function* of which Sullivan spoke," writes an art critic, "was the spirit in search of substance." "That which exists in spirit ever seeks and finds its visible counterpart in form," Sullivan said, "its visible image." "Form follows function," but Sullivan was speaking of the "functions of the rosebud and the eagle's beak."[28]

Sullivan learned something about the use of materials from Richardson. The movement toward organicism represented in Sullivan's work, however, had prior sources, particularly in Emerson and Whitman, whose words animate the writings of Sullivan and Wright. Sullivan had been as a youngster a devoted student of botany, a fact that shows up in the glorious leaf and flower forms in many of his buildings. Then the powerful influence of Darwin in the late nineteenth century seemed to corroborate the theory of organic form which was buzzed about in Sullivan and Wright's Chicago. Like the transcendentalists and like the Darwinians, Sullivan and Wright thought of architecture as growth, process. Buildings, of course, stand still (though Japanese metabolists seventy years later would show ways of correcting that too); but architects continue to change and adapt. A useful idea in Chicago at the turn of the century.

Organicism would necessarily require considerations of the relationship between the insides and the outsides of buildings. Too much American architecture had worked from the outside in: Sullivan and Wright began to think about inner space. Why could not interior space "come through and button on the outside"?[29] This question would be a preoccupation with later architects all over the world.

Muscular, brawly Chicago, "inhabited," said Rudyard Kipling, by "savages," was curiously enough the first American city whose leading architects were strongly influenced by well-bred Japanese. The Chicago Columbian Exposition of 1893 was chiefly marked by a craven display of spurious monumental copies of classical forms. The only American who contributed a fresh architectural experience was Louis Sullivan, who designed the gorgeous Transportation Building. Another sight new to most visitors, including architects, was Masamichi Kuru's adaptation of the famous eleventh-century temple Hōō-den,

Phoenix Hall. Sullivan's drawings for homes were changed after 1893, to reflect, among other things, the horizontal lines he saw in the three structures that constituted Phoenix Hall. Even more profoundly affected was Frank Lloyd Wright.

Phoenix Hall embodied Wright's ideas of organic architecture perfectly, and whetted his appetite to study Japanese architecture in its own setting—which he did, of course, and built in Japan the famous Imperial Hotel, now razed, and a residence near Kobe, now threatened. (The Imperial Hotel, as probably most people know, withstood the terrible Tokyo earthquake of 1923, and was first used as a soup kitchen, to feed the homeless and hungry victims of that disaster.) His praise of Japanese art in general, and architecture in particular, was unceasing and unstinted: the Japanese home, he said, is "a supreme study in elimination—not only of dirt, but the elimination, too, of the *insignificant*."[30] His most important compliment to Japan was his imitation of many of the abstract principles of Japanese architecture.

Many Wright residences are, like Japanese residences, dominated by their low, wide-eaved roofs, and by other horizontal lines which rhythmically repeat the roof line and the flat prairie on which they stand. He almost always avoided symmetry; a cube, he said, was unfit for human habitation. Like the Japanese, he preferred to use building materials in their natural state; his hand in harmonizing the artifact with its setting was wonderfully deft, and he often aided his cause by incorporating into his structure stone or rough timber from that setting. He modulated light, so that the feeling inside many Wright buildings is reminiscent of the interior of a Japanese home with the shoji closed. Perhaps most important of all was his remarkable inventiveness in the use of space. This in part defines what he meant by the elusive term *organic architecture*. Wright said he discovered that that originated in China of the Chou Dynasty: "Although I did not know it then, the principle now at the center of our modern movement was very clearly stated as early as five hundred years before Christ by the Chinese philosopher Lao Tze. . . . that the reality of a building consisted not in four walls and a roof but inhered in the space within, the space to be lived in . . . my own recognition of this concept had been instinctive."[31] The inner uses of a Wright building are legible from the outside; and often the outside is carried in, as with the use, primitively, of the rough exterior wall surface in the interior. Further—and this is particularly comparable to the best Japanese interiors— the interior space moves, so to speak: it has a dynamic quality, spaces interpenetrate. His studied use of planes beyond planes, curious intersections, and rhythmic horizontals make of his interiors what Tange said of Japanese architecture: "it is an architecture of vistas." Perhaps not enough has been made in art of man's delight in arranged surprise: his expectation overturned, but overturned in a manner proved by the artist to be logical, even inevitable. Wright was a man of astonishing originality; like such other American geniuses as Herman Melville and Charles Ives who were largely without appreciation among a people who have been timid and conservative about the arts, he was cranky. But, working quite alone (except, one presumes, with the memory of his great teacher), he helped Le Corbusier, Mies van der Rohe, and Walter Gropius invent "modern" architecture, the first great change in the Western esthetics of building, I suppose, since the Middle Ages.

Some thoughtful critic has said that three buildings in the twentieth century have revolutionized all subsequent thought and feeling about architecture: Le Corbusier's Chapel of Notre Dame du Haut at Ronchamp; Tange's Yamanashi Press and Radio Center; and Wright's Falling Water, the Kaufmann House at Bear Run, Pennsylvania. Concerning the last: Clay Lancaster is author of a copious, learned, and sensitive book, required reading for anyone interested in our present subject, *The Japanese Influence in America*, which chiefly treats of architecture. Between each of his lines, we must understand that he had in mind comparisons in abstract principle with classical Japanese architecture. His analysis of Falling Water is a splendid one, which I will depend upon here.[32] Behind it lies his study of how powerfully the abstract principles of Japanese architecture worked on Wright.

Its site, over a waterfall and a deep ravine, required great technical ingenuity, which Wright matched with original esthetic form. To vertical stone piers rising from the stony stream are anchored smooth, horizontal concrete slabs, "suspended in space." Rock and concrete, vertical and horizontal, balance harmoniously, yet contrast. As at Ise, the illusion of great simplicity conceals subtle craft. One feels, strangely, both a sense of lightness and a sense of solidity at the same time. The form is "functional though somewhat elusive and unreal. Conventional house parts — wall and window, door and roof — have been laid aside for ascending and hovering solids of pure design. The design imitates and continues in abstraction the forms that Nature has provided here. The building is so well suited to the setting that it becomes an integral part of it." "Falling Water is spacious without being roomy"—a comment Morse made on Japanese houses. The main living space shades off into recesses. A natural stone hearth, freestanding, faces the entrance. Beyond that, the room seems "dissolved into glass," then opens out onto a terrace. Every bedroom has its balcony (as does each apartment in the Japanese high-rises). Now Lancaster begins to make more explicit his recollections of Eastern architecture, then to remind us of Giedion's remarks on the modern sense of space. A two-dimensional floor plan of Falling Water would give no sense of it. "The unusual site of the Kaufmann house is like that of certain buildings in the Orient, recalling a Lamaist monastery perched high above a mountain pass, a pagoda with roofs fluttering over a sea of cherry blossoms, the Phoenix Hall on an islet in a lake, or a Cantonese merchant's mansion on a navigable waterway. The dramatic impact of Falling Water is three-dimensional, involving the integration of inside volumes with outer forms and the spatial relation of the house to surrounding landscape." The last sentence, he says, would apply equally to other buildings of "Farther Asia, or, one might say, for organic architecture wherever it happens to be." He opposes the "dynamic and even romantic" quality of this building to the "static" building usual to the West.

Finally, he cites the last surprise. The poet, said Robert Frost, inserts the blade into us, then twists it a bit. Lancaster wonders about the purpose of a suspended staircase descending from the living room to the stream below. "With the waterfall at the edge of the house on the left, a boat could not be used here, and the swimming pool, a few feet away, has its own steps from the balcony between the stone walls farther to the right." Perhaps a Japanese prototype exists for this enigma, he surmises, in the "Flying Cloud" Pavilion, built in Kyoto in the sixteenth century. "The stairs can be reached only by boat. One comes up into the *funairi-noma* (entrance hall) through sliding panels in the floor. . . . The suspended staircase of the house at Bear Run is evidence that the late phase of organic architecture was not wholly within the realm of functionalism, however much the two may seem to correspond."

I cannot resist citing one further comparison between Wright's architecture and the best of Japan's at Ise, even though we are here in the realm of subconscious response. Tange, analyzing the cool and stately Ise, must perhaps struggle some to prove that it embodies not only the Yayoi heritage, which is clear, but the Jōmon as well, which is considerably less obvious. To manage the latter, he emphasizes the setting of the buildings, the prodigious forest. The small buildings, he says, avow their puniness among those symbols of dark and dangerous procreative forces which the Jōmon people acknowledged so thoroughly. Vincent Scully, for years a student of Wright's work, writes:

We ask ourselves about the clients, Did they know what they had, or what swallowed them? . . . What did the clients see here? Why did they want it? They saw peace, surely, and utter calm and dim quietness and warmth, and marvelous functional flexibility despite the general order, and plenty of unexpected discoveries, and even a few witty asides. These things probably induced them to put up with some feeling of oppression and the occasional real darkness, and the sense of an "utterly competent leader" directing it all.[33]

The sense through architecture of something below it all takes different forms in these two reactions; but the feeling that architecture can achieve so profound an emotion is the same.

Ironically, Wright has had few successful followers in the United States. Early in his career, a number of Europeans, many of them at the Bauhaus, admired his work greatly, however (he did not return the compliment). And a number of these men, Jewish or leftist, fled to the United States as the Nazis began to harass the Bauhaus. On America these immigrants had a great impact. The greatest of them were Walter Gropius and Ludwig Mies van der Rohe. (Le Corbusier visited the United States—"A Journey to the Country of Timid People," he called it—only twice, rather joylessly, but his mark upon Americans as upon Japanese was great.)

The work of Gropius and Mies van der Rohe bears little resemblance to that of Wright. It is too simple to say that in the ancient debate between pragmatic functionalists in architecture and estheticians, Wright was on the latter side, the other two on the former. All three would say they achieved appropriate compromises between use and beauty. Gropius and Mies, however, worked out of very scientistic ideas about space. Mies's concentration was on ordered space, interchangeable "universal space," extreme simplicity. "Less is more" was his favorite dictum—Zen-sounding enough, one would guess, to please any Japanese. One important Japanese architect, however, is critical: Mies is too impractical; his beauty is "not of architecture or of buildings, but of abstract existence."[34] Someone else has said that the success of his buildings depends on his focusing his attention on only a few of their functions. Gropius, as architect and teacher, continued to insist upon the importance of the machine as the proper model of the architect. (Le Corbusier moved from his early definition of a house as *la machine a habitée* to the sweeping concrete forms of the Ronchamp chapel.)

Both preoccupations led to unrelieved right-angle architecture of a sort Wright deplored. They led also to imitation, and soon to cliché. Mies's soaring glass Seagram Building was a glory, but dozens of buildings like it around the United States begin to seem trite (and mirror glass is interfering with air-conditioning systems in neighboring buildings). Lewis Mumford, that most demanding of all architectural critics in the United States, thought the United Nations buildings already clichés in 1950. Certainly these pure and clean forms reflected the Puritan "plain style" in their stripped-down quality, but not necessarily so in their sheen and scope.

The work of Gropius and Mies meant that lesser designers could do creditable work. It also meant that Americans, who long resisted "modern" architecture, were won over fairly rapidly: no one would think now of topping a skyscraper with a Gothic cupcake. The success of their work also led to revolt against the severe functionalism of Gropius and the clean cubes of Mies by architects more interested in evocative surfaces, such as Edward Stone, Philip Johnson, and the lyric, American-born Minoru Yamasaki. American architects who wish new solutions, however, are very much less adventuresome than their Japanese (or Italian) counterparts in the use of reinforced concrete.

Certainly American governments, always having felt more secure with neutral building, are not ready for daring buildings. Perhaps not even corporate clients are. The business corporation, however, was converted to some forms of contemporary work, perhaps believing that the vast, shining billboards bearing their names advertised them as advanced but not *reckless* thinkers.

Architects themselves became corporations, a characteristically American move, and large firms such as Skidmore, Owings, and Merrill have made important contributions, both in office buildings and on college campuses. It has been in the SOM offices particularly, in recent years, that engineers continued to devise new systems for reaching further and further into the sky—110 stories, at the time this was written. We know the quarrels people have with skyscrapers, how they steal other people's sunlight, dwarf the pedestrians in the caverns they make of streets, cause traffic congestion, and turn skylines into jagged graphs bespeaking fierce competition. These arguments (except in a few instances such as recently in Florence) have rarely won out over high downtown land prices and perhaps powerful men's need to advertise their power. For those were the structures that received the most attention from serious architects. A few of the most gifted worked on airports and shopping centers, a few on churches and temples.

Domestic buildings received little attention, after Wright died: housing for those who could afford their own was largely left to private developers; housing for the poor, in multi-unit "projects," was a continuing national scandal. Emphasis among architects was generally on big buildings or clusters. A few of the best of the individuals and firms submitted city plans, to be filed away by governmental agencies, but only recently in the United States as in Japan have architects talked much about building in some larger social, economic, and geographical context.

I have never heard the term *American style* used to differentiate the work of Americans following the international style. The most distinctive of their structures in that style may be those which derive from the vernacular, such as Albert Kahn's workable but perhaps deliberately frumpish factories, or Robert Venturi's pop-art conceits. The term *Japan style*, however, has had currency since the 1960s. The Japanese architecture I have focused on until now is in what Robin Boyd calls "Tourist Traditional,"[35] and it clearly derives from the Yayoi tradition, in Tange's terms. Postwar Japanese architecture derives from the

Jōmon style: bold, massive, sometimes even phantasmagorical. In the crucial ways, the Japan style was like other international architecture; it was modular, it showed structure openly with unmasked materials, it studied space to assure its interpenetration, and it gloried in new technical possibilities. None of these ways of thinking, except the last, were new to the Japanese: Tange dates them from Ise, and Wright remarked that traditional Japanese architecture was very modern. Japanese modern also retains the ancient discomfort in symmetry and in the straight line unchallenged by the curve. Japanese curves, by the way, have not traditionally been deduced from geometry; rather, they have inhered in materials, as for example the curve of a long batten held at both ends. The Japanese, several of whose leaders in architecture have worked with Le Corbusier, have been more receptive than Americans to his later, more primitive works, when he used rough materials, absolutely original forms, and massive proportions.

The young Japanese architects are a brash lot, judging from their writing and many of their projects. One of their elders calls them "shameless," but approvingly. For their elders brought them up to be assertive. Architects Kiyonori Kikutake and Kurokawa Noriaki and critic Noboru Kawazoe were in their thirties when they formed the metabolism group in 1960. At the heart of their theory lay an idea long also at the heart of the esthetic theory of many Americans: process. Architecture must continually grow. Some of the younger architects discuss growth against the backdrop of the Japanese tradition; others seem never to mention the past. Many more Japanese than Americans have addressed themselves to the acute problem of urban crowding—more acute in Japan than in the United States, of course. Some of their projects for expanding usable space in the Tokyo area are amazing, almost breathtaking: huge helixes twisting high into the sky, allowing light and air at all parts; tall, round columns, with bridges containing apartments joining them, again with plenty of space between; tall cylinders floating on enormous concrete rafts in the bay; or submarine apartments floating beneath its surface. Many of the forms are absolutely new in construction, not to mention the ideas about using space. The rather stuffy governmental bureaucracies appear far from ready for such plans, and indeed they're daring enough to give almost anyone pause. Yet everything indicates that solutions which are short of daring will soon be inadequate; meanwhile, those plans exist, and young men, some still in their twenties, continue to add to the stock.

The metabolists have actually erected structures which illustrate one of their most interesting ideas. Much of what we do as working people, they say, will remain unchanged; other functions will change as technology inevitably changes. So buildings such as Kiyonori Kikutake's bizarre Miyakonojo Civic Center house functions thought to be permanent in reinforced concrete, and others subject to change in perishable metals. Some structures are built with exposed bolts which would permit easy change to a new element attached to the old base. Tange has made use of certain of these ideas in the revolutionary Yamanashi Press and Radio Center, alluded to earlier, and in a smaller version of it on the Ginza, the Shizuoka Building. In form, these remind us of the basic Japanese structure: massive cylindrical posts, supporting squared horizontals. The shapes announce the work that takes place within: service functions such as plumbing, heating, and elevation take place in the cylinders, while the presses, studios, and offices are housed in the squared horizontals. Free spaces exist between the members; it is hoped that they can remain, but if necessary, new work can be housed by filling them in.

I have been speaking of a few architects who have built a few fine buildings which spot Japan's landscape. Interestingly, much of their best work has been on town halls and civic centers, in contrast to the Americans' emphasis on office buildings. Not that office buildings haven't had their share of attention too, in an equally commercial Japan; but while the best American architects seldom get government commissions, excepting Skidmore, Owings, and Merrill for their fine Air Force Academy campus, the Japanese, particularly in the provinces, often ask a successful native son to come home to design a civic center or some such public building.

A few buildings: the general look of most parts of most Japanese cities is dreary. They had to rebuild quickly after the war, using whatever materials they could lay their hands on, and a number of these jerry-built structures remain. Some city fathers, such as those in Nagoya and Sendai, planned well and provided wide, orderly streets to rebuild on, but most cities, like Tokyo, are a snarl. Even in newer residential districts, the appearance is less than lovely. Staggering land prices have forced a domestic architecture which, for ordinary citizens, requires abandonment of the traditional horizontal look and acceptance of what is to my eyes a rather ungainly vertical look, with walls of some sort of stucco.

The architects are aware of this. The pages of the *Japan Architect*, the English-language version of a leading journal, are full of strident talk of change, of wonderfully imaginative plans for multifamily housing and regional development. The same is true of the pages of the American *Architectural Record* and *Architectural Forum*, but less frequently and less urgently. Large numbers of people in both countries live in housing that is too cramped—in Japan, two small rooms serve many a family—and without decent amenities. Until recently, few architects, apparently, have addressed the problem of large-scale low-cost housing. I have noted recent efforts in Japan. In the United States, more or less anonymous designers of "mobile homes" have probably done more than anybody else to ease the situation. About fifteen million families live in these cleverly planned units. They are often almost as large as a small tract house; they cost about half as much. More care has recently been given to planning the "parks" in which these homes are grouped. Scarcely ever mobile after they arrive at their site, they nevertheless contain a lingering echo of the restless mobility which has marked the American culture. They in some measure fulfill the old dream of inexpensive mass-produced housing for the many, and they embody once again a triumph of sorts for the American builder without the academic training which is intended to fit him for that calling. Multifamily housing provided by both governments is on the whole grim and unimaginative, though in Japan it is still so much preferable to what most people can afford that the odds of winning the lotteries by which potential dwellers are chosen are very long. The Tokyo metropolitan government does better than the national government: in Tama New Town, for example, where their apartment buildings stand side by side as if to welcome comparison, Tokyo's provide more amenities, and their use of the site is much more organic. (I was delighted to look at drawings, in 1971, made by elementary school students who had recently moved to Tama from downtown Tokyo: "Sunlight!" the drawings said, "Space!")

Similarly, the state of New York has built housing developments strikingly more humane than those produced by the federal government in its forty-year history; New York hires such first-rate architects as Paul Rudolph, and it accepts their plans.

The architects in both countries are studying Finnish and English plans and are drawing their own; possibilities exist; but few politicians seem to share the enthusiasm or the sense of urgency of the architects.

The strokes I have used to suggest the present state of architecture have been too broad. Some Japanese, for example, very conscious of the Japanese tradition, have deftly adapted new materials and methods to retain something of the feel of that tradition. The new reinforced concrete offices for the Ise shrines, unobtrusively half-hidden in a grove, refuse to challenge in shape or tone the hallowed buildings they serve. Few of the prize-winning houses in recent issues of the *Japan Architect* are without at least one tatami room, and many preserve other traditional elements. All retain the Japanese respect for materials in their natural state. Even when the forms are distinctly "modern," the psyche that shaped them often seems Japanese. For example, of massive stone cylinders which Yamamoto Tadashi designed for a folk-history museum, he writes, "Another step in the direction of harmony with nature was the use of stone excavated from the site in the buildings and in the gardens. Stone that slept underground for long ages has assumed new life and strength as a result of sudden contact with sunlight and air. Piled in huge masses, it became nature that has been altered and set in a new position but that has not been destroyed."[36] I don't believe an American would be likely to think of stone in that manner.

The Americans generally, as I have hinted, seem more timid than the Japanese. A recent survey by *Architectural Record* of the attitudes of architects under thirty-five generally suggests that their profession is still circumscribed by their old white, upper-middle-class limitations. Yet there are signs that many Americans have heeded many of Japan's architectural lessons for the West as enunciated by Harada, in such ways as the use of natural materials, the harmonious use of setting, and (extrapolating a bit from him), a more dynamic sense of interior space.

Two further hopeful signs for our artificial environment appear in the recent journals in both countries. Brief allusions earlier suggested one: a growing sense of architecture seen in a larger context than the individual building or cluster, a sense that the building must consider its neighborhood, its region, even the whole planet. Second, many young architects think more about conserving old works of art, restoring them, and planning new construction in a way that does not affront contiguous old. The *Japan Architect*, which ordinarily runs a series on architecture considered in some larger perspective, began a series in the early 1970s on provincial folk festivals, and the incidental role architecture plays in them. This corroborates a growing interest in both cultures in the past, in continuity, which in turn may well reflect a growing distrust of that magic word *progress*. (At the same time, increasingly more attention is paid to the design of second homes, for the wealthy who can retreat to the mountains or the sea, and to hotels and shopping centers, designs for which are always lively, and sometimes vulgar.)

Will the new symbols nourish souls? Evidence exists showing that Americans want individual family homes, with grass surrounding them, and in fact most Americans have that now. What of the others? And what of the prospects for the vitality, the variety and choice, and the other urbane values which are implied in those preferences? Japanese polls indicate a similar preference at least for less crowded urban life, and traditions suggest a similar predisposition for separate family quarters. Yet geography, and the relentless shift of population to the Tokyo-Nagoya-Osaka strip, probably indicate that many Japanese must make do with very large multi-unit housing.

Can concrete replace wood in our affections? Does the television set in the tokonoma do the job of the flower arrangement? In the United States, as I said in an earlier chapter, young people object to the sterility of the suburbs—what there is for them to do is distant, bicycles are dangerous on the freeways getting there, automobiles, when they can get them, cost more and more to operate, and they appear increasingly to be left with hanging around the shopping center or watching television. Fortunately, the increasing fondness of thoughtful young Americans for the small town can presently be accommodated. We haven't seen much evidence yet that Mr. Tanaka's internationally advertised decentralization of the Japanese archipelago has begun, in order that like-minded citizens of Japan can be similarly accommodated.

The human animal has proven himself over the past century or two to be a wonderfully adaptable creature. One guesses that in the future his symbolic life will get less nourishment of the sort his family home has traditionally granted him. New images have appeared on the landscapes, many of them very beautiful; but it is easier to understand how one's spirit can relate to home and temple than it is to office, airport, or shopping mall. Schools and community centers seem more likely objects of affection. Yet the first priority in these two wealthy nations, one would suppose, should be housing all of their citizens in a condition of dignity.

For a purpose which may be capricious, I wish to return briefly to the traditional hope in Japanese gardening and architecture to suggest further space beyond what one sees. Could this be an even more wondrous phenomenon than it at first appears to be? Could this be a strategy by a very crowded people (even a long time ago) to gain space in the imagination through the ingenuity of art? Does this also explain, as well as Zen doctrine does, the empty spaces which the Japanese have preferred in literature and painting? Conversely, perhaps, the early Americans gained the security of a sense of order through closing out the unaccustomed vastness of their environment, with walls that became as artificial as possible as soon as possible? A boy in Willa Cather's *My Ántonia*, having grown up in Virginia, describes his first impressions of Nebraska, which was to be his new home: "There was nothing but land: not a country at all, but the material out of which countries are made. . . . Between that earth and that sky I felt erased, blotted out." Many of the earliest settlers of Virginia and Massachusetts have left records of similar emotions.

Traditional architectural forms in both places gave sanction to both kinds of impulses, but I am asking if environmental conditions may not have reinforced movement in certain directions. In the United States of a century ago, John Brinckerhoff Jackson concludes, the "characteristically American organization of space" demonstrated "emphasis on the linear process," with specialized functions along the line.[37] He had studied such early evidences as grid-line roads, cattle runs in stockyards, and railroads; later developments of assembly lines, and highways, corroborate his conclusion. Then I am reminded of a tour de force by John Kouwenhoven a few years ago. What, he asked, did chewing gum, *Huckleberry Finn*, soap operas, skyscrapers, comic strips, the *Leaves of Grass*, and jazz all have in common? American, of course, in origin, though many others have taken them up. More importantly, a series of modules with no necessary beginning or end, going on for as long as artist or sponsor wishes, with no esthetic reason for choosing one or another place for ending. Very much unlike Aristotle's rules, but approaching the Japanese esthetic.

CHAPTER 8

The Nurture of the Young

No matter what perspective one uses in examining the cultures of Japan and America, his glance must ultimately rest on how they train the minds and sensibilities of their young people. Obviously the tone and strength of the cultures in the future are in important ways being shaped in their schools and colleges. (Informal education is another matter; I cannot here wrestle with the protean question of education which issues from parents, peers, churches and temples, Boy Scout leaders, judo instructors, and television tubes.) National budgets reveal that both peoples cherish more deeply priorities other than education. Americans spend about seven times as much for the military as for elementary and secondary education. The Japanese spend much more for education than for national defense—12.2 percent of the state budget as opposed to 7.7 percent in 1970—but only 4 percent of Japan's gross national product goes for schooling, as opposed to 6.5 percent in the United States.

Yet, quantitatively speaking, the two school systems must be considered successful: the Japanese have achieved almost universal literacy, and the Americans aren't far behind; and the strength of the two economies indicates success by that gross measure, as well. Acknowledging the achievement of those minimal goals, we must now inspect the quality of those two systems. Do they encourage the kind of imagination necessary to cope with ailments peculiar to postindustrial cultures: anomie, alienation, cultural entropy, and, most importantly, ecological disaster? Schools inevitably tend to inculcate in students the traditional values of the culture; can they manage to test those values against the changing necessities of life? How well do schools perform their critical social role in the two democracies, that of keeping open to each citizen the opportunity for an education equal to that of each other citizen? Then schools have another kind of problem in a mass democracy: are the kinds of ideas, values, and modes of behavior which are consciously or unconsciously rewarded only those of the tepid middle? Is democratic education, in other words, doomed to mediocrity? In some part, this is a question concerning the nature of the public control of the schools.

In considering these matters, we will necessarily touch on frailties that have been endemic to the two systems for a long time. In Japan, these include three that are interrelated: an apparently indestructible pyramid of prestige, which is responsible for the well-known "examination hell" into which youngsters are thrown; a somewhat intractable Ministry of Education; and a method of teaching which rather generally violates the following precept enunciated by Jacques Barzun. The pupil, he says, "wants to open a door or spell 'accommodate.' The would-be helper has two choices. He can open the door, spell the word; or he can show his pupil how to do it for himself. The second way is harder and takes more time, but a strong instinct in the born teacher makes him prefer it."[1] American education has all too often succumbed to the mean undercurrent of anti-intellectualism which has plagued Americans throughout their history, with the result that a humanely conceived and well-balanced curriculum has often been sacrificed to a vague notion of training for "good citizenship," rather than for sound thought and heightened sensibility. Such flaws in these two excellent educational systems inhere in their histories, which we must now glance at.

Education in both countries was, in the beginning, lodged in religion. Learning in Japan before the Tokugawa period, mostly centered in courts and monasteries, originated in China and was meant for courtiers and their priestly retainers. The situation was similar in medieval Europe. During the seventeenth Christian century, education opened up to commoners in both cultures.

In the early Tokugawa period, few even of the samurai, later a well-educated class, were literate. During the course of that long period of peace, however, government leaders encouraged the broadening of education, and it progressed rapidly. Rich daimyo—lords—sponsored some schools, large cities others. As the popular base broadened, attendant changes occurred. The classical curriculums consisted of the Chinese *bu* (the military arts) and *bun* (civil studies), the literary arts, and general intellectual pursuits; these curriculums may be compared to the ancient Western *trivium*—grammar, logic, and rhetoric—and *quadrivium*—geometry, arithmetic, astronomy, and music—which were the bases of the idea of liberal arts education inherited by the Americans. Some of the newer Tokugawa schools, however, increasingly open to the sons of the wealthy middle class and farmers, taught writing, arithmetic, and etiquette as well as traditional Chinese military and moral studies. Samurai and commoners began to teach, joining the monks and priests. Another change of perhaps even greater import accompanied these. The English anthropologist Ronald P. Dore writes, "a new word appears in fief edicts announcing the establishment of schools or redefining educational policy. The word is *jinzai*—human talent."[2] Notice the democratic implications in this. To make men "useful in public service" became an avowed aim of education. Commoners had become wealthy and important; why not enlarge their talent, improve their capacity for public service? The curricular emphasis remained on literacy and on moral training, but by the end of the eighteenth century, a note we would call "vocational" was sounded with increasing frequency: more and more *terakoya* were opened, schools of reading, writing, arithmetic, and practical wisdom intended to increase men's efficiency in their hereditary occupations. Measured by our simplest yardsticks, these efforts were immensely successful. In 1710, Japan had 600 publishers and booksellers; in 1809, 656 lending libraries did business in Tokyo alone. In 1837, barely one British child in four or five ever entered a school. By the end of Tokugawa in the middle of the nineteenth century, Japan perhaps approached 50 percent literacy among boys, and 10 percent to 20 percent among girls (Dore, who has made this estimate, reminds us that data are so scarce as to make it a risky one).

The achievement of the northern colonies in America during the same period was equally praiseworthy, and the motives behind offering schooling underwent a somewhat similar shift. The Puritans' reason for establishing schools very early in their "errand into the wilderness" was that everybody had to be able to read the Bible. The hated Roman Catholic church, in opposition to which the Puritans formulated many of their attitudes and beliefs, interpreted religious truth through its hierarchy of churchmen; the Puritans (and other sects such as the Quakers) believed each church member should himself study what was held to be infallible scripture. A Massachusetts law of 1647 required that every township with a population over fifty should hire a teacher of reading and writing, in order to outwit "that old deluder Satan." Harvard College was founded for the training of ministers six years after the colonists landed in the wilderness; legend has it that the first students could hear the wolves howl as they studied. Nothing in these religious beliefs excluded the teaching of science, but its importance was subordinate to religion.

Soon, however, the same secular tendency which we saw in Tokugawa Japan set in. Benjamin Franklin, one of the early great apostles of public education, argued in 1740 for more emphasis on modern foreign language, on mathematics, and on "natural and mechanic philosophy." Particularly he urged the study of English. Pennsylvania, with a large population of Germans, was already experiencing what the "nation of immigrants" was to struggle with through much of its history: many of its people were incompetent in the language in which it managed its affairs. Further, the sly Ben suggested, "While they are reading natural history, might not a little *Gardening, Planting, Grafting, Inoculating,* etc. be taught and practiced; and now and then excursions made to the neighboring plantations of the best farmers, their methods observed and reasoned upon for the information of youth? The improvement of agriculture being useful to all, and skill in it no disparagement to any."[3] That other great apostle of public education, Thomas Jefferson, shared Franklin's emphasis on the practical—though neither excluded a solid grounding in the Latin classics and perhaps some Greek. Furthermore, Jefferson's interest in education was part and parcel of his political thought: "It is an axiom in my mind that our liberty can never be safe but in the hands of the people themselves, and that, too, of the people with a certain degree of instruction."[4] His design for free public education was to provide elementary education for all white people, then select out, at various stages, the more able, the *most* able, to go to a free public university (Japan's pattern today, though imperfectly executed). In this way, Jefferson reasoned, the experimental republic would assure itself a sound leadership, an ever-renewed "natural aristocracy" of "virtue and talent" (recall the Tokugawa talk of *jinzai*). The South has always lagged in education: certainly Jefferson's Virginia, with its influential gentry who preferred private tutors for its sons, then England for their higher education, was far from ready for his plan. America generally still balks at the provision which was the capstone of his plan—free tertiary education for the very brightest—but it soon, at Jefferson's urging, laid the political and economic foundation for the rest of his plan. The Ordinance of 1787, remarkable in many ways, stipulated that a portion of all new land opening up north of the Ohio River should be given over to the establishment of public schools. The priorities set by the legislators were ambiguous: "Religion, morality, and knowledge being necessary to good government and the happiness of mankind, schools and the means of education shall forever be encouraged." Clearly, not necessarily education for the sake of education. Jefferson's political emphasis shows, but it is not exclusive.

Opposition to such ambitious plans for the education of all citizens at public expense came, curiously, from opposite directions. Many people, with colonial "pauper schools" in mind, felt ashamed to send their children to schools which charged no fees. At the other pole, the well-to-do, not unexpectedly, opposed paying for the education of the children of the less affluent. The famous patrician Edward Everett declared that one might as well pay a student's tailor. Such attitudes were suffused with class bias: education should not be opened to those who "were better suited to their station without it." Nevertheless, under pressure from the infant trade unions and from such persuasive propagandists as Horace Mann, the vision began to be realized. In 1825, there were few public schools. In 1850, almost half of all Americans aged five to twenty were in school, most of them learning only reading and writing from teachers barely more erudite than themselves. (The ratio of men to women in school was 49 to 44; of whites to nonwhites was 56 to 1.8.)

Education in Japan during Tokugawa, I repeat, was roughly commensurate in quantity, and similarly mixed between the practical and the high-minded in purpose. The jolt of the Restoration after 1868 tipped it abruptly toward the practical. The plans were bold. There shall be "no uneducated families in a community and no uneducated members in a family," declared the Meiji oligarchy in 1872, when it was also stipulated that science be included in the elementary curriculum, as in the West. On the level of higher education, teachers from the West were brought to Japan and promising students were sent abroad, "to England to study the navy and merchant marine, to Germany for the army and for medicine, to France for local government and law, and to the United States for business methods."[5] Some Japanese fell into slavish imitation of Western ways, to the amusement and consternation of their fellow citizens, but on the whole the borrowing was selective. We should not be surprised to learn that the experiment did not succeed immediately. It could not be adequately financed. Teachers were scarce, particularly people who could teach the Westernized curriculum. Conservatives resisted strongly, particularly some pious Buddhists. Schools were burned, and students, especially young women, stayed home from school in large numbers. By trial and error, educational leaders chose and rejected various models. First French models seemed most appropriate, though the Japanese went a step beyond the Napoleonic system and made elementary schools public (they weren't tuition-free in France until 1881). Decentralized control on the American model resulted in reduced class attendance, so the educational leaders turned to Prussian models, which gave the national government more control. The Prussians identified the goals of education with the goals of the state, as did Confucian precedents. (Recall that Americans did this only ambiguously.) These were the 1880s, a time, we have seen, of reaction against hook-line-and-sinker Westernization of the sort some earlier Meiji educational leaders had proposed.

All this educational ferment culminated in the famous Imperial Rescript on Education, in 1890. This was posted in all the schools, in awe and respect. Notice its Confucian tone; it begins: "Our Imperial Ancestors have founded our Empire on a basis broad and everlasting, and have deeply and firmly implanted virtue." "Virtue" is defined as "loyalty and filial piety." This virtue is "the source of our education." "Ye, our subjects, be filial to your parents, affectionate to your brothers and sisters; as husbands and wives be harmonious; as friends true, bear yourselves in modesty and moderation; extend your benevolence to all; pursue learning and cultivate arts, and thereby develop intellectual faculties and perfect moral powers; furthermore, advance ˌpublic good and promote common interests."[6] As in the Northwest Ordinance of a century before, education for its own sake doesn't seem to be the point; rather personal morality is good for the nation-state. The earlier document, however, does include "the happiness of mankind" in the mix; the later document seems rather more uncompromisingly centered on virtue.

Nationalist sentiments in the two countries during the nineteenth century led to debates about the study of their own cultures. We have noticed several times before that learned Americans have felt their culture to be inferior to Europe's, and that learned Japanese have felt the same way about themselves in respect to the Chinese—and, later, the Westerners. The political and economic nationalism of the American Revolution was soon followed by a wave of cultural nationalism. Noah Webster published reading and spelling books in the "American" language. Patriots called for an American literature, American manners. Historians such as George Bancroft began creating a history which pictured the "Great Experiment" as the divinely ordained final reward for men who had long struggled against the shackles of European tyranny; schoolbooks soon followed his lead. In 1837, Emerson wrote, "our day of dependence, our long apprenticeship to the learning of other lands, draws to a close." Yet college curriculums were chiefly borrowed from Europe until the end of the nineteenth century, no serious study of American literature was published until 1878, and no professor of American literature existed until the 1920s. American studies, generally, did not gain respectability until after World War II, when, following the familiar pattern, their validity was recognized by foreign scholars.

The corresponding Japanese history of cultural nationalism in the schools was more cyclical. Toward the end of the eighteenth century, *Kokugaku*, Japanese studies, began to challenge *Kangaku*, Chinese studies. The most forceful leader in this movement was Motoori Norinaga; of him a historian has said that he "could be compared with such a person as Herder or Jakob Grimm. It is a general phenomenon that the awakening of national feeling is to be seen preceding the formation of a modern state, where the memory of the past becomes alive."[7]

When that state came to life, in Meiji, this new feeling for the old Japan was useful: the emperor was reinstated as its symbol, and was also, incidentally, very active in formulating educational policy. (The present emperor and his brother are scholars, one might add.) As we have noticed, the original slogan of Meiji suggested learning Western science while maintaining "Japanese spirit," but during the first decade or so of this period, the practical emphasis among the learned seemed to be on the Western. A German doctor who was teaching medicine in Tokyo wrote, "In the 1870's . . . Japan went through a strange period in which she felt a contempt for her own native achievements. Their own history, their own religions, their own art, did not seem to the Japanese worth talking about, and were even regarded as matters to be ashamed of." Japan's foreign minister, Inouye Kaoru, said, "It is my opinion that what we must do is to transform our Empire and our people, make the Empire like the countries of Europe and our people like the peoples of Europe."[8] The great Mori Arinori, later to become a rather conservative minister of education, suggested that Japan adopt the English language. Wits of the period loved to poke fun at their fellow countrymen who adopted, with little grace, they said, Western clothing, furniture, and manners.

Twenty years later, few were joking; men were crying "shame." Groups of patriots formed to dedicate themselves to "the preservation of the national essence." But they went further: "there is no doubt," said one publication in 1891, "that the Japanese are burdened with the great responsibility of exerting their special talents, making up for the imperfections of the white races, and advancing the world to a state of perfect happiness."[9] The less nationalistic 1920s gave way, as everybody knows, to outright chauvinism in educational policy during the late 1930s. In this mood, the Imperial Rescript quoted above was perverted to ends which were political, not educational. The other side of the coin is of course that the press for public education was successful, not only in creating general literacy, but also in creating excellence, at least in science, technology, and the arts of organization.

Any evaluation of American education during the same period would probably be similar. The opposition to public education that was alluded to earlier was slow to melt. Massachusetts passed a compulsory education law in 1852, New York ensured that education would be free in that state in 1867. Not until 1872 was the legality of public support for some 300 high schools in the United States validated by the Supreme Court. In 1862, the Morrill Land Grant College Act became law. The Japanese historian of education Michio Nagai, whose perspective is international, considers that act "revolutionary," since it admitted the offspring of humble folk to the arcana of higher education.[10] At the same time, the purposes of public education seemed to remain as much civil as intellectual. The "practical wisdom" that was taught in the late Tokugawa schools fills the pervasive McGuffey's readers of the American nineteenth century; Benjamin Franklin was a hero in the textbooks of both cultures during the latter half of the nineteenth century—in Japan even after many of the other Western figures had disappeared. American textbooks were otherwise as chauvinistic as Japanese. Here is one sample out of many possibilities. The author is saying that the very fact that Washington and Franklin existed proved the unique virtue of the American civilization.

At the grand and soothing idea that this greatest instance of human perfectibility, this conspicuous phenomenon of human elevation and grandeur should have been permitted to rise first on the horizon of America, every citizen of these states must feel his bosom beat with rapturous and honest pride, tempered with reverential gratitude to the great author and source of all perfection. . . . He will be penetrated with astonishment, and kindled into thanksgiving when he reflects that our globe had existed six thousand years before a Washington appeared on the theatre of the world; and that he was then destined to appear in America.[11]

In the standard McGuffey's readers, such patriotic boasts appeared alongside anecdotes illustrating prudential wisdom, as in some of the Tokugawa and Meiji reading books. Patriotism was not merely a lesson taught: the fact of the existence of "free schools" was in itself a source of political pride. The Massachusetts system, declared Horace Mann, "knows no distinction of rich and poor, of bond and free. . . . Without money and without price, it throws open its doors, and spreads the table of its bounty, for all the children of the State. Like the sun, it shines not only upon the good, but upon the evil, that they might become good."[12]

. It was Mann who most effectively set about improving the quality of teaching in these free schools. In 1857, two-thirds of Pennsylvania's teachers were under twenty-five and two-fifths of them had fewer than three years' experience. That was the year when the organization now known as the National Education Association was formed, marking a step in the direction of professional attitudes toward the art of teaching. The NEA subsequently gained enormous power over the content of formal public education. That its influence has been wholly benign may be doubted; at least I will try to make that point later.

Perhaps it is unnecessary to point out that most of the foregoing remarks about the history of education are germane only to males. Definitions of the roles of women in both cultures have shaped the character of the education available to them. Not that either culture has assumed women to be uneducable: we recall those highly cultivated ladies of the Heian court, and the likes of Anne Hutchinson, Abigail Adams, and Phillis Wheatley in seventeenth- and eightcenth-century America. Among the most important advocates of public education in Japan and the United States, the Emperor Meiji and Thomas Jefferson held that women should be included. The Emperor Meiji, for example, said, "Due to the inadequate provisions for the education of women in our country, most of them are not able to understand the meaning of civilization. . . . It is obviously desirable for men who go abroad to take their wives and sisters with them."[13] The 1872 education act provided for the education of women, as we have seen. Nevertheless, Meiji was a traditionalist as well as a reformer, and the tradition was that women's education be particularly concerned with the arts and with *ninjo*, the workings of the human heart. And so, for example, he (or perhaps he spoke for the oligarchy) opposed the appointment of a military man to preside over the Peer's School for Girls: "Women's education is not the same as men's. The position of President of the Girl's School would have been more appropriately filled by a person of calm, rather than active disposition. . . . A person of greater composure should have been selected to direct the education of girls."[14] Opinion among most thoughtful Japanese of the time, in fact, was that learning should lead to the increased wisdom of women in motherhood.

By 1920, only 37 percent of Japanese girls had made it through middle school. A report in 1918 of the Special Council on Education suggested that higher education be encouraged for women, but that document was considered "premature." Already some women had been admitted to universities, however, and to women's colleges. In the free air of the 1920s and early 1930s they might be encouraged at such places to read Ibsen and struggle for their intellectual fulfillment. Only very exceptional women then demanded that their higher education be the same as that provided men. A woman in some families must still muster a bit of boldness to elect exactly the same studies as a man.

Parallels in the United States are apparent. Secondary education for most women was expected earlier in the United States than in Japan; and about two-fifths of the students presently in higher education are women. It has not ordinarily been thought the same process as for men, however: in America too, the ends of education for women have usually been considered different from those for men. Even that authentic visionary Thomas Jefferson, writing to his daughter, had this to say: "The acquirements which I hope you will make under the tutors I have provided for you will render you more worthy of my love; and if they cannot increase it, they will prevent its diminution." Then he lays out her curriculum: music, dancing, drawing, French, and English composition—all the ladylike refinements, undertaken to please men, like those of a character out of *The Tale of Genji*.[15] The academies in New England stressed marital training rather more than Japanese schools, as might be expected. Mary Lyon and Emma Willard established academies in the 1830s which gradually became colleges with curriculums identical to those in men's colleges. Oberlin College became coeducational in 1833. Nevertheless it would not be surprising if there were still some parents in the United States whose hopes in sending their daughters to college are that they'll catch husbands there; and in the professional schools, women are nudged in the direction of certain specialties, such as gynecology in medicine and family affairs in law, and there are almost no female engineers. In 1971, 403 of the 50,357 bachelor of engineering degrees awarded in the United States went to women. The women's liberation movement has begun to break some of those barriers.

Of blacks in the United States, old theories about their uneducability persist in various ugly corners, evidence to the contrary notwithstanding. Educational opportunities for this one-eighth of the population are improving, perhaps more rapidly than for American Indians, Mexican-Americans, and Puerto Ricans; but on the average, they are not as good as those for whites. The same is true of opportunities for Japanese *burakumin*—those of the caste anciently banished from all but the "unclean" jobs such as slaughtering and tanning livestock. This injustice in Japan is not, of course, based upon racist theory; perhaps it is related to the fact that little education has been deemed necessary for their hereditary dirty jobs. This caste is much smaller than that of the American black, but I am confident that that provides very little satisfaction to any given member of it.

In both Japan and the United States teachers mostly prefer not to be assigned work in schools for children of the poor. The significance of this fact is that very persuasive evidence exists that the quality of teaching correlates closely with the teacher's sense of whether he or she is in a "good" school. Schools, which are intended to help overcome poverty, unwittingly sometimes reinforce it.

Both national governments make some attempt to compensate for inequalities in education that occur because regions are poor, but equalization funds are inadequate, and in fact a student from a wealthy state such as New York or prefecture such as Tokyo has a distinct advantage over one from Arkansas or Hokkaido. In the United States, moreover, the diminishing but heavy dependence on local property taxes requires many people whose children have long since left home and whose interest in education may have waned to support the schools; the failure of many school-bond elections has been attributed to this fact. In Japan the very complex system of national, prefectural, and local taxation may be somewhat more equitable.

Inequities exist, yet the two systems are fairly successful, *comparatively* speaking, at making good on their promise of a fair chance for all. Japan and the United States lag far behind France and West Germany in kindergarten attendance, but ahead of the United Kingdom. About 80 percent of the students in both cultures continue education beyond what is required by law—middle school graduation in Japan, and age sixteen in most states, standards that are about equal. (In the United States 83 percent of the white students graduate from high school, 65 percent of the blacks.) The enormously ambitious expansion of the Japanese university systems following World War II, and the American GI Bill, which subsidized the education of veterans of that war and later ones, plus the growing affluence of both societies during that same period, widened dramatically the opportunity for higher education. Japan has a college and university population of about one and a half million; the United States, with double the total population, has seven and a half million people in tertiary education. Some able students are priced out of college in both places, but in the United States about 80 percent of those who graduate in the top quarter of their high school class make it on to college. The Ministry of Education admitted in the late 1960s that qualified students were excluded from higher education because there wasn't enough room for them; a white paper on education in 1972 established 40 percent as the proportion of university-age people who ought to be enrolled in universities, and said that construction of new facilities toward that end was too slow. What the eager young Japanese and Americans find when they get to college, of course, is another matter. In the whole complex history of university unrest in Japan and the United States in the 1960s, one common denominator may be found, besides the hatred of war: the impersonality of the large university. The scale which makes such impersonality more or less inevitable, however, represents success measured by a different standard: equality of opportunity. The high quality of education in Tokugawa Japan was in large part responsible for the rapidity with which the country became "modern," when it was imperative that it do so; the same imperative necessitated broadening the popular base of higher education. Meiji slogans that encouraged individual initiative were reinforced by the successful translation of Samuel Smiles's *Self-Help* and by many rags-to-riches biographies of such men as Benjamin Franklin, Abraham Lincoln, and the peasant who became ruler of Japan, Toyotomi Hideyoshi. The plea that merit rather than rank be the basis for national leadership had already begun to succeed during Tokugawa. Now the necessity to learn Western techniques rapidly gave that argument special urgency, since the social waste which results from restricting the pool of prospective talent became unconscionable. Japan was on the road to becoming what is called there a "meritocracy," with public education supporting a very high degree of social mobility. As praiseworthy as that is, it has nevertheless led to a chronic problem in the Japanese educational system: its sharply hierarchic structure. Also in the name of democracy, Americans have perennially insisted upon local autonomy of public schools, and control of colleges and universities by specially chartered corporations or by committees named by state governments. This history has also left educational institutions vulnerable to flaws inherent in the system. We will look at them later.

It is time now to step back and see how these histories, and also more recent developments, have shaped the nature of formal education for the two peoples. First, what do they think they should be doing? Many of the earlier objectives we have already noticed, of course, remain. Their avowed aims have necessarily straddled the dilemma posed by the wish to help individual human beings toward fulfillment and the inevitable other aim, acculturization. The basic Japanese law of 1947, for example, says:

Education shall aim at the full development of personality, striving for the rearing of the people, sound in mind and body, who shall love truth and justice, esteem individual value, respect labor, and have a deep sense of responsibility, and be imbued with the independent spirit, as builders of a peaceful state and society. . . .

In order to achieve the aim, we shall endeavor to contribute to the creation and development of culture by mutual esteem and cooperation, respecting academic freedom, having a regard to actual life and cultivating a spontaneous spirit.[16]

The stereotypical view is that the Japanese stress the social, while the Americans stress the individual. The official statement above seems to me rather forthright in its emphasis on personal development. Of course the wording of Occupation documents was very often provided by the Americans, but these words were apparently taken very seriously by a number of parents and teachers. To corroborate other evidence that this is so, a 1974 article in the *Japan Interpreter* documents the frustrations felt by several Japanese teachers because their classes are too large to allow them to give attention to individuals and because administrators are too intractable to brook imaginative pedagogy.

Conversely, the following, from the American National Education Association, as near an official statement as one could find, weighs social goals as heavily as personal:

The purpose of democracy is so to organize society that each member may develop his personality primarily through activities designed for the well-being of his fellow members and of society as a whole. . . .

Consequently, education in a democracy . . . should develop in each individual the knowledge, interest, ideals, habits, and powers whereby he will find his place and use that place to shape both himself and society toward ever nobler ends.[17]

The NEA made that statement, part of what was called the *Report on the Cardinal Principles of Secondary Education*, in 1918, but it was reaffirmed by that body through the Council of Chief State School officers, in 1969. "*The Cardinal Principles*," said that body, "were a revolutionary departure from the old knowledge conception of education." (I shall not pause to try to explain the council's slovenly use of the English language, though that would be a fruitful exercise.) They elaborate. The first of two "broad purposes growing out of fundamental needs" they see for elementary schools is "to develop the basic skills and understandings essential to the effective use and comprehension of the arts of communication." That, presumably, means "teach them to read and write," a praiseworthy goal. The second is "to promote the development of character and right social conduct through activities that give satisfying experiences in cooperation, self-control, and fair play."[18] The point is that people who make American educational policy themselves seem suspicious of teaching disciplined thought and refined sensibility, and all too eager to substitute for them what they call "life adjustment."

Arthur Bestor is a distinguished historian and a strong critic of this sort of attitude. In *Educational Wastelands* he comments on a publication of 1947 by Teachers College at Columbia University, a center of the life-adjustment ideology, which states that curriculums should be built around "basic problems . . . of everyday living"; one of its chapters is entitled "Life Situations Are the Curriculum; Organized Bodies of Subject Matter Are Resource Areas." Bestor chafes at that kind of disdain for traditional studies in such courses as history, English, and mathematics; he's acid enough in commenting on a similar group of educators who wish to undermine public respect for those disciplines: " 'Traditional subjects are logically organized,' it [the group of educators] had to admit, and the contrast with what it was proposing was all too obvious. 'Effective teachers are enthusiastic about the subjects they teach,' the Commission lamented." The public persists in protecting their old ways: " 'There are enormous continuing pressures for teachers and principals to continue doing the things they do well'—a hopelessly old-fashioned attitude that would require a good deal of propaganda to eradicate." The enlightened educators confess that they see no panacea for curing such attitudes. Another such group reports that it is their wisdom that social science should address itself primarily to "reduce the tensions . . . of children and youth." Bestor's retort is that young people probably ought to practice hard thinking very diligently in order to learn how to prevent, in the world, the causes of some of these tensions. The life-adjustment educators, however, say that "if we neglect the tensions . . . we run the risk of being academic."[19]

Matters could be even worse. The optimism which is behind the whole idea of universal public education may have disappeared among those responsible for proffering it. A report by the United States Office of Education in 1945 informs us that vocational schools can prepare only one-fifth of their pupils for skilled occupations and another one-fifth for college. The remaining three-fifths, it says, must settle for "life adjustment," and even that booby prize (the phrase is mine, not the office's) will fail to materialize unless administrators recognize the necessity that it should do so.[20] The Office of Education has no power comparable to Monbushō, its Japanese counterpart, but the report represents the thinking of what Bestor calls the "interlocking directorate of professional educationists," those products of and professors in teachers colleges who administer the schools, choose textbooks, write certification standards for teachers, and so on. One might protest: do not the local school boards hold the ultimate power? But these boards tend to defer to the "experts" on all issues save budget; nor are the parent-teachers associations ordinarily a serious force. In fact, educators discuss among themselves modes of "engineering consensus" for their wishes. We must return to the politics of education shortly.

One hopes not to exaggerate. Cries for quality in education have increased during the decades since World War II—by individuals (including many educators) and by associations. Strangely enough, the Russians helped these protesters when they launched Sputnik into an atmosphere of Cold War fearfulness. Nevertheless, that massive 1969 NEA publication which was cited earlier gives the critics very little to celebrate. In 1840, Alexis de Tocqueville wrote of his concern that mass democracy might lead to a culture of mediocrity.

These, then, are the aims of public education as enunciated by those entrusted to formulate them in Japan and the United States. One need not question their sincerity if he notes that from political and economic points of view, universal education provides both nations an intelligent and disciplined working force, graded in such a way that those who must do the menial work have not been awakened intellectually to the extent that they become overly bored and distraught. Seen from this angle, the two educational systems appear wonderfully successful.

Perhaps, though, the word *education* is inappropriate in this context. Ronald Dore's distinction between "education" and "qualification" is important to our purposes. "Education," he says, "involves changing people: it depends on awakening, and sustaining by a continuous process of partial satisfaction and further stimulation, curiosity and the desire for self-development, the desire to understand, the desire to achieve, and the desire to master." "Qualification," on the other hand, is merely "instrumental," "the passive absorption of ready-made answers in order to become qualified, certified, and entitled to a job, a salary, and social status. Education results from the desire to learn; qualification results from the desire to be certified as having learnt. Education is learning as an end in itself or as a means to action; qualification is the merely instrumental *use* of learning, not to do, but just to be."[21] Dore's distinction helps us get at the hierarchical structure in Japanese education, the rigidity of which seems impervious. Japanese businesses and governmental offices, in their understandable effort to recruit the likeliest young men, have encouraged an emphasis on qualification rather than education. The former imperial universities, Tokyo foremost among them, followed by Kyoto and Hitotsubashi, have traditionally admitted a smaller percentage than other universities of those who have taken the institutions' entrance examinations. Employers have assumed that the select few who are admitted there have proved their intelligence and diligence, and have recruited from those places first. Therefore, high school graduates continue to prefer going to one of the "big three," which then receive more applicants from which to choose, so that employers may indeed be accurate in considering those students most intelligent and diligent; and thus the circle remains closed—almost irrevocably, it seems. From these universities, one descends the ladder of prestige through some private universities to the newer prefectural universities.

The system obviously works in some rough and ready manner: Japan is by any standard a success. Certain side effects are just as obviously harmful. It is an open secret that Japanese university students need work very little—much less in the best institutions there than Americans in the best American institutions. It is their *admission* that counts to employers, who presently begin to recruit even sophomores—"cutting the rice green," they say. The system guarantees that future leaders of Japan are qualified as intelligent and very industrious, but it does not necessarily guarantee that they are educated. That their primary and secondary schools move faster toward the acquisition at least of what Alfred North Whitehead calls "inert facts" is very clear. On an international UNESCO mathematics test, Japanese youngsters proved to be the best in the world. Two of my young Japanese friends were clearly handicapped when they returned home after spending a year in my little city's schools, which are probably no better or no worse than the national average.

But some things are plainly wrong. First, the sharpness of the hierarchy itself may be counted a disadvantage. Given the lifetime system of employment, a young person's future may be rather permanently cast when he is nineteen or twenty years old—in fact, earlier, as we shall see. Second, several other of the universities which are conduits to good jobs are in Tokyo, so half the student population of Japan is there. Presumably, then, much of the booming "prep school" industry is there. These are cram schools, intended to prepare students for the all-important examinations. Seventy percent of a recent freshman class at Tokyo University spent at least one year in a prep school, and I have heard that some young people remain *ronin*—masterless samurai—for as long as seven years, readying themselves for the magic Tokyo University. Further, some prep schools have their own entrance examinations, so there are prep schools for prep schools. Obviously, this costs money, and erodes the chances of the less affluent to enter the most prestigious places.

Further, the examination system tempts the schools to teach that material which is useful for examinations—to drill it into them, regardless of their understanding. Each lower school gains its reputation from its success in escalating its students to higher schools, those whose reputations have been gained in a similar way. So the whole system coagulates. The competition for auspicious seats on the ladder of classrooms remains fierce, despite continuous cries for reform.

Those cries become more intense as it is increasingly clear that children who are ambitious or are the offspring of ambitious parents quite literally lose their youth, from about twelve years on, until they enter college. To the burden of long and anxious study is added, for some, the decision about what kind of career to pursue. Entrance into specialized faculties requires specialized preparation, so one must think of entrance into senior high schools which give such training. Japan's suicide rate has been often overstated, compared with that of other peoples, but the tension that accompanies "examination hell" may account for an abnormally high rate at the exam-taking age level in Japan.

It is hard on the mothers as well. In the middle classes especially their success or failure *as mothers*—the most important aspect of their role as people—is in large part judged by success or failure of their children on those examinations. In families of that rank, fathers may see very little of their children: it's up to mama. Has she coached them thoroughly enough after school? Nourished them properly, instilled disciplined study habits? The standard jokes about *Kyōiku-mamas*—exam mamas—showing up at the examination halls to tender vitamin pills and a massage have more of pathos than of humor about them; a great deal really *does* ride on those exams: the whole course of a child's life.

The standardized test scores in the United States carry much less freight. Admissions officers in the colleges and universities generally find them less accurate predictors of success than high school grades and perhaps than less tangible factors, such as evidence of high motivation. The pressure on students is thus transferred to day-by-day performance in the classroom. That of course could be bad enough, if it weren't for the fact that most parents and most employers recognize that colleges less prestigious than Harvard or Yale do the job very well, perhaps better. Large careers, in fact, are not uncommonly launched from pads of small repute. I surmise, after having talked with many students at a number of colleges and universities over the years, that the pressure on American young people is not ordinarily as great as the popular press says it is. An American student who is willing to settle for a college or university of middling stature can get in and through it with no perceptible pressure whatever at any point along the line, though perhaps nothing much happens inside his skull bone.

Japanese schools, to repeat, through secondary, are generally better than American, in the sense at least that they deposit more information faster than do their American counterparts. The best Japanese colleges and universities seem to me inferior to the best American in their teaching of undergraduates. Michio Nagai, a critic of the Japanese system, complains that it creates "compartmentalized" selves, and he longs for "general education, liberal education, and reorganization of the curricula"; neither students nor professors, he agrees, work very hard in Japanese colleges and universities.[22] (My own observation is that some students and some professors, particularly of science faculties, work quite hard, but that the average expenditure of energy is less than in the best American institutions.) In perhaps fifty American colleges and universities, undergraduates must work hard and can get a liberal arts education, a heritage from their Greek and Roman past and their English ancestors at Oxford and Cambridge. And if I may be indulged a bit of self-pity, teaching at such an institution is enormously demanding. Two facts may help account for the alleged laziness of some Japanese professors: salaries are so low that many of them must moonlight, some holding as many as three jobs; and Japanese universities are as incestuous as Harvard was until recent years, preferring to hire their own graduates onto their faculties. Once there, their jobs are quite secure, if they don't criticize their seniors too much.

Returning to the use of schools in preparing an intelligent and disciplined work force, graded to perform the tasks the economy requires: surely no conscious conspiracy among teachers and administrators exists to pervert their missions toward this end, but the results often seem the same as though one did. (Technical and vocational courses and schools, of course, are another matter, but I won't discuss them here.) They seem so because bureaucrats who organize the work of schools and school systems behave, not surprisingly, like other bureaucrats. Their dearest hope is that nobody rocks the boat. Charles Silberman has reached the dismal conclusion that much of what goes on in American schools has the effect of rewarding docility. Almost every attribute of thought and sensibility which one associates with the learning process is discouraged in the name of order. Clocks: Silberman cites instances of teachers being reprimanded when their students become so interested that they stay overtime. Silence: it's taboo for students to show too much interest in or dissent from what is being said, particularly if teacher is speaking. Motion: whether its purpose is to relieve boredom with the class, or to demonstrate excitement about it, or simply to meet a child's kinetic necessities, movement is discouraged. In a sense, insofar as wiggling in the school-desk is impeachable on grounds of violation of decorum, the teacher is as liable to censure from above as the students, as Silberman has shown when he speaks of a teacher who took off his jacket and tie to delve all the more enthusiastically into a demonstration of dissection.[23] Even requiring a "lesson plan"—certainly not evidence of a plot to undermine education as Dore defined the term—can stultify learning. If genuine concern should develop in the classroom, must the teacher really remain loyal to his lesson plan? Administrators who visit classrooms think so.

It is equally clear that the pattern of education in Japan creates an ideal working force. While kindergarten and elementary school classrooms are free and open, the serious business begins in middle school, and the serious business is passing examinations. Inevitably, scores on the National Achievement Tests formulated by the Ministry of Education reflect on a teacher's ability, so even teachers who oppose the tests, as many do, must feel some pressure to direct their efforts toward them. The curriculums, also designed by Monbushō, are full; one critic charges that Monbushō's hope, in making them so, is that leftist teachers will have no time to spread their ideas.[24] Social studies are presented as definitive bodies of material to be absorbed without debate. Generally, questioning and discussion are minimal in Japanese classrooms. I have found that even at the university level students generally had not developed the skill of questioning *in the classroom*, though they certainly did so outside; others have had the same experience.[25] The habit of quiet receptivity in the classroom seems to have become hardened. A college student reports of his university experience at Tokyo, presumably the best, as follows: "In spite of the fact that our classes are as small as twenty in number, there is something in the atmosphere of the classroom that discourages discussion with our professors, who give us lectures as though they were disregarding our presence." As we know, he and his classmates studied very hard to be admitted there, only to find that "those who are really interested in study are compelled to study on their own." "We are utterly disappointed," he concludes.[26]

We must of course understand that circumstances and traditions conspire against a less passive mode of education. Of enormous importance in this respect, given the incredible burden on teachers, is the fact that the average Japanese public school classroom holds about fifty pupils, as opposed to about thirty—too many—in the United States. The Japanese teacher goes to work along the path of the ancient tradition of the sensei—teacher, leader, elder friend, almost guru. How can he live up to this awesome role, given fifty kids to respond to and strong control, direct and indirect, from Monbushō? What opportunity has he to follow the precepts enunciated in *The Aims of Education* by Alfred North Whitehead: "Let the main ideas which are introduced into a child's education be few and important, and let them be thrown into every combination possible. . . . From the very beginning of his education, the child should experience the joy of discovery. The discovery which he has to make, is that general ideas give an understanding of that stream of events which pours through his life, which is his life."[27]

Other obstacles to less passive education exist. Professors, if they moonlight, can have little time for preparation of classes; and their careers, even more than in the United States, I believe, are measured by success in publication rather than in teaching. Many university students live in such squalid circumstances in their rooming houses that their health is affected: the tuberculosis rate among college students is higher than the national average. Most important, perhaps, is a less tangible cultural fact. The Japanese began buying that American export, the cult of youth, as early as the 1920s. But even though the advertising men hawk it energetically today, schools, with their students in seemly uniforms, appear little affected; at any rate, the youth cult must be grafted onto an ancient tradition of respect for elders. This habit of respect may well reach no deeper than manner, but it reinforces another trait that has been attributed to Japanese. They wish not to compete with their friends openly, it is said. (The system of examinations for university admission accommodates this characteristic, of course.) The class is a unit which should function harmoniously, without disruption. I have read somewhere of a student who was angry with his teacher because of a low mark, but, not wishing to disrupt the class, waited until after school to assault him. This loyalty to the group, of course, is of further benefit to the economy. Making decisions in Japan is very much a group affair, and the *batsu*, or cliques, formed in college may remain in a given business or government bureau for decades. "The old school tie" is known in certain American institutions, but not so persistently or so importantly as in Japan.

The Japanese culture may inhibit dynamic education of the sort Whitehead described, but Monbushō must bear much of the responsibility for a system of rote learning. One scholar, we recall, has charged that in requiring a very full curriculum, the ministry assures that teachers have little free play, and that students keep their noses in the textbooks approved in Tokyo. The national testing program reinforces cramming the material in those books. Certainly Nikkyōso, the large and powerful teachers' union, is constantly charging Monbushō with preventing more open pedagogical techniques. (The smaller Kyoshikai, which corresponds closely to the NEA in that its members oppose Nikkyōso's identification with workers, seldom opposes Monbushō's policies forcefully.) Finally, Monbushō is simply a very conservative bureaucracy which has generally served a conservative political party, so a bureaucracy's usual resistance to change is compounded. Michio Nagai states the case clearly. The Japanese bureaucrat's method of *shingikai hōshiki*, deliberative consultation, "by its very . . . nature abandons long-range planning and the responsible implementation of far-reaching proposals and seeks instead to balance and harmonize the opinions and influences of various interest groups." Bureaucracies subsist on rules and regulations; the result is that Nagai reports the same stifling of spontaneity in the Japanese classroom that

Silberman found in the American, "in the beautiful name of school unity." "Today's educational world sacrifices respect for the convictions of the individual teacher."[28]

Officials of the American Occupation decentralized control of the Japanese schools, acting on the assumption that centralization *in itself* was partially responsible for wartime jingoism in the schools. Monbushō regained control in 1950, against very strong opposition from Nikkyōso. In fact I have always felt that the influence of the Occupation on the school system in Japan has been overstated; the switch to the 6-3-3-4 system seems to me rather technical, especially in light of the standard joke that it has become, allowing for indefinite periods of time out for cramming for exams, a 6-X-3-X-3-X-4 system (referring to the number of years in elementary and middle schools, then junior and senior high, the X's indicating time out for cram school).

Nor am I thoroughly persuaded by the theory that local control is in itself a guarantee of freedom of expression in the classroom. Here we encounter once again Tocqueville's observations about the tyranny of the majority in a democracy of the masses. Instances in which books are burned and teachers fired in the name of "decency" are not rare—and "decency" at such times is ordinarily defined in sexual terms rather than in terms of violence, for example, or more complex moral issues. Beyond that, if nationalism is a substitute for religion, the assumption that local control prevents propagandistic schooling is a fiction. It is probably true that American schools have been freer of political control than is ordinary in the history of the world. But patriotism has always, in one way or another, been part of the curriculum of most American schools. For example, elementary school children open their days with a pledge of allegiance to the flag. (When Prime Minister Tanaka advocated in 1974 that schoolchildren daily sing the national anthem, which few of them know, and witness a flag-raising ceremony, he caused a furor.) Most American high schools require a course which used to be called "Civics," but which is now more commonly called "American Government," and these courses are often taught as lessons in patriotism rather than analyses of the workings of government. Following is "The American's Creed," which is printed on the frontispiece of a standard textbook for such a course, often revised and reprinted since 1917:

I believe in the United States of America as a government of the poeple, by the people, for the people, whose just powers are derived from the consent of the governed . . . a sovereign Nation of many sovereign States . . . established upon those principles of freedom, equality, justice and humanity for which American patriots sacrificed their lives and fortunes.

I therefore believe it is my duty to my country to love it, to support its Constitution, to obey its laws, to respect its flag, and to defend it against all enemies.[29]

In the same book, the following paragraph appears:

One need only to look at the great achievements and the standard of living of the American people to see the advantages of our economic system. We view the trends toward nationalization and socialism in other countries with grave misgivings. We believe that a well-regulated capitalism—a free-choice, individual incentive, private enterprise system—is the best guarantee of the better life for all mankind.[30]

Blind patriotism is not the only block to free inquiry in the American system. A distrust of the intellect, deriving perhaps from the frontier, on the popular level, and from romanticism, among the learned, has clouded American education for a century and a half. The theme of "the contrast," alluded to on a couple of earlier occasions, identified the problem of the decadent European as, among other things, his excess of learning. American schoolbooks of the nineteenth century contained lessons advising against this flaw. "She is a strange child," one moral tale concluded. "She will take a book and read it while the boys and girls run and play near her. I fear she reads and thinks too much." Or "Manhood is better than Greek. Self-reliance is better than Latin."[31] The twentieth-century American citizen generally applauds the high school athletic star or the chic cheerleader who supports him far more heartily than the good scholar. The taxpayers who support the schools are poorly entertained by the latter and perhaps even challenged in disquieting ways. I have conferred with many people about whether such a distrust of the intellect exists in Japan, and we find no evidence of such.

Flaws also inhere in a system of centralized control as exercised by Monbushō. Just as the old McGuffey's readers of the American nineteenth century contained heavy doses of homely wisdom so the common schools of Tokugawa Japan, following aristocratic Chinese models, were full of homily. This tradition of moral education became chauvinistic indoctrination in the hands of the war party, and the American Occupation forbade it. Moral education came to life again in the 1960s, however, despite the earnest protest of Nikkyōso. Perhaps because of teachers' strong opposition, the courses seem harmless enough, if not boring. Very young children are taught to keep clean and guard their books; older children are taught to respect their families and develop a "large mind." One young informant has told me that he gets to watch a considerable amount of television in the classroom during the time set aside for these lessons. At the same time in 1974 when Prime Minister Tanaka advocated patriotic exercises in the schools, he suggested that these required courses drill into the children that they should cherish people, nature, home, things, and "our country and society," moral principles at least four of which one would be reluctant to quarrel with; he also, in what Japanese wryly called his "ten commandments," recommended they be taught to eschew vices such as being finicky with food and careless of traffic regulations,[32] matters of somewhat lesser magnitude than those that troubled Moses.

One further point emerges from the foregoing. We are concerned here with freedom of inquiry in the schools, the only condition which will assure their producing citizens with the lively, quarrelsome, and imaginative minds and sensibilities which these convulsive times require. Monbushō is at least faced with a countervailing power, the potent teachers' union. That mix may produce a more productive dialogue about the aims of education than the more tepid atmosphere of the United States, in which the "interlocking directorate" of the NEA tells what it wants, and local school boards reply by saying how much of that they can afford. One further ingredient must be recognized in this mix: teachers and professors in Japan generally speaking carry more status than Americans in their profession. Further, at all educational levels, there are in Japan more men teaching than women. Both of these conditions are changing, but not rapidly enough to alter the fact that Americans of either sex who teach, when they state their opinions, have a less attentive audience than Japanese. At the beginning of the twentieth century, Thorstein Veblen observed that public school teachers often came from petit bourgeois origins and therefore

worried about their public acceptance, with the result that they be-
haved very timidly in the classroom. Even allowing for change, that
may still be the situation, so that teachers do not wish to press
strenuously their complaints or their aspirations. Once again overstatement is possible. Some classrooms in the United States as in Japan
(especially in the lower grades) are observably animated, earnest, and
instructive.

Public policy which skimps on education would appear to the most
cursory glance to be lamentably shortsighted. In the United States, it is
said that a surplus of teachers exists, and in fact some promising young
people who are trained to teach must find other work. Yet classrooms
are too full for effective teaching—though not so full, as we noticed, as
Japanese classrooms. The Japanese and the Americans apparently do
not value the education of their young as highly as do some
cultures.

Yet more public money is not the whole answer. If a majority of
Americans, including members of the NEA, entertain a lingering
suspicion of matters esthetic and intellectual, if Monbushō remains
stodgy and frightened of teachers, if the status of certain universities
remains so high that no relief of "examination hell" is possible, if
leadership in both countries is more interested in training a work force
than in enhancing human life through enlarging the horizons of the
mind, and if social snobbery is unabated, money won't help. A Japanese friend has made an analogy between the Japanese educational
system and a skyscraper: given a base that is limited in breadth, it has
gone about as high as it can go, and what is wanting is a broader
philosophical basis. American public education, it has often been said,
tries to cover too much, from driver's training and home economics to
Latin, and is thus unable to do any of it well. (I am not alone in
observing a decline in reading and writing skills among high school
students: every professor I know agrees.)

Yet countertendencies exist. Ronald Dore exemplifies them in
Japan by reporting the contents of a monthly magazine named *Snow
and Firefly Days*, published for cram school students. Among many
helpful hints about taking examinations is, for example, "an article on
a well-known 13th century diary by a Buddhist recluse entitled *How to
Read, and How to Savor, the Tsure Zure-Gusa*."[33] And in the United States
as well, in enclaves within certain universities and in good small

colleges, ancient wisdom which can help clarify the present is honored. As for new knowledge, nobody worries, I would suppose, about the health of the natural sciences in Japan and the United States.

When Japan reopened its doors to Western learning during Meiji, it had already achieved a good base of education for commoners. Its leap since then to universal literacy in Western and Japanese learning seems as miraculous as its postwar economic boom. The United States pioneered in universal public education, once thought a folly. If American education is a failure, said one English observer, it is one of the most magnificent failures in history.

CHAPTER 9

In Concluding

Trying to estimate the usefulness to the twentieth century of ingrained ways of thought and feeling in Japan and the United States is sure to be a matter of hunch and conjecture, but it seems important to try. The Japanese have of course proven themselves wonderfully adaptable to new circumstances. The Americans' earlier history of similar skills is almost as remarkable, considering the depth of the frontier and the numbers of immigrants; if, in recent decades, they have seemed somewhat stodgy and set in their ways, a widespread awareness of the criminality of the Indochinese adventures and the liberation from the dung-heap of Watergate could catalyze a national self-examination similar to that occurring in Japan.

In Chapter 1 I touched briefly on the fact that each people has a massive problem that is endemic to its history: space, in Japan, and racism, in the United States. The individual families of Japan have done what they could to solve its particular problem, few of them begetting more than two children. The engineers of Japan have demonstrated marvelous skills; can science help them take the next necessary step, and check pollution? Can philosophers or politicians persuade people to disperse from the jammed Tokyo-Nagoya-Osaka strip? Can architects construct multifamily housing in which people can live with dignity? Can economists show means of accomplishing these things without placing the cost of them entirely upon ordinary citizens? The demon racism—irrational, stubborn, and vicious—will surely someday be expelled from the American body politic, where it has fed for so long. Since World War II, some progress has been made in reducing the ill effects of the disease, and, I believe, in curing the disease itself, particularly where Jews and black people are concerned. Yet very large numbers of people are still caught in a circular trap the circumference of which is defined by bad nutrition, bad housing, bad education, bad jobs, and thus on around, generation after generation. Statesmanlike laws are not without results; but, though the Japanese may laugh at those who husk rice a grain at a time, the ultimate solution is the enlightenment of each citizen, which can occur only through patient, careful, thoughtful, and sensitive work by every agency of education, from the school to the television studio. Elements have been present in the culture to support that work, from the beginning of America's history.

For the solutions to each people's particular problem, then, we turn again to education, to the responsive mind. And so do we as we consider problems common to mass industrial societies in the twentieth century. Kenneth Boulding cites three "traps" which such societies must avoid: war, overpopulation, and entropy.[1] The Japanese, to repeat, have largely solved the second of these, and the American birthrate is declining rapidly, so we probably need consider here only war and entropy.

The Japanese learned more painfully and decisively than any other people the lesson of nuclear war, and every poll taken during the past two decades demonstrates that the meaning of the lesson doesn't fade. Antiwar sentiment has always existed in the United States, and it asserted itself (though ineffectually for many years) during the Indochina wars. Most Americans now think those wars were a mistake; but the strength of their peaceable intentions has not been tested further. What are the kinds of emotions which feed a people's willingness to suffer warfare?

Let us return to the sentiment of nationalism. Signs are clear that in both countries people began early in the 1970s to examine their own histories with a new ardor. In the United States, this was encouraged by the advent of the 1976 bicentennial. Committees formed to plan celebrations sometimes seemed at a loss to know how to do so, but that in itself forced them to study history; on the other hand, some agencies found ingenious means of publicizing the revolutionary years. Fond and careful restoration of old buildings and villages had been under way already, as it had also in Japan. When some high school students in Georgia began investigating the dying arts and crafts of their rural elders, their findings, published in the magazine *Fox Fire* and in two best selling anthologies, found enthusiastic readers all over the country, especially young ones. Strong interest among young people in folk music is matched by older persons' widespread interest in genealogy, antiques, and such vernacular arts as quilting and weaving.

In Japan, the current runs even more swiftly. In 1972, more then forty books of serious national self-examination were published, in what the social psychologist Hiroshi Minami calls an "introspection boom."[2] I was told early in the 1970s that thoughtful young Japanese were making pilgrimages to their ancestral villages, from the same motives that inspired young Americans to explore rural areas, and even their family homes in Europe, Asia, and Africa. Some Japanese journals reflect this tendency; and interest has been revived in the folklorist Kunio Yanagida, founder of a non-Western school of folk-lore study.[3] The interest among young Japanese in folk music parallels that of Americans, except that Japanese know American songs, while the reverse would be true only in the rarest cases.

And so on. Such evidence, and more, indicates that Japanese and Americans are replacing their emotional attachment to political and economic nationalism with cultural nationalism, a much more benign condition. Further, to the extent that much of this new historicism looks to regions and neighborhoods, the focus moves away from the nation-state itself.

Explanations for this new interest in cultural history are complex. The astonishingly regular cyclical shift in Japan, from adaptation of foreign ways, often required by circumstances, to reevaluation of native ways, moves again to the latter position. Japan's understandable loss of confidence during the 1970s in the United States as a political, economic, and technological model, and the concomitant rise in respect for China, where modern Western ideologies were reconciled to indigenous patterns of thought and where social reforms which many Japanese long for have been accomplished, have influenced this wave of introspection. So have the revisitations of ghosts from the

1940s, such as Yukio Mishima's romantic talk before his suicide of the "True Japan," and the return of old soldiers from the battle zones of those days.

I have mentioned the bicentennial celebration as a corresponding cause of national self-evaluation in the United States. The Watergate scandals reawakened interest in the study of holy writ, the Constitution, with an accompanying rise in respect for a kind of political fundamentalism in certain political figures. Perhaps in both cultures this slight shift in focus from the nation-state to the region and the locality is touched with sentimental nostalgia. Perhaps also it is rational enough. First, no future alternative seems to exist for either people to living more simply, more in the style of the preindustrial days, so the desire to learn how one's grandparents managed to cope with such conditions makes sense. Second, some retreat from the long-unquestioned mystique of the "modern" is reasonable when that faith has shown itself to be flawed, as the air itself palpably testifies.

It is easy to be thrilled by the vision of Margaret Mead and others that an opposite and complementary shift in people's loyalty might take place, toward all humankind who share the blessings and burdens of our only planet. That vision, she knows, is as old as the major religions, but recent developments make it more plausible. Her own discipline, anthropology, is crucial to mutual understanding; television, that genie that is capable of so much intelligence as well as so much banality, could be its agent. Professor Mead proposes that votaries of the "faith for the twentieth century" would celebrate throughout the world on Earth Day, at the vernal equinox, joining in "delight in the world that the Lord has made, and delight in the light in the sky, and delight in the spring."[4] The strange provincialism we have noticed among the Japanese and the Americans might suggest that they would not in large numbers be among the first converted. The metamorphosis would indeed be radical. Edwin O. Reischauer reminds us, to our utter chagrin, that the following rhyme could have currency only a few decades ago.

> Little Indian, Sioux or Crow,
> Little frosty Eskimo,
> Little Turk or Japanee,
> O! don't you wish that you were me? . . .

> You have curious things to eat,
> I am fed on proper meat;
> You must dwell beyond the foam,
> But I am safe and live at home.[5]

The Englishman Robert Louis Stevenson was guilty of that one, but Japanese and Americans have in the not-so-distant past displayed the same mind-boggling ethnocentrism. Further, the preoccupation with themselves that was discussed above doesn't mark them as likely candidates for the faith. Yet, in a perverse way, study of themselves may lead them to some deeper understanding of their fellows of the human species. When I was growing up in Indiana, I was told by people who ought to know that if I dug a deep enough hole in my backyard, I would wind up in China. Beyond that, I already know plenty of Japanese and Americans, young and old, whose allegiances range well beyond their national boundaries.

The great black scholar W. E. B. DuBois made an eloquent plea for pluralistic culture when, in 1903, such was an unfashionable position. For his antiquated concept of "race" we must today read "culture"; and we must recognize that his perspective was not then as global as it would become later, when the Treaty of Versailles cut the world pie in the old prewar manner, for the white men and for the Japanese. "Work, culture, liberty," DuBois urged, "striving toward that vaster ideal that swims before the Negro people, the ideal of human brotherhood, gained through the unifying ideal of Race, the ideal of fostering and developing the traits and talents of the Negro, not in opposition to or contempt for other races, but rather in large conformity to the greater ideals of the American Republic, in order that some day on American soil two world-races may give each to each those characteristics both so sadly lack."[6] If each culture were to be aware of itself and true to itself, but aware as well of the strengths and weaknesses of other cultures, they could in concert generate beauty and truth the vitality of which could make the breath come fast: we have seen this in Henry James and Sōseki, in Wright and Tange; we have seen it at gatherings of diverse people who have met in the spirit of open acceptance of one another.

A further important point must be added about Japanese nationalism in the 1970s. The Japanese are intensely aware that they are undertaking an experiment of momentous importance to the history of the world since the advent of the nation-state: they are a great economic power without being a great military power. Conservatives among them feel that this situation can be maintained only under the American nuclear umbrella—and conservative Americans want them to violate their Constitution in order to share the cost of such weaponry. A good many Japanese, however, feel that the American military presence is, if anything, a threat to them. With American bases there, a hostile power might have reason to bomb Japan. Without them, who would bother? With virtually no natural resources and with little arable land, with nothing but a technical plant that could easily be destroyed by any one of the powers, why, they ask, would any other of them want Japan? The question is difficult to answer.

An ingredient in this mix of new Japanese attitudes and ideas is a measure of disappointment. The nobility of their experiment seems not to be noticed by others, or to be understood. Their efforts to create, in East Asia, a counterpart to the American Peace Corps often meet rebuffs because of old wartime animosities (not that Americans aren't also sometimes denied welcome). They are saddened: if the American Revolution excited the world's imagination in the last century, why should not the attempt to be a power without guns do likewise in this?

As we ponder the danger of future war, we must consider the kindred danger of ideology. The "true believer" has proved himself century after century a man to beware of. Ideologues supported the Japanese war party as the Manchurian incident was expanded into the horrendous Pacific war. Many Americans were able to justify the Indochinese wars on ideological grounds, as anti-Communist crusades, neglecting even to distinguish among kinds of communism. Perhaps that unaccountable lack of confidence in their own cultures which we have noticed so often leaves the Japanese and the Americans particularly vulnerable to the kind of national self-justification that can lead to a penchant for ideology.

Again we find counterpoint. Both peoples are known for their pragmatism, their respect for the concrete fact. Yet the opposite is also true. "Over the last century," says Ronald Dore, "the Japanese have shown a rare passion for every new idea. In the 19th Century, they were quick to catch on to liberalism, positivism, utilitarianism, evolutionism, romanticism, realism. In the 20's and 30's, there came anarchism, socialism, democracy, communism, fascism, racism, etc."[7] Similarly, in the several aspects of American culture we have glanced at, it seems astonishingly abstract and theoretical. A mind given to abstraction is not necessarily the mind of an ideologue, though it has made a necessary move in that direction. Faith in such abstract ideas as progress and the harmony of interests falls short of ideology, though, to repeat, the late-nineteenth-century belief in laissez-faire economics was a dogmatic one. The American Constitution is a rather pragmatic document, on the whole; and generally Americans have distrusted programmatic thinking such as that of socialists, even when homegrown, and particularly when foreign-born. The Japanese imagination, as we have seen especially when we studied it in novels and in attitudes toward nature, seems by contrast quite existential.

A third state of mind underlying a people's willingness for war has been identified by Erich Fromm in *Escape from Freedom*. The burdens of freedom, particularly for people reared in an ethic of work and success, are great, and may cause collapse when the economy forces them into positions of lower status than they are accustomed to. Feeling powerless and frustrated, they seek power through identification with a bellicose nation-state. Societies which proclaim themselves "classless" do indeed put a heavy strain on the citizenry, if their culture defines worth as success and chiefly rewards a few who win power or money. "Status anxiety" may be muffled somewhat in Japan by old habits of accepting the inevitable; many Americans have learned similar skills, in spite of a longer history of grandiose expectations. Legislation can reduce the number of disappointed lives, but I suspect that the belief in both cultures that money can buy satisfaction in the form of owning things must undergo considerable revision. I refer again to the predictions of economists of an ecological bent. The hardship of doing with less, however, may not be severe: most people seem somehow to have managed, in the days before the two economies became so dependent on the sale of marginal consumer goods. As everyone knows, the outrageous gap between the standard of living of the rich nations and the poor must somehow be narrowed, soon.

Regarding expectations, including those for neat resolutions of problems, I wish to repeat the question: do such esthetic patterns of Americans as symmetry, climax, and resolution influence attitudes toward their own ordinary day-by-day living? Then I wish to repeat the assertion that some strains in the American esthetic tradition resemble, in their emphasis upon process as form, the Japanese patterns more than European antecedents would lead one to expect.

My confidence that the concept of entropy is a fruitful one in the study of contemporary culture is strong. Heavily dependent upon Norbert Wiener, among others, I have given a good deal of attention to ways in which we might better understand mass industrial cultures through the use of this analogy to thermodynamics and information theory.[8] I have used the following paragraph to try to describe the feel of tepidity, the lack of distinctiveness, and the hackneyed quality of many aspects of the American culture.

Suppose some man—let us call him Mr. K. He has spent five days reading essays by high school seniors from all over the United States, for their College Board exams. The question they were asked to write on, about status symbols, invited pious homilies, so only 5 percent of them were good enough to be interesting, and only 5 percent bad enough to arouse curiosity. The rest were so nearly identical and so dreary in content that they merged and faded into the smoggy miasma of his anticonsciousness. Then he headed home, four days on the Interstates, toward Denver: Standard Oil stations, Stuckey's signs, Holiday Inns. That's about it: no Burma Shave signs, no town squares, no wrecks, no regional differentiation. He took to driving too fast, naturally, burned out his engine, and was forced into a Holiday Inn for three days and nights. Somebody who looked like Anita Bryant was at the desk. The "food" and "lodging" there was a perfect embodiment of the "uniformity of decent competence" that Crèvecoeur had remarked in American life two centuries earlier. There were no books to be bought in the town, except from the rack at the drugstore. The content behind the hundred-odd titles there was reducible to maybe a dozen formulas, so Mr. K. watched television for many hours, and began to worry about his mind's inability to make distinctions, between commercials and contests, spy-heroes and cowboys, war movies and news clips from a battlefront. He listened to a certain chief of state explain his policies to his people, but Mr. K. sensed that the man had chosen all his words from the most crowded area of a probability curve, and then let them soak for a while in a mild bleach. The usual torpor of the atmosphere in that inn was somewhat unsettled by the fact that a number of its guests had been citizens of Fort Wayne, Indiana, Peoria, Illinois, Des Moines, Iowa, and Lincoln, Nebraska, and were suffering from a sense of vague disorientation: some wag in the night had switched those cities around, without telling anybody which he had put where; the people couldn't tell much difference, and didn't much mind, but became irritable when asked where they were from. Mr. K. spent some time reading the brochure the management had left in his room, and what he found there added nagging fear to his growing nervousness. Certain names appeared and reappeared on the pages, and all of them seemed to be reinforcing one another in ways that were subtly unsettling: Billy Graham, Norman Vincent Peale, Bob Hope, some Eisenhower, some Nixon, Arnold Palmer, Pat Boone, Anita Bryant. Were they some interlocking directorate of the culture, approved by the chain of inns, plotting to freeze the culture at fifty-eight degrees Fahrenheit?

We needn't follow Mr. K. further—his collapse from what Dr. Welby diagnosed as "boredom fatigue," his decision to fly home, his experiences at the airport, and so on.[9]

I have discussed the manner in which the brilliant Thomas Pynchon has dealt with cultural entropy in *The Crying of Lot 49*. Despite my contention that Kobo Abé was also concerned with the matter in *Woman of the Dunes*, I am persuaded that cultural heat death is nowhere near as imminent in Japan as in the United States. Mass production of things, images, and ideas has surely eroded the distinctiveness of local and regional forms in Japan, but they are more deeply rooted in time than American forms, and thus presumably firmer. The Americans, I repeat, have had a longer experience than anybody else with mass culture.

Here, a word must be said about modes of variety. The first impression a foreigner receives in Japan is of homogeneity. After a while, though, he may be reminded of something like the tradition of the English sonnet, in which long history has set up expectations which so completely govern one's reading that small variations make large difference. So it is in Japan: one soon feels great diversity, in small ways. In the United States, very wide differences exist in kinds of people and modes of behavior, but they have been only recently foregathered, and so little ordered by insight and art that they seem analogous to random music rather than variations on a theme. Paradox again: on the one hand we speak, as Tocqueville did, of tepid similarity which admits of little distinctiveness in America; on the other, of unassimilated differences. The Japanese, diverse in local ways of being and behaving, have long been one people so that local differences have mostly been respected and even cherished.

The stay against entropy is ordered diversity, diversity articulated in such a manner that differences generate new forms, in the dialectical manner. Paradox may lead to stalemate or loggerhead, or it may lead to new understanding. Debate that achieves synthesis out of thesis and antithesis must be grounded in language that is understood by all parties. The self-educated runaway slave Frederick Douglass taught us in the 1840s that black men may have an opposite sense of the meaning of critical words from what the white man has. The vast gulfs separating many Americans from one another are in part understandable in that nation of immigrants, but economic distances cannot be readily explained. Contraries in a culture cannot refresh or renew if no dialogue exists. The radical student movement in Japan is formidable, but, as has often been remarked—excepting the activities of its murderous Red Army fringe—its "demos," throughout their long history since elite students of the Meiji period protested, have the look of ritual, with students and policemen playing their expected roles. The animosity between the left and the right in Japan is not to be minimized, but it is acted out on the same field. Language barriers between Spanish-Americans and "Yankees," the impalpable but real ghetto walls around most blacks, the invisibility of the Appalachian poor whites, and the boundaries of the reservations in which many native Americans live, all reduce the possibility of the dialectic working fruitfully.

The discussion so far has been negative, mostly, about avoiding traps. What can be said more positively, about maintaining life humanely? Surely no further commendation need be made here of the esthetic skills of the Japanese which grace almost everything they do, humble people as well as the highly trained. Many Americans have such skills, too, but the tradition is not so deeply embedded. Americans do not recognize some of their own ways of telling stories or of designing their surroundings as artful, and would perhaps be embarrassed by the notion that such is the case. Certainly their skills are often roughhewn, a quality some of the best professionals exploit, but Jōmon or "redskin" art has its virtues, too; and of course the more learned "paleface" or Yayoi tradition is alive as well in America. All kinds of arts and crafts in all kinds of places have been capable of vulgarity. Now, of course, vulgarity is mass-produced, so that vigilant critics and sensitive teachers must help us maintain our capacity to discriminate.

No one need worry that well-educated people in Japan and the United States will be unable to find ways of using their leisure that refresh and satisfy the spirit. (They have had, incidentally, more chance to practice at it than most people on earth.) But of course many people in both places are much less well educated than they should be. The flawed systems of education may be blamed also for the unfair distribution of labor in the two cultures. Tracking systems and providing poor schools for the children of the poor tend—though not at all absolutely—to determine a child's future long before anybody could properly assess his potentiality. We know certainly that talent is woefully wasted, presently. Governments could, if they wished, change the practice of providing poor schooling to the poor. As to tracking, why should not *all* the young receive both humane and vocational learning, say, through high school? That this would require more years in school is clear enough. The high unemployment rate in the United States would seem to meet that objection. The labor shortage in Japan is in part a problem of underemployment, and is further influenced by the system of early retirement. That such education would cost more is also clear enough, but other nations manage to allocate more of their resources to the nurture of the young than do these two. Why should not all citizens, during certain periods of their lives, share the drudgery and the dirty work? Probably both Japan and the United States, in their different ways, are at present too deeply committed to a hierarchical society to justify our devoting too much attention to that question here.

Is it too early in history to ask another question? Jefferson wished to define "progress" as "life, liberty, and the pursuit of happiness." Ōkuma Shigenobu, the founder in 1882 of the Progressive party in Japan, defined it as "the realization of the eternal happiness of the entire people."[10] One need not believe that a person's life is ever likely to be without sorrow in order to believe that those political goals are worthy ones. The leaders of both peoples, however, have chosen instead a political and economic definition of "progress." Perhaps, given the weakness of the United States during its infancy and of Japan during the Restoration and again following World War II, that was the most expedient definition. At any rate, those same leaders have shown that it is possible to produce all the material goods, and more, necessary to happiness. The idea of progress itself, so defined, can now be seen to contain dangerous explosives. We now know how gingerly it must be handled. But redefined, in the humane manner of Jefferson and Ōkuma, and handled suspiciously, it may still render service to the liberal tradition to which the two peoples are committed.

Critics who attack the idea of liberal democracy from the left speak as do the old liberals from programs of economic growth which have not adapted themselves to projections of worldwide shortages of resources. The traditional humanistic thought of the Japanese and the Americans, since it is diverse, gives promise of more flexibility in choosing goals and priorities. More specifically, in both places, motifs have always been audible, sometimes very clearly, which tell what can be gained by simplicity.

Nor can one dismiss lightly the ancient faith in maintaining the free circulation of ideas and information. That a very great Russian novelist should be hampered, in some of his considerations, by stereotypes, seems a large loss. Further, the simple technical capacity to exchange information must not be taken for granted. Information about the condition of life among, for example, people living on the widening fringes of the Sahara is not automatically available to every citizen of the world, but practically every Japanese and American can know about it. And their memories might recall ancient teachings, in each tradition, which declare that such suffering must not occur. Looking on the baroque skyline of Tokyo or New York, many of them have already thought of simplifying things, and more must. If we should decide that we can do without some of our hardware, however, that which actually helps us in our attempts to exchange information should surely be spared from the discard pile.

Japan and the United States are blessed with many skilled and conscientious people. That fact, and the dialectic quality of the two cultures, make more plausible the old faith that arduous debate might yield ways to adapt to contemporary conditions more surely than ideology can. No one could expect dramatic resolution to such tough new questions. Jets don't really speed us on man's old plodding voyage, though they must harden his resolve to keep on with it.

This is not a political essay; I have no special competence in such matters. No citizen dare ignore politics, however. (It is a political decision of momentous importance, for example, to decide that this child should not study art, or that that artist's work should be "realistic.") Anyhow, the politicians are finally no more important than the artists and prophets who make us smell the rot in what's decadent and see the brightness of what's possible, and no more important than the teachers and publicists who make available to everybody these sensations. The foregoing cursory look at the two cultures suggests, I hope, something about which is what in each of them.

"Same Difference"

In the neighborhood where I grew up, we were quite certain that we knew what was what in this world. Yet our block wasn't impervious to challenge from outside agitators, or even from among our ranks. Our cherished beliefs about cars, about girls, and about the queer habits of people in other neighborhoods were constantly under attack, but didn't die easily. Most important to us were our sports heroes.

None of us would ever see Babe Ruth play defense in the outfield, for example, but we wished to believe in his skill and zeal in that capacity. When cynics gave us incontestable evidence that he dogged it out there, it hurt. So we shrugged our shoulders and said, "Same difference—he gets the job done at the plate." And so with our other articles of faith: if we could see some larger truth that was undisturbed by the wiseacres, we could say, "Same difference," and adjust to adversity. The phrase served us well; it was a small neighborhood, and we had to live together.

Men and women of more consequential responsibilities than we had then could do worse.

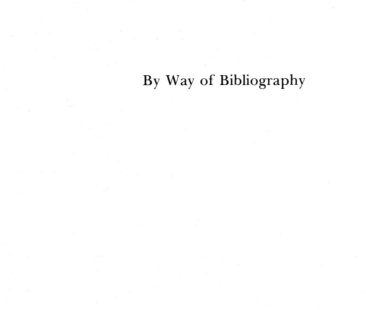

By Way of Bibliography

By Way of Bibliography

My dependence on other scholars in this volume is so great, particularly as I discuss Japan, that the first typescript had a fly-specked look, from too many footnote numbers. Therefore I decided to cite sources only of direct quotations (excepting quotations from American novels and from other books published in the United States in many editions, such as Emerson's *Nature*) and of ideas clearly not in the public domain. In compensation there follows here an attempt to mention the titles that apply generally to the volume, and then, for each chapter, a note on my sources for that topic. Perhaps nobody knows which of the ideas he takes to be his own are really appropriations; the following books are influences I know about.

The clearest influences, probably, come from the work of three of my former teachers: Ralph Gabriel, *The Course of American Democratic Thought* (New York: Ronald, 1940); Henry Nash Smith, *Virgin Land* (Cambridge, Mass.: Harvard University Press, 1950); and Leo Marx, *The Machine in the Garden* (New York: Oxford University Press, 1964). Although it is no longer fashionable to do so, I often find myself referring to Charles and Mary Beard, *The Rise of American Civilization* (New York: Macmillan, 1930), and to Merle Curti, *The Growth of American Thought* (New York: Harper, 1943). Lewis Mumford's work has had a large impact on me, especially *Technics and Civilization* and *The Culture of Cities* (New York: Harcourt, 1934 and 1938). A model for practitioners in American Studies is Alan Trachtenberg, *Brooklyn Bridge* (New York: Oxford University Press, 1965). A most solid cross-cultural study is Lawrence W. Chisholm, *Fenellosa: The Far East and American Culture* (New Haven, Conn.: Yale University Press,

247

1963). Enough has been said of F. S. C. Northrop's admirable *The Meeting of East and West* (New York and London: Collier, 1946).

Perhaps the best two short histories of Japan in English are John Whitney Hall, *Japan from Prehistory to Modern Times* (New York: Dell, 1970; originally published as *Das Japanische Kaiserreich*, Frankfort: Fischer Bücherei, 1968), and Edwin O. Reischauer, *Japan, the Story of a Nation* (New York: Knopf, 1970), entitled in earlier editions *Japan, Past and Present*. Hall is fuller on pre-Meiji history, Reischauer on the post–World War II period, during part of which time, of course, he served as the United States ambassador to Japan. The former is probably preferable for the classroom, the latter for the home library. I have found myself on less good terms with Richard Storry, *A History of Modern Japan* (Baltimore: Penguin, 1970—a Pelican original). I have depended heavily on essays in three volumes in particular of the splendid Princeton University Press series Studies in the Modernization of Japan: Marius B. Jansen, ed., *Changing Japanese Attitudes toward Modernization* (1965); Ronald P. Dore, ed., *Aspects of Social Change in Modern Japan* (1971); and Donald H. Shively, ed., *Tradition and Modernization in Japanese Culture* (1971); and also on a product of the East-West Center in Honolulu, Charles A. Moore, ed., *The Japanese Mind* (1967). A useful collection of historical documents is William T. DeBary, ed., *Sources of the Japanese Tradition* (New York: Columbia University Press, 1964 ed.), vol. II.

Western and Japanese thinking about Japan has been strongly influenced by Ruth Benedict, *The Chrysanthemum and the Sword* (Boston: Houghton Mifflin, 1946); and by Chie Nakane, *Japanese Society* (Berkeley: University of California Press, 1970). I prefer the more pluralistic brand of anthropology in Kazuko Tsurumi, *Social Change and the Individual* (Princeton, N.J.: Princeton University Press, 1970). Ronald P. Dore's *City Life in Japan* (London: Routledge, 1958) has staying power which I will mention later.

Donald Keene is one of America's great authorities on Japanese literature; and he moves into the general culture in *Living Japan* (London: Heinemann, 1959) and *Landscape and Portraits* (Tokyo and Palo Alto, Calif.: Kodansha, 1971). R. H. Blyth is an older English counterpart who also relates literature to the general culture; see, for example, *Haiku*, vol. I: *Eastern Culture* (Tokyo: Hokuseido, 1949, 1962), and *Japanese Life and Character in Senryu* (Tokyo: Hokuseido, 1960).

Daisetz Teitaro Suzuki's *Zen and Japanese Culture* (Princeton, N.J.: Princeton University Press, 1970) is already standard reading.

A number of books intended for the general public seem to me to be excellent. Fosco Maraini's *Japan: Patterns of Continuity* (Tokyo and Palo Alto, Calif.: Kodansha, 1971) is gorgeous to look at and appealing in its thesis, which is that cultural continuity will continue to be imbedded in the Japanese language. His earlier *Meeting with Japan* (New York: Viking, 1959) is also a sophisticated book. Oliver Statler's *Japanese Inn* (New York: Random House, 1961) and Bernard Rudofsky's *The Kimono Mind* (Garden City, N.Y.: Doubleday, 1965) are worthy books in this category, and so, particularly, is the lesser known James Kirkup's *These Horned Islands* (London: Collins, 1962). Sacheverell Sitwell, poet and architectural critic, produced as sensitive a job as we would have expected in *The Bridge of the Brocade Sash* (Cleveland: World, 1959). (Japan seems to bring out the best in sensitive foreigners: notice also those novels by two of the world's best, Nikos Kazantzakis's *The Rock Garden* and Arthur Koestler's *The Lotus and the Robot*.)

Everybody should read Okakura Kakuzo's *The Book of Tea* (1906), available in several editions, including the handsome one by Charles E. Tuttle, Tokyo and Rutland, Vt. (1956).

The standard periodicals about Japan in English are these: the scholars' *Journal of Asian Studies*; the more popular *Japan Interpreter* (formerly *Journal of Social and Political Ideas*), published by the Japan Center for International Exchange, Tokyo; and *Japan Quarterly*, published by the Asahi newspaper organization. Asahi from 1954 until 1971 published a beautiful annual, *This Is Japan*, which contained useful, if popularized, articles on a number of subjects.

Chapter 1. The Problem

David Potter's *People of Plenty* (Chicago: University of Chicago Press, 1954) is almost a handbook of the thought about national character expressed up to the time of its publication. George DeVos and others' *Socialization for Achievement* (Berkeley: University of California Press, 1973) discusses, from the point of view of a "psychological anthropologist," the manner in which culture maintains continuity even though political, economic, and educational institutions change.

Leo Marx's *The Machine in the Garden* discusses earlier essays on the dialectic nature of the American culture. See also the essays by scholars from many disciplines in Michael Kammen, ed., *The Contrapuntal Civilization* (New York: Crowell, 1971). Okakura Kakuzo stresses contradiction in the Japanese culture in his essay on Tao and Zen in *The Book of Tea*, as does R. H. Blyth in his many translations of and commentaries on Japanese poetry. Kenzo Tange sees contradiction as inextricably built into the culture—see *Ise: Prototype of Japanese Architecture* (Cambridge, Mass.: MIT Press, 1965). Kazuko Tsurumi in *Social Change and the Individual* demonstrates dramatically the struggles of Japanese to switch from wartime ways of thinking to postwar ways of thinking. Hiroshi Minami's *Psychology of the Japanese People,* tr. Albert R. Ikoma (Tokyo: University of Tokyo Press, 1971) was written in

1953 but did not become available in translation until recently; he, too, emphasizes contradiction.

Chapter 2. The Wilderness Zion and the Land of the Gods

A standard study of the modern nation-state which remains interesting is Hans Kohn, *The Idea of Nationalism* (New York: Macmillan, 1948).

The American mythology mentioned here, skewed a bit to fit southern culture, is at the heart of William Faulkner's "The Bear" (included in *Go Down Moses*, 1942). I must mention *Virgin Land* and *The Machine in the Garden* again, as well as R. W. B. Lewis's *The American Adam* (Chicago: University of Chicago Press, 1955), a book which is more exclusively literary than the other two. Constance Rourke's *American Humor* (New York: Harcourt, 1931) tells about "the contrast."

My information about Japan for this chapter comes mainly from Hall, Reischauer, the Princeton series, Leonard Mosley, *Hirohito, Emperor of Japan* (Englewood Cliffs, N.J.: Prentice-Hall, 1966), and the Moore and DeBary collections.

Chapter 3. The "Crass Materialists" and the "Economic Animals"

Ronald P. Dore's *City Life in Japan* has, in spite of its age, been cited as recently as January 1975 by a leading Japanese urbanist, Shibata Tokue, as retaining its validity insofar as it applies to metropolitan Tokyo.

There are two excellent works in English on the economic history of Japan: William W. Lockwood, *The Economic Development of Japan* (Princeton, N. J.: Princeton University Press, 1968), and Seymour A. Broadbridge, *Industrial Dualism in Japan* (Chicago: Aldine, 1966).

The classic works on religion and capitalism in the West, of course, are Max Weber, *The Protestant Ethic and the Spirit of Capitalism* (New York: Scribner, 1930, 1956), and R. H. Tawney, *Religion and the Rise of Capitalism* (New York: Harcourt, 1926). Robert N. Bellah, *Tokugawa Religion* (Glencoe, Ill.: Free Press, 1957), does the same job concerning Japan, corroborated by Byron Earhart, *Japanese Religion: Unity and Diversity* (Belmont, Calif.: Dickenson, 1969)—though the central purpose of the latter book is of a different nature. George DeVos and others' *Socialization for Achievement* focuses on child-raising and family patterns and helps define the culture by examining what it considers deviant behavior. Joseph Dorfman's three-volume *The Economic Mind in American Civilization* (New York: Viking, 1953) is monumental. Dorfman has also worked on Thorstein Veblen, whose economic and cultural interpretations of the American culture still seem to me to be the most brilliant of all—so much so that John Kenneth Galbraith comes in second. *The Affluent Society* by Galbraith (Boston: Houghton Mifflin, 1958) has probably insinuated itself into this work more often than his other books have.

For contemporary attitudes about material possessions, I have relied mainly on periodicals—especially, concerning Japan, the *Japan Interpreter*. Ezra and Suzanne Vogel, *Japan's New Middle Class* (Berkeley: University of California Press, 1963; 2nd ed., by Ezra Vogel, 1971), is invaluable. It is matched in excellence, in my opinion, by Herbert Gans's *The Levittowners* (New York: Pantheon, 1967), the best of a whole literature about the postwar American suburbs. Robert and Helen Lynd's *Middletown* (New York: Harcourt, 1929; my ed., 1956) remains a sensitive and solid study.

Chapter 4. The Old Environment: Nature

Beyond Smith, Marx, and R. W. B. Lewis, A. Whitney Griswold's *Farming and Democracy* (New Haven, Conn.: Yale University Press, 1952) deserves more attention than it gets. John Brinckerhoff Jackson's *American Space* (New York: Norton, 1972) focuses on the years 1865–1876; it is a wonderfully ingenious book in that it gives us clues to American culture by way of the manner in which it organizes space. Paul Shepard's *Man in the Landscape: A Historical View of the Esthetics of Nature* (New York: Knopf, 1967) does very well what its subtitle suggests.

Testimonials to the love of nature of the Japanese, and analyses of their relationship to it, are legion. See especially Kenzo Tange (with Noboru Kawazoe), *Ise: Prototype of Japanese Architecture*, and Walter Gropius, Kenzo Tange, and others, *Katsura: Tradition and Creation in Japanese Architecture* (New Haven, Conn.: Yale University Press, 1960); these books contain dazzling photographs and provide fascinating insights into the cultural roots in nature of Tange, that architect of urban buildings. See also Langdon Warner, *The Enduring Art of Japan* (New York: Grove, 1952); Isamu Kashikie, *The ABC of Japanese Gardening*, tr. John Nathan (Tokyo and Rutland, Vt.: Japan Publications, 1964); and, especially, the books by Blyth and Suzuki.

Chapter 5. Workaday and Holiday

The most profound studies of the industrial culture of the West are, in my opinion, Mumford's *Technics and Civilization* and Siegfried Giedion, *Mechanization Takes Command* (New York: Oxford University Press, 1948). Also useful in more limited ways are John Kouwenhoven, *The Arts in Modern American Civilization* (New York: Norton, 1967),

originally titled *Made in America* (1948); and Paul and Percival Goodman, *Communitas: Means of Livelihood and Ways of Life* (Chicago: University of Chicago Press, 1947). Thorstein Veblen nourishes one's
thoughts endlessly; I am most familiar with his *Theory of the Leisure
Class* (New York: Viking, 1899). Norbert Wiener, *The Human Use of
Human Beings: Cybernetics and Society* (Boston: Houghton Mifflin,
1954), is almost as rich. My understanding of Staffan Linder's *The
Harried Leisure Class* (New York: Columbia University Press, 1970) is as
yet inadequate, but it seems a very useful updating of Veblen. Most
readers know about John Kenneth Galbraith, *The New Industrial State*
(Boston: Houghton Mifflin, 1967).

Ronald P. Dore, as usual, is extraordinarily learned and sensitive.
His *City Life in Japan* has been mentioned; *British Factory—Japanese
Factory* (Berkeley: University of California Press, 1973) has historical
as well as contemporary dimensions. Robert E. Cole's *Japanese Blue
Collar* (Berkeley: University of California Press, 1971) implies compar-
isons with American factories; Arthur M. Whitehill, Jr., and Shin-ichi
Takezawa's *The Other Worker* (Honolulu: East-West Center, 1968)
makes comparisons systematically. *Minor Industries and Workers in
Tokyo* (Tokyo: Tokyo Municipal Library, 1972) is one of an excellent
series in English by the Tokyo government.

The Elton Mayo studies lie behind all empirical studies of the
American industrial worker. In addition Charles Rumford Walker's
Steeltown (New York: Harper, 1950) and his *The Man on the Assembly
Line* (Cambridge, Mass.: Harvard University Press, 1962); Ely Chin-
oy's *Automobile Workers and the American Dream* (Garden City, N.Y.:
Doubleday, 1955); and *Work in America: Report of a Special Task Force to
the Secretary of Health, Education, and Welfare* (Cambridge, Mass.: MIT
Press, 1973) are invaluable.

Ezra Vogel's *Japan's New Middle Class*, 2nd ed., and Herbert Gans's
The Levittowners pair off nicely as studies of suburban life. Gans's
earlier *Urban Villagers* (Glencoe, Ill.: Free Press, 1962) suggests certain
similarities between an Italian-American community in Boston and
what Dore reports about Tokyo.

Studs Terkel's interviews, recorded in *Division Street, America* (New
York: Pantheon, 1966) and *Working* (New York: Pantheon, 1972,
1974), provide a direct sense of what ordinary Americans think and
feel about their lives. Bill Moyers's *Listening to America* (New York:
Harper, 1971) does almost as well the same job. Tsurumi's *Social
Change and the Individual* helps us hear a few Japanese in the same
direct way, as do occasional interviews in the English-language newspapers of Japan—the *Japan Times, Asahi, Yomiuri*, and *Mainichi*; for a
while the *New York Times* had a reporter, Takashi Oka, who was skillful
at such interviews in Japan, but he is no longer with the *Times*.

On the whole, I find most work on leisure, except those general works cited above, disappointing; this includes David Plath, *After Hours: Modern Japan and the Search for Enjoyment* (Berkeley: University of Calfornia Press, 1964). I have relied heavily on current periodicals for my generalizations in this chapter and on personal observation. Hidetoshi Kato, ed., *Japanese Popular Culture* (Rutland, Vt., and Tokyo: Charles E. Tuttle, 1959) is still not hopelessly outdated, and the *Japan Interpreter* carries on where he left off—in fact, he sometimes contributes to that journal. Many American works on mass media and popular culture exist.

Chapter 6. Fiction and the Popular Imagination

As American literature is the field among those represented here that I am most familiar with, it is the most difficult one in which to detect my own borrowings. I am aware of a debt to F. O. Matthiessen, *American Renaissance* (London: Oxford University Press, 1941); Constance Rourke, *American Humor*, already cited; and Richard Chase, *The American Novel and Its Tradition* (New York: Doubleday, 1957). A critical theory which fits very well the needs of the interdisciplinary scholar is in Kenneth Burke, *The Philosophy of Literary Form* (Baton Rouge: Louisiana State University Press, 1941; revised abridged ed., New York: Vintage, 1957).

Critical works about Japanese literature are scarce. I cite again the many translations and commentaries of R. H. Blyth and Donald Keene. Scattered introductions and essays by Edward Seidensticker, Ivan Morris, Earl Miner, and Father Mathey are very useful. Keene's concise *Japanese Literature: An Introduction for Western Readers* (London: Murray, 1953) is the best primer, but the August 20, 1971, issue of the *Times Literary Supplement* (London) includes some splendid introductory essays.

Masao Miyoshi's *Accomplices of Silence: The Modern Japanese Novel* (Berkeley, Los Angeles, and London: University of California Press, 1974) came to my attention after my manuscript was completed, but a quick skimming of it suggests that it is extremely useful.

Chapter 7. Shelter and Symbol

The best general histories of American architecture are James Marston Fitch, *American Building* (Boston: Houghton Mifflin, 1966); John Burchard and Albert Bush-Brown, *The Architecture of America* (Boston: Little, Brown, 1966); and Edgar Kaufmann, Jr., ed., *The Rise of an American Architecture* (New York: Praeger, 1970), especially the Vincent Scully essay, "American Houses: Thomas Jefferson to Frank Lloyd Wright." Oliver Larkin's hoary *Art and Life in America* (New

York: Rinehart, 1949) still contains much information, particularly about popular architecture, that is not available elsewhere, as does John Kouwenhoven's *The Arts in Modern American Civilization.* William A. Coles and Henry Hope Reed, Jr., eds., *Architecture in America: A Battle of Styles* (New York: Appleton-Century-Crofts, 1961), is a good collection of original documents about debates concerning particular buildings, but it is now out of print. My admiration for Siegfried Giedion's *Space, Time, and Architecture,* 5th ed. (Cambridge, Mass.: Harvard University Press, 1967) must be obvious.

Nor have I neglected to praise Clay Lancaster's *The Japanese Influence in America* (New York: Walton H. Rawls, 1963), the best cross-cultural work I know not by an anthropologist excepting perhaps Chisholm's *Fenellosa.*

The charm of Edward S. Morse's *Japanese Homes and Their Surroundings* (first published, 1886; reprinted, New York: Dover, 1961) has not, I hope, been overstated. Kenzo Tange's *Ise* and *Katsura* are required reading. The George Braziller (New York) series on architecture has provided us with these useful volumes: William Alex's *Japanese Architecture* (1967) and Robin Boyd's *New Directions in Japanese Architecture* (1968); I have made much use of these books here. Of the many good issues of the *Japan Architect,* that of June 1964 is the best from the historical point of view, but I have used issues on contemporary work as well.

Of individual American architects, Louis Sullivan has inspired at least three American men of letters to thoughtful books: Sherman Paul, Hugh Morrison, and John Szarkowski. Their volumes are *Louis Sullivan, an Architect in American Thought* (Englewood Cliffs, N.J.: Prentice-Hall, 1962); *Louis Sullivan: Prophet of Modern Architecture* (New York: Norton, 1962; originally published, 1935); and *The Idea of Louis Sullivan* (Minneapolis: University of Minnesota Press, 1956). Like Tange, Frank Lloyd Wright can speak very well for himself; perhaps the best book by him and about him to read first is *A Testament* (New York: Horizon, 1957). The most recent bibliography of works about him that I have seen filled three pages.

Chapter 8. The Nurture of the Young

For my sense of Japanese education, I depended again on Ronald P. Dore, not only upon his *Education in Tokugawa Japan* (London: Routledge, 1965) but also upon a number of essays by him in various places, as well as on Michio Nagai, *Higher Education in Japan,* tr. Jerry Dusenbury (Tokyo: Tokyo University Press, 1971)—a rather theoretical work—and several essays by him elsewhere; Herbert Passin, *Society and Education in Japan* (New York: Bureau of Publications, Teachers College, Columbia University, 1967), which takes a rather conventional view of education; and Theodore Brameld, *Japan: Culture, Education, and Change in Two Communities* (New York: Holt, Rinehart, 1968), which in many places gives a very direct sense of what the system means to individual students, parents, teachers, and administrators. Several essays in the Princeton series discuss education. Some passages in David and Evelyn Thompson Riesman's *Conversations in Japan* (New York: Basic Books, 1967) and in Tsurumi's *Social Change and the Individual* reveal students' attitudes toward their education. Newspapers and journals are full of the subject; the coverage is much fuller than in the United States.

Robert Ulich's *The Education of Nations* (Cambridge, Mass.: Harvard University Press, 1961) is the best comparative study I know; it is, I'm afraid, rather technical or legalistic in its thinking about education and does not include Japan; other comparative studies that I have found which do treat Japan do so only in an external way—laws, statistics, and so on.

Books about American education tend to be a bit contentious, either selling the "progressive" orthodoxy or opposing it. An exception is Merle Curti's *The Social Ideas of American Educators* (Paterson, N.J.: Pageant, 1959). Probably the most intelligent statement from the progressive camp, following the much-misunderstood John Dewey, is George Counts's *Education and American Civilization* (New York: Teachers College Press, 1952). Bestor and some other opponents of the progressives are cited in the footnotes to this chapter.

Notes

Notes

Chapter 1. The Problem

1. Bernard Rudofsky, *The Kimono Mind* (Garden City, N.Y.: Doubleday, 1965), p. 134.

2. Marius B. Jansen, "Three Slogans of Modernization in Japan," *Report of the International Conference on the Problems of Modernization in Asia* (Seoul: Asiatic Research Center, Korea University, 1965), p. 275.

3. Okakura Kakuzo, *The Book of Tea* (Rutland, Vt., and Tokyo: Charles E. Tuttle, 1956; originally published, 1906), pp. 7–8.

4. The folklorist Kunio Yanagida, quoted in Tadakoro Taro, "What We're Reading Now," *Japan Quarterly*, 19(No. 2): 209 (April–June 1972).

5. Ferdinando Basabe, "Attitudes of Japanese Students toward Foreign Countries," *Monumenta Nipponica*, 21:61–87 (1966).

6. *Asahi Evening News*, March 17, 1971; responses on March 18.

7. *Ibid.*, April 6, 1971.

8. Eto Jun, "Japan's Shifting Image: Reflections from the Local American Press, 1969–1971," *Japan Interpreter*, 8(No.1):70 (Winter 1973).

9. *New York Times*, August 15, 1971, E, p. 3.

10. Yonosuke Nagai, "The United States Disintegrating," *Psychology Today*, May 1972, pp. 24–26.

11. Lionel Trilling, *The Liberal Imagination: Essays on Literature and Society* (New York: Viking, 1951), p. 9.

12. Arthur Koestler, *The Lotus and the Robot* (New York: Harper, 1960).

13. Robert Huntingdon, in *Monumenta Nipponica*, 23:476–477 (1968).

14. Douglas G. Haring, "Japanese National Character: Cultural Anthropology, Psychoanalysis, and History," *Yale Review*, 42(No. 2):382, 392 (December 1952).

15. Ajita Ogiwara, "Japan and America; Some Contrasts," *Orient/West*, 10 (No. 1):370 (1966).

16. F. S. C. Northrop, *The Meeting of East and West* (New York and London: Collier, 1946), pp. 136, 344–345.

17. Keyes Beech in *Tokyo Daily Yomiuri*, June 20, 1972, p. 5. Gilles Anouil, "Les Jeunes, Changeront-Ils le Japon?" *Realités*, November 17, 1972, p. 82. Kazuko Tsurumi,

259

260   Japanese and Americans

Social Change and the Individual (Princeton, N.J.: Princeton University Press, 1970).

18. See Tetsuo Najita, "Restorationism in the Political Thought of Yamagata Daini," *Journal of Asian Studies*, 21(No. 1):27–28 (November 1971); David Elkind, " 'Good Me' or 'Bad Me,' " *New York Times Magazine*, September 12, 1972, pp. 18–19.

19. Harold Stewart, tr., *A Chime of Windbells: A Year of Japanese Haiku in English Verse* (Rutland, Vt., and Tokyo: Charles E. Tuttle, 1969), p. 57.

20. Kenzo Tange (with Noboru Kawazoe), *Ise: Prototype of Japanese Architecture* (Cambridge, Mass.: MIT Press, 1965), pp. 16, 30.

21. David Potter, *People of Plenty* (Chicago: University of Chicago Press, 1954), pp. 21–24, 27, 30.

Chapter 2. The Wilderness Zion and the Land of the Gods

1. Samuel Sherwood, quoted in Robert Middlekauff, "The Ritualization of the American Revolution," in Lawrence Levine and Middlekauff, eds., *The National Temper* (New York: Harcourt, 1972), p. 107.

2. Kato Shuichi, "Japanese Writers and Modernization," in Marius B. Jansen, ed., *Changing Japanese Attitudes toward Modernization* (Princeton, N.J.: Princeton University Press, 1965), pp. 443–444.

3. Van Wyck Brooks, *Fenellosa and His Circle* (New York: Dutton, 1962), p. 26. See also Lawrence W. Chisholm, *Fenellosa: The Far East and American Culture* (New Haven, Conn.: Yale University Press, 1963).

4. From the *New York Morning News*, quoted in Richard Current and John Garraty, eds., *Words That Made American History*, 2 vols. (Boston: Little, Brown, 1965), I, 437–445.

5. From *Our Country* (1885), quoted in *ibid.*, II, 132–133.

6. Quoted in Richard Hofstadter, *Social Darwinism in American Thought, 1860–1915* (Philadelphia: University of Pennsylvania Press, 1945), p. 154.

7. In *Harper's New Monthly Magazine* (1885), quoted in Perry E. Gianakos and Albert Karson, eds., *American Diplomacy and the Sense of Destiny*, 4 vols. (Belmont, Calif.: Wadsworth, 1966), I, 19.

8. *Kokutai no Hongi*, ed. Robert King Hall, tr. John Gauntlett (Cambridge, Mass.: Harvard University Press, 1949), p. 183.

9. *Ibid.*

10. *Ibid.*, p. 94.

11. Leonard Mosley, *Hirohito, Emperor of Japan* (Englewood Cliffs, N.J.: Prentice-Hall, 1966), p. 181.

12. *Ibid.*, p. 270.

13. Okakura Kakuzo, *The Book of Tea* (Rutland, Vt., and Tokyo: Charles E. Tuttle, 1956; originally published, 1906), p. 5; Kenzo Tange (with Noboru Kawazoe), *Ise: Prototype of Japanese Architecture* (Cambridge, Mass.: MIT Press, 1965), p. 19.

14. E. M. Forster, *A Passage to India* (New York: Harcourt, Brace, 1926), p. 322.

Chapter 3. The "Crass Materialists" and the "Economic Animals"

1. Nakamura Hajime, "Basic Features of the Legal, Political, and Economic Thought of Japan," in Charles R. Moore, ed., *The Japanese Mind* (Honolulu: East-West Center, 1967), p. 160.

2. Byron Earhart, *Japanese Religion: Unity and Diversity* (Belmont, Calif.: Dickenson, 1969), p. 7.

3. Tejima Toan (1773), quoted in Hiroshi Minami, *Psychology of the Japanese People*, tr. Albert R. Ikoma (Tokyo: University of Tokyo Press, 1971), pp. 102–103.

4. Quoted by Nakamura, in Moore, ed., *The Japanese Mind,* p. 160.

5. Quoted by Nakamura, "Suzuki Shosan, 1579–1655, and the Spirit of Capitalism in Japanese Buddhism," tr. William Johnston, *Monumenta Nipponica*, 22:3 (1967).

6. *Ibid.*, p. 6.

7. Nakamura, "Some Features of the Japanese Way of Thinking," *Monumenta Nipponica*, 14:32 (1958–1959).

8. Quoted in Perry Miller, *The American Puritans* (Garden City, N.Y.: Doubleday, 1956), pp. 172, 173, 175.

9. See Ralph Gabriel, *The Course of American Democratic Thought* (New York: Ronald, 1940), p. 149.

10. Ihara Saikaku, *The Eternal Storehouse of Japan*, tr. G. W. Sargent, in Donald Keene, ed., *Anthology of Japanese Literature* (New York: Grove, 1955; citations from Evergreen ed., 1960), quotations from pp. 357–362. One edition of Saikaku's book is entitled *The Way to Wealth*, tr. Soji Mizuno (Tokyo: Hokuseido, 1955).

11. Kamo no Chōmei's "An Account of My Hut" is found in Keene, ed., *Anthology of Japanese Literature*, pp. 197–213.

12. Sato Nobuhiro in William T. DeBary, ed., *Sources of Japanese Tradition*, 2 vols. (New York: Columbia University Press, 1964 ed.), II, 50–73.

13. Quoted in Minami, *Psychology of the Japanese People*, pp. 92–93.

14. *Kokutai no Hongi*, ed. Robert King Hill, tr. John Gauntlett (Cambridge, Mass.: Harvard University Press, 1949).

15. J. Hector St. John Crèvecoeur, *Letters from an American Farmer* (New York: Dutton, 1957 ed.; originally published, 1782), pp. 35–36.

16. Alexis de Tocqueville, *Democracy in America*, vol. II (1840), Chapter 27.

17. Abraham Lincoln, speech at New Haven, Conn., March 6, 1860. The observation about the persistence of the phrase "bettering one's condition," especially in Jackson and Lincoln, is Professor Alan Jones's, in a lecture at Grinnell College, October 1974.

18. Abraham Lincoln, debate with Stephen Douglas, Alton, Ill., October 15, 1858.

19. Robert and Helen Lynd, *Middletown* (New York: Harcourt, 1929); Ezra and Suzanne Vogel, *Japan's New Middle Class* (Berkeley: University of California Press, 1963; 2nd ed., by Ezra Vogel, 1971).

20. Herbert Gans, *The Levittowners* (New York: Pantheon, 1967), p. 270 and n. 45.

21. Vogel, *Japan's New Middle Class*, 2nd ed., p. 81.

22. *Ibid.*, p. 239; italics his.

23. Gans, *The Levittowners*, p. 419.

24. Eli Chinoy, "The Tradition of Opportunity and the Aspiration of Automobile Workers," *American Journal of Sociology*, 57:453–459 (March 1952).

25. John H. Boyle, "Idioms of Contemporary Japan," *Japan Interpreter*, 7(No. 1):62–63 (Winter 1971).

26. "Japan-ness," *Japan Quarterly*, 16(No. 3):264–267 (July–September 1969).

27. Vogel, *Japan's New Middle Class*, 2nd ed., p. 276.

Chapter 4. The Old Environment: Nature

1. Yukawa Hideki, "Modern Trend of Western Civilization and Cultural Peculiarities in Japan," in Charles A. Moore, ed., *The Japanese Mind* (Honolulu: East-West Center, 1967), p. 63.

2. Fosco Maraini, *Japan: Patterns of Continuity* (Tokyo and Palo Alto, Calif.: Kodansha, 1971), p. 14.

3. Kishimoto Hideo, "Some Japanese Cultural Traits and Religion," in Moore, ed., *Japanese Mind*, p. 111.

4. Paul Shepard, *Man in the Landscape: A Historical View of the Esthetics of Nature* (New York: Knopf, 1967), *passim*. Daisetz Teitaro Suzuki, "Reason and Intuition in Buddhist Philosophy," in Moore, ed., *Japanese Mind*, pp. 66–109.

5. Kishimoto, in Moore, ed., *Japanese Mind*, p. 110.

6. Shepard, *Man in the Landscape*, pp. 67–68.

7. J. Hector St. John Crèvecoeur, *Letters from an American Farmer* (New York: Dutton, 1957 ed.; originally published, 1782), p. 42.

8. Takenishi Hiroko, review of Karaki Junzo's *Nihonjin no kokoro no rekishi* in *Japan Interpreter*, 2(No. 7):231 (Spring 1971).

9. Nakamura Hajime, "Some Features of the Japanese Way of Thinking," *Monumenta Nipponica*, 14:32 (1958–1959).

10. Yasunari Kawabata, *Japan the Beautiful and Myself*, tr. Edward G. Seidensticker (Tokyo and Palo Alto, Calif.: Kodansha, 1969).

11. I am using Nobuyuki Yuasa, tr. and ed., *The Narrow Road to the Deep North and Other Travel Sketches* by Bashō (Baltimore: Penguin, 1968; these translations first published, 1966).

12. Shepard, *Man in the Landscape*, pp. 117, 125.

13. Harold Stewart, tr., *A Chime of Windbells: A Year of Japanese Haiku in English Verse* (Rutland, Vt., and Tokyo: Charles E. Tuttle, 1969), p. 60.

14. Robert Frost, *Selected Poems of Robert Frost* (New York: Holt, Rinehart, 1965), p. 138.

15. Robert N. Linscott, ed., *Selected Poems and Letters of Emily Dickinson* (Garden City, N.Y.: Doubleday, 1959), p. 88.

16. Umemoto Seiichi, *Japan Here and There* (Tokyo: Hokuseido, 1959).

17. Kenzo Tange (with Noboru Kawazoe), *Ise: Prototype of Japanese Architecture* (Cambridge, Mass.: MIT Press, 1965), pp. 20–22.

Chapter 5. Workaday and Holiday

1. Fosco Maraini, *Meeting with Japan* (New York: Viking, 1959), p. 12.

2. Marius B. Jansen, "Three Slogans of Modernization in Japan," *Report of the International Conference on the Problems of Modernization in Asia* (Seoul: Asiatic Research Center, Korea University, 1965), p. 273.

3. Donald H. Shively, "Nishimura Shigeki: A Confucian View of Modernization," in Marius B. Jansen, ed., *Changing Japanese Attitudes toward Modernization* (Princeton, N.J.: Princeton University Press, 1969), pp. 193ff; I also borrow from other essays in that book.

4. Ely Chinoy, "The Tradition of Opportunity and the Aspirations of Automobile Workers," *American Journal of Sociology*, 57:453–459 (March 1952).

5. Charles Rumford Walker, *Steeltown* (New York: Harper, 1950).

6. Samuel P. Hays, *The Response to Industrialism* (Chicago: University of Chicago Press, 1957), p. 35.

7. Hyman Kublin, *Asian Revolutionary: The Life of Sen Katayama* (Princeton, N. J.: Princeton University Press, 1964), p. 111.

8. Shizuo Matsushima, "Labour Management in Japan," *The Sociological Monograph #10, Japanese Sociological Studies* (Keele, Staffordshire: University of Keele, 1966), p. 70.

9. Quoted in Jonathan Norton Leonard, *Early Japan* (New York: Time-Life Books, 1968), pp. 130–133.

10. *Work in America: Report of a Special Task Force to the Secretary of Health, Education, and Welfare* (Cambridge, Mass.: MIT Press, 1973), pp. 12–13.

11. Takashi Oka, "Japan's Workers," *New York Times*, November 15, 1970, III, 1. See also "Japanese at Work," *New York Times*, March 19, 1972, p. F3.

12. Arthur M. Whitehill, Jr., and Shin-ichi Takezawa, *The Other Worker* (Honolulu: East-West Center, 1968).

13. Oka, "Japan's Workers"; " 'Spirit of Work' Still Much Alive," *Daily Yomiuri*, June 20, 1972.

14. Keyes Beech, in *Daily Yomiuri*, June 20, 1972, p. 5.

15. Hiroshi Minami, *Psychology of the Japanese People* (Tokyo: Tokyo University Press, 1971), especially early sections on Japanese soldiers; Kazuko Tsurumi, *Social Change and the Individual* (Princeton, N.J.: Princeton University Press, 1970), especially the chapter "The Impact of the War on Women"; Robert E. Cole, *Japanese Blue Collar* (Berkeley: University of California Press, 1971), *passim*.

16. Ralph Orr, "Money Issues Take Back Seat Early in Auto Talks," *Detroit Free Press*, July 29, 1973, p. 6-A.

17. *Work in America*, p. 37.

18. Cole, *Japanese Blue Collar*, p. 141.

19. Jo Thomas, "The View from the Good Time Bar," *Detroit Free Press*, July 15, 1973, p. D1.

20. Kobo Abé, *Woman of the Dunes*, tr. E. Dale Saunders (New York: Vintage, 1964), pp. 97–98.

21. Tsurumi, *Social Change and the Individual*, p. 277.

22. Quoted in Studs Terkel, *Division Street, America* (New York: Pantheon, 1966; citations from Avon ed., 1967), pp. 41–42.

23. Cole, *Japanese Blue Collar*, p. 85.

24. Ely Chinoy, *Automobile Workers and the American Dream* (Garden City, N.Y.: Doubleday, 1955), p. 50.

25. Cole, *Japanese Blue Collar*, p. 108.

26. Chinoy, *Automobile Workers*, p. 126.

27. Cole, *Japanese Blue Collar*, p. 108.

28. But a 1972 publication of the Tokyo Metropolitan Library, *Minor Industries and Workers in Tokyo*, says that statistics concerning small enterprises are extremely difficult to compile because of the large number of back-alley factories, "wind-blown accumulations of unsuccessful entrepreneurs."

29. Chinoy, *Automobile Workers*, p. 124.

30. Cole, *Japanese Blue Collar*, p. 132.

31. *Ibid.*, p. 173.

32. *Work in America*, pp. 29–30.

33. Terkel, *Division Street, America*, pp. 204–206.

Chapter 6. Fiction and the Popular Imagination

1. Quoted by G. H. Healey in the introduction to Akutagawa Ryūnosuke, *Kappa*, tr. Geoffrey Bownas (Rutland, Vt., and Tokyo: Charles E. Tuttle, 1971).

2. Ivan Morris, "Why Read Japanese Literature?" *Times Literary Suplement*, August 20, 1971, p. 1002.

3. Donald Keene, *Landscapes and Portraits: Appreciations of Japanese Culture* (Tokyo and Palo Alto, Calif.: Kodansha, 1971), Chapter 1.

4. Donald Keene, ed., *Modern Japanese Literature* (New York: Grove Press, 1956), p. 13 of Keene's introduction.

5. Marius B. Jansen, "Three Slogans of Modernization in Japan," *Report of the International Conference on the Problems of Modernization in Asia* (Seoul: Asiatic Research Center, Korea University, 1965), p. 275.

6. David Dilworth, "The Initial Formation of 'Pure Experience' in Nishida Kitaro and William James," *Monumenta Nipponica*, 24:94 (1969).

7. Sōseki Natsume, *Kokoro*, tr. Edwin McClellan (Tokyo: Charles E. Tuttle, 1969).

8. Yasunari Kawabata, *Snow Country*, tr. Edward G. Seidensticker (New York: Berkley, 1964).

9. Yukio Mishima, *After the Banquet*, tr. Donald Keene (New York: Berkley, 1963).

10. Kenzaburo Oë, *A Personal Matter*, tr. John Nathan (New York: Grove, 1968).

11. Kobo Abé, *Woman of the Dunes* (New York: Random House, 1964).

12. Dazai Osamu, *No Longer Human*, tr. Donald Keene (New York: New Directions, 1973).

13. Keene, *Landscapes and Portraits*, pp. 186–203.

14. M. M. Liberman, *Katherine Anne Porter's Fiction* (Detroit: Wayne State University Press, 1971), p. 31.

15. Keene, *Landscapes and Portraits*, p. 205.

16. Yasunari Kawabata, *The Sound of the Mountain*, tr. Edward G. Seidensticker (New York: Berkley, 1970).

17. Kenneth J. Gergen, "The Healthy, Happy Human Being Wears Many Masks," *Psychology Today*, May 1972, pp. 31–35, 64.

Chapter 7. Shelter and Symbol

1. Walter Gropius, Kenzo Tange, and others, *Katsura: Tradition and Creation in Japanese Architecture* (New Haven, Conn.: Yale University Press, 1960), p. v. The critic Udo Kultermann verifies this reading in *New Japanese Architecture* (New York: Praeger, 1960), p. 9.

2. Vincent Scully, "American Houses: Thomas Jefferson to Frank Lloyd Wright," in Edgar Kaufmann, Jr., ed., *The Rise of an American Architecture* (New York: Praeger, 1970), p. 165.

3. Quoted in William A. Coles and Henry Hope Reed, Jr., eds., *Architecture in America: A Battle of Styles* (New York: Appleton-Century-Crofts, 1961), pp. 14–15.

4. John Burchard and Albert Bush-Brown, *The Architecture of America* (Boston: Little, Brown, 1966), p. 16.

5. Julian P. Boyd, ed., *Papers of Thomas Jefferson*, vol. XI (Princeton, N.J.: Princeton University Press, 1955), p. 226.

6. Scully, "American Houses," pp. 169, 184.

7. Quoted in Oliver Larkin, *Art and Life in America* (New York: Rinehart, 1949), p. 175.

8. *Ibid.*

9. Quoted in John A. Kouwenhoven, *The Arts in Modern American Civilization* (New York: Norton, 1967), p. 52.

10. Siegfried Giedion, *Mechanization Takes Command* (New York: Oxford University Press, 1948), pp. 389ff, 512ff.

11. Siegfried Giedion, *Space, Time, and Architecture*, 5th ed. (Cambridge, Mass.: Harvard University Press, 1967), pp. 365–366.

12. Kenzo Tange (with Noboru Kawazoe), *Ise: Prototype of Japanese Architecture* (Cambridge, Mass.: MIT Press, 1965), p. 16.

13. I depend here for a discussion of Harada's work on Clay Lancaster, *The Japanese Influence in America* (New York: Walton H. Rawls, 1963), pp. 166–169.

14. Edward S. Morse, *Japanese Homes and Their Surroundings* (New York: Dover, 1961; originally published, 1886), p. 227.

15. Lancaster, *Japanese Influence in America*, p. 166.

16. Gropius, Tange, and others, *Katsura*, p. 31.

17. *Ibid.*, p. 23.

18. Ichirō Haryū, "The Toshogu at Nikko," *Japan Architect*, 39:87 (June 1964).

19. Gropius, Tange, and others, *Katsura*, pp. 23ff.

20. Morse, *Japanese Homes and Their Surroundings*, quotations from pp. 114–117.

21. Gropius, Tange, and others, *Katsura*, pp. 26–30.

22. Noboru Kawazoe, "The Metabolism I," *Japan Architect*, 44:107–108 (December 1969).

23. Larkin, *Art and Life in America*, p. 172.

24. Tange, *Ise*, pp. 30, 33, 51.

25. Norman Carver, *Form and Space of Japanese Architecture* (Tokyo: Shokokusha, 1955), p. 130.

26. Giedion, *Space, Time, and Architecture*, pp. 435–436.

27. Gropius, Tange, and others, *Katsura*, p. 28.

28. John Szarkowski, *The Idea of Louis Sullivan* (Minneapolis: University of Minnesota Press, 1956), pp. 25, 26.

29. Quoted in *ibid.*, p. 24.

30. Quoted in Giedion, *Space, Time, and Architecture*, p. 405.

31. Quoted in Lancaster, *Japanese Influence in America*, pp. 159–160.

32. Lancaster, *Japanese Influence in America*, pp. 160–161.

33. Scully, "American Houses," pp. 193–195.

34. Noboru Kawazoe, "Metabolism II," *Japan Architect*, 45:97 (January 1970).

35. Robin Boyd, *New Directions in Japanese Architecture* (New York: Braziller, 1968), p. 7.

36. Yamamoto Tadashi, "How the Final Form Emerged," *Japan Architect*, 49:28 (January 1974).

37. John Brinckerhoff Jackson, *American Space: The Centennial Years* (New York: Norton, 1972), p. 239.

Chapter 8. The Nurture of the Young

1. Jacques Barzun, *Teacher in America* (Boston: Little, Brown, 1945), p. 17. Barzun approves of lecturing but finds its use mainly in inspiration.

2. Ronald P. Dore, *Education in Tokugawa Japan* (London: Routledge, 1965), p. 44.

3. Quoted in Robert Ulich, *The Education of Nations* (Cambridge, Mass.: Harvard University Press, 1961), p. 228.

4. *Ibid.*, p. 231.

5. Edwin O. Reischauer, *Japan, the Story of a Nation* (New York: Knopf, 1970), p. 135.

6. Quoted in William T. DeBary, ed., *Sources of the Japanese Tradition* (New York: Columbia University Press, 1964 ed.), II, 139.

7. Kentaro Hayashi, "Tradition and Modernization in Japan," *Report of the International Conference on the Problems of Modernization in Asia* (Seoul: Asiatic Research Center, Korea University, 1965), p. 264.

8. Donald H. Shively, "The Japanization of Middle Meiji," in Shively, ed., *Tradition and Modernization of Japanese Culture* (Princeton, N.J.: Princeton University Press, 1971), pp. 81, 91.

9. *Ibid.*, p. 103.

10. Michio Nagai, *Higher Education in Japan*, tr. Jerry Dusenbury (Tokyo: Tokyo University Press, 1971), p. 238.

11. Ignatius Thomson, *The Patriot's Monitor, for New Hampshire* (Randolph, Vt., 1810), p. 70, quoted in Ruth Miller Elson, "American Schoolbooks and 'Culture' in the Nineteenth Century," *Mississippi Valley Historical Review*, 46:430 (December 1959), p. 430.

12. Quoted in Ulich, *Education of Nations*, p. 240.

13. Michio Nagai, "Westernization and Japanization: The Early Meiji Transformation of Education," in Shively, ed., *Tradition and Modernization in Japanese Culture*, p. 47.

14. *Ibid.*, p. 45.

15. November 28, 1783, in William B. Parker, ed., *Letters and Addresses of Thomas Jefferson* (Buffalo, N.Y.: Jefferson Society, 1903), p. 32.

16. Quoted in Herbert Passin, *Society and Education in Japan* (New York: Bureau of Publications, Teachers College, Columbia University, 1967), p. 302.

17. Quoted in Ulich, *Education of Nations*, p. 243.

18. *Education in the States: Nationwide Development since 1900* (Washington, D.C.: NEA, 1969), p. 220.

19. Arthur Bestor, *Educational Wastelands* (Urbana: University of Illinois Press, 1953), pp. 82, 83–88, 99, 492–499.

20. Quoted in *ibid.*, p. 82.

21. Dore, *Education in Tokugawa Japan*, p. 492.

22. Michio Nagai, "University Problems in Japan," *Bulletin* of the International House of Japan, April 1969, pp. 13, 18, 23.

23. Charles Silberman, *Crisis in the Classroom* (New York: Random House, 1970), pp. 113–157.

24. Theodore Brameld, *Japan: Culture, Education, and Change in Two Communities* (New York: Holt, Rinehart, 1968), p. 255.

25. See, for example, David and Evelyn Thompson Riesman, *Conversations in Japan* (New York: Basic Books, 1967).

26. Kazuko Tsurumi, *Social Change and the Individual* (Princeton, N.J.: Princeton University Press, 1970), p. 327.

27. Alfred North Whitehead, *The Aims of Education* (New York: New American Library, 1951 ed.; originally published, 1929), p. 14.

28. Nagai, *Higher Education in Japan*, pp. 236, 239.

29. William A. McClenaghan, *Magruder's American Government* (Boston: Allyn and Bacon).

30. *Ibid.*, p. 20.

31. Elson, "American Schoolbooks," p. 121.

32. *Time Magazine*, June 17, 1974, p. 45.

33. Ronald P. Dore, "The Importance of Educational Traditions: Japan and Elsewhere," *Pacific Affairs*, 45:506 (Winter 1972–1973).

Chapter 9. In Concluding

1. Kenneth Boulding, *The Meaning of the 20th Century* (New York: Harper, 1964).

2. Hiroshi Minami, "The Introspection Boom: Whither the National Character?" *Japan Interpreter*, 8:159 (Spring 1973).

3. Tsutomu Kano, "Why the Search for Identity?" *Japan Interpreter*, 8:155–156 (Spring 1973).

4. Margaret Mead, "A Twentieth Century Faith," *Journal of Current Social Issues*, 10:4–5 (Spring 1973).

5. Quoted in Edwin O. Reischauer, *Toward the Twenty-First Century: Education for a Changing World* (New York: Random House, 1974), pp. 174–175; the rhyme is from *A Child's Garden of Verses*.

6. W.E.B. DuBois, *The Souls of Black Folk* (originally published, 1903). In John Hope Franklin, ed., *Three Negro Classics* (New York: Avon, 1965), p. 220.

7. Ronald P. Dore, "New Ideas and Old Habits," *Bulletin* of the International House of Japan, August 1965, p. 32.

8. The basic text is Norbert Wiener, *The Human Use of Human Beings* (Boston: Houghton Mifflin, 1954); Henry Adams, however, said early in the century that entropy was the clue to recent history, in his introduction to *The Degradation of the Democratic Dogma* (1919), edited by his brother Brooks.

9. From a paper read to the spring meeting of the Midcontinent American Studies Association at Park College, Missouri, 1973.

10. Quoted in William T. DeBary, ed., *Sources of the Japanese Tradition* (New York: Columbia University Press, 1964 ed.), vol. II; the quotation I have used actually fuses characterizations of "progress" on pp. 185–186.

Index

Index

"J" in this index denotes Japan; "US" denotes the United States

Abé, Kobo: on quality of life in J, 107–108, 112; *The Face of Another* and masks, 156, 165; *Woman of the Dunes* discussed, 158–161; on cultural entropy in J, 239–240; mentioned, 168

Adams, Abigail, 212

Adams, Henry, 15, 153

Adams, John, 35

Addison, Joseph, 132

Adler, Dankmar, 188

Adventures of Augie March, The (Saul Bellow), 153–155

Adventures of Huckleberry Finn, The (Mark Twain): attitude toward nature in, 71–74; formal looseness of, 129–130; influence of, 130; and esthetic of process, 201; mentioned, 36, 68, 127, 155, 160

Adventures of Tom Sawyer, The (Mark Twain), 36

Advertising: in J, 49, 54, 106–107, 123; in US, 49, 106–107

After the Banquet (Yukio Mishima), 153–155

Age of Reason, *see* Enlightenment

Agrarianism, in US, and "stages of civilization" theory, 63

Agriculture
In J: diminishing importance of, 58; and attitudes toward nature, 59
In US: Jefferson on, 48; diminishing importance of, 58; and space, 59

Agriculture, US Department of, 175

Aiken, Conrad, 125

Aims of Education (Alfred North Whitehead), 224

Akarui seikatsu, as contemporary slogan in J, 123

Akutagawa Ryūnosuke, Chinese influence on, 126

Alaska, 81

Alger, Horatio, Jr., 39

Alienation, and education in J and US, 203–204

Amaterasu, and myth of origins of J, 20

Ambassadors, The (Henry James), discussed, 133–138

American, The (Henry James), 43, 131

American Federation of Labor, 95

"American Plan," 103

American Revolution: and nationalism, 19; influence of abroad, 24–25; as myth and symbol in US, 34; mentioned, 88

269

Andalusia (Biddle mansion), 175
Anomie, and education in J and US, 203–204
Anti-intellectualism, in US, and schools, 227
Antinomianism, in US, 15
Appliances, desire for polled in J, 54
Architectural Forum, as reflection of architects' concerns, 198
Architectural Record, as reflection of architects' concerns, 198, 199
Architecture
    In England, 199
    In Finland, 199
    In Germany, contrasted with that in US, 177–178
    In Italy, 194
    In J: Chinese influence on, 59; and international style, 153, 170, 178, 193, 196; and literature, 161, 185; materials for, 170, 171, 178–179, 180, 182–184, 185, 196, 199, 200; and nature, 170, 171, 179, 180, 184; principles of, 171, 179–180, 190; influence of on US, 172, 178, 190; and new needs during Meiji, 178; use of space in, 178, 179–180, 182–184, 185; and vernacular tradition, 179, 181, 182, 184, 185; sukiyu style in, 181–182, 184; shoin style in, 181, 182; shinden style in, 181–182; symbolism and, 182, 186, 187–188, 200–201; boldness of contemporary, 194, 196; and ecology, 195; "metabolists," 196; for government and business, 197; tradition in contemporary, 196, 199; and housing problems, 231
    In US: and European origins, 23; and skyscrapers as innovations, 36, 188; and international style, 170, 193–196; and nature, 170, 171–172, 192; materials for, 170, 172–173, 174, 176–177, 185, 188, 189, 190, 191–192, 194, 199, 200; and symbolism, 171–172, 174, 175, 177, 188, 200–201; principles of, 171–178, 180, 185–186, 188, 191–193; eclecticism in, 171–178, 185–186; as corporation, 172, 194–195, 197; in colonial and early republic periods, 172, 173, 174; Chicago School, 172, 176–177, 188–189; use of space in, 174, 177, 178, 183–184, 185, 189, 190, 199; and monumentality, 174, 175, 189, 194–195; vernacular tradition in, 176–177, 180, 185, 195, 198; and education, 177, 185, 206; and religion, 179, 185; and government, 185, 194, 195; shingle style in, 188; Japanese influence on, 188; recent timidity of, 193, 194, 199; and ecology, 195, 200
    International style of: distinctive form in J, 153, 170, 196; in US, 170, 193, 196; precedents in J, 178
Aristotle, and Western esthetics, 130, 134, 144, 202
Arnold, Matthew, on US, 23
Art
    In China, respect for in J, 21
    In J: and space, 16, 201; Western surprise at quality of, 21; foreign influences on, 21, 22, 51; appreciation of in US, 22; and cultural nationalism, 35; and people, 36, 115–116; mentioned, 18, 114
    In US: and lack of self-confidence, 12, 22, 23, 176; innovations in, 18, 36; European criticism of, 23; popular importance of, 116
Artisans, in J, 40, 88. See also Workers, in J
Asahi Shinbun, and poll of life goals in J, 54-55
Asia: and imperialism in J, 30–31; J's new role in, 236
Asia, Southeast, fear of J and US imperialism in, 6
Asians, US wars against, 27–28
Assistant, The (Bernard Malamud), discussed, 156, 161–163
Athens, Greece, 58, 125
Automation, and job security in J and US, 99–100
Automobiles: popular desire for in J and US, 49–50, 107; and pollution, 81; and conquest of nature in US, 81; dependence on in US, 200
Automobile workers, in US, 103–104, 107

Bancroft, George, and nationalistic history, 209
Barth, John, and *Giles, Goat Boy,* 152
Barton, Bruce, and *The Man Nobody Knows,* 33
Barzun, Jacques, on teaching, 204
Baseball, in US: and pastoralism, 59; lore of in fiction, 120
Bashō: and paradox in haiku, 14; and antimaterialism, 44; attitude toward nature compared with Twain's, 68–75; memory of visits alive in rural J, 77; and economy of experience, 108, 134
Bathing, in J, and national character, 9–10
Bauhaus, 193
Bear, The (William Faulkner): attitude toward nature in, 68; mythic quality of, 151; mentioned, 127
Beard, Charles, 6
Beaudelaire, Charles, 161
Beech, Keyes, 13
Bellah, Robert, *Tokugawa Religion* cited, 111
Bellow, Saul: longing for nature in *Henderson, the Rain King,* 80; compared with Mishima, 153; and tradition of seeker, 156; humor in, 168; mentioned, 155
Benedict, Ruth: *The Chrysanthemum and the Sword* cited, 10, 39; critiques of book, 103, 165–166
Beowulf, as warrior-hero, 25
Bestor, Arthur, on education in US, 217–218
Bigelow, William Sturgis, 180
Biltmore (Vanderbilt mansion), 175
Birth control, in J, 16
Blacks, in US: and racism, 6, 232; and literature, 15, 65, 67; and economic attitudes, 39; and labor force, 90; and education, 213–214; mentioned, 59, 235. *See also* Racism, in US
Blue-collar workers, *see* Workers
Boccaccio, Giovanni, 125
Bode, Wilhelm, on architecture in US, 177–178
Bolivar, Simon, and American political thought, 24
Books, in J and US, production of and best sellers, 119
Boston, Mass.: and tourism in US, 77; architecture of, 183–184; mentioned, 35, 133

Bostonians, The (Henry James), satire in, 133
Boulding, Kenneth, on twentieth-century problems, 232
Boyd, Robin, and "tourist traditional" architecture in J, 195
British Broadcasting Company, and J's NHK, 118
Brown, Charles Brockden, 129
Bryce, James, Viscount, and legalistic mind in US, 15
Buddhism, in J: and materialism, 40; and nature, 61; and Christianity, 65; and influence on Bashō, 69; recent best seller on, 119; holidays, 122; and architecture, 181; and education during Meiji, 208; mentioned, 151. *See also* Zen Buddhism
Bulwer-Lytton, *see* Lytton, Edward George
Bunraku, and cultural nationalism, 35
Burakumin, and inequality of opportunity, 214
Bureaucracy, and organization of life in J and US, 84
Burroughs, William S., and erotic themes in *Naked Lunch,* 152
Bushido, 26, 29
Business
    In J: fear of in US, 4, 13; education for in US during Meiji, 21; and religion, 40; and bookkeeping, 84; and organization of work, 92 ff; and lifetime employment, 92; family as model for during Meiji, 92; and personnel recruitment, 106, 219; and advertising, 107
    In US: and fear of competition from J, 4, 13; public subsidies of, 6, 12; and nationalism, 33; and religion, 41; regulation of, 48; bookkeeping in, 84; and organization of work, 89ff; theoretical basis of, 92; and advertising, 107; and architecture, 185

Cable, George Washington, 70
California, 5, 160–161
Cambridge University, 222
Cane (Jean Toomer): and nature, 68; compared with Kawabata's work, 140
Capitalism, *see* Business
Carnegie, Andrew, 39, 86

Carver, Norman, on architecture in J, 186
Catch-22 (Joseph Heller), humor in, 160
Cathedrals, architecture of, 171, 179
Cather, Willa, My Ántonia quoted, 201
Centaur, The (John Updike), myth in, 156
Cervantes, Miguel de, 125
Chapel of Notre Dame du Haut, Ronchamp (Le Corbusier), 191
Chase, Richard: on dialectic in literature of US, 7; on differences in literature in England and US, 129–130
Chevalier, Michel, on social mobility and restlessness in US, 91, 115
Chicago, Ill., 32, 66, 85, 108, 109, 113, 155, 189
"Chicago School" of architecture, 172, 176–177, 188–189
Chicago World's Fair of 1893, and architecture of J and US, 177, 189–190
Child labor, in J and US, control of, 6
Child raising, in J and US, and national character, 9
China: attitudes toward in J, 3, 20, 21, 29, 185, 209; leaders' fear of militarism in J, 6; J seen as heir to, 30; influence of on gardens and architecture in J, 59, 78, 171, 181; war with J, 93; influence of on literature of J, 126, 132; influence of on education in J, 204–205, 228; mentioned, 11, 190
China trade, and culture of US, 11, 19
Chou En-lai, and fear of renewed militarism in J, 6
Christianity, in US: and imperialism, 24, 27–28, 30; and economic theory, 33, 92; and materialism, 33, 40, 52; and Asian religions, 65, 131; mentioned, 81, 89, 90, 122, 166, 171. See also Religion, in US
Chrysanthemum and the Sword, The (Ruth Benedict): cited, 10, 39; critiques of, 103, 165–166
Churchill, Winston, 52
Cinema, see Mass culture
"Circles," in J, 117
Cities
    In J: vulnerability of, 15; as new environment, 83; appearance of, 197–198
    In US: vulnerability of, 15; as new environment, 83

City Life in Japan (Ronald Dore), on psychology of Japanese, 165–166
City planning, in J and US, and contemporary trends, 196, 197–198
Civil War, US, and dual sovereignty, 19
Class, social, see Social mobility, Social structure
Clemens, Samuel Langhorne (Mark Twain): and theme of "contrast," 23–24; fictional form in works of, 36, 129–130, 144; as symbol in US, 36, 39; antimaterialism of The Adventures of Huckleberry Finn, 44; image of frontiersman in, 63; attitudes toward nature compared with Bashō, 68–74; and economy of experience, 108, 134; pessimism of late period of, 129; on use of masks in narration, 142, 166; influence of on Faulkner, 143; distinctiveness of humor of, 160, 168; mentioned, 68, 77, 168
Climate: of J, and architecture, 178, 181; of US, and architecture, 180
Clubs, in J and US, and leisure, 117
Cole, Robert, cited on workers in J, 101, 103, 111
Cole, Thomas, paintings of and "stages of civilization" idea, 64
Columbia University Teachers College, and aims of education, 217
Columbian Exposition of 1893, and architecture of J and US, 177, 189–190
Comedy, stage, in J, and Faulkner, 142
Communal life, of J, and rice culture, 113
Communication, in J and US, increasingly impersonal nature of, 112–113
Communism, in J, opposition to in Kokutai no Hongi, 46
Communist party of J, and labor movement, 96
Communitas (Paul and Percival Goodman), on quality of leisure in US, 112
Community, sense of in J and US, see Housing, Neighborhoods, Workers
Confessions of a Mask (Yukio Mishima), 165
Confucianism, influence on culture of J, 29, 40, 45, 88, 89, 208
Congress of Industrial Organizations, 95
Constitution of J: Seventeen Article, and national virtues, 48; present, and

pacifism, 236
Constitution of US: symbolic importance of, 15; and nationalism in US, 19; antilabor interpretations of, 92; and Watergate, 234; mentioned, 63, 237
Consumerism, in J and US, *see* Materialism
"Contrast," theme of in US, 23–24, 227
"Convergence theory": and attitudes toward nature, 81; and literature, 157
Conwell, Russell H., on Christianity and capitalism, 41
Cooper, James Fenimore: and antimaterialism of Leatherstocking tales, 44; image of man in nature, 63; influence of Scott on, 129. *See also* Leatherstocking tales
Cotton, John, on Christianity and materialism, 41
Cowboys, as popular heroes in US, 25, 34–35
Credit buying, in US, and materialism, 50
Crèvecoeur, Hector St. John de: *Letters from an American Farmer* and American boosterism, 22; and US economy in colonial period, 46; image of frontiersman, 63; mentioned, 71
Crying of Lot 49, The (Thomas Pynchon), compared with Ábe's *Woman of the Dunes*, 158–161
Cubism, and modern architecture, 187

Daisy Miller (Henry James), and American innocence, 167
Darwin, Charles, as influence on Louis Sullivan, 189
Darwinism, social, and American imperialism, 27–28
Dazai Osamu: and antiheroes in *No Longer Human* and *The Setting Sun*, 152, 156; use of masks by, 156; *No Longer Human* compared with Malamud's *The Assistant*, 161–165; mentioned, 44, 153
Death of a Salesman (Arthur Miller), and consumers' desires, 54
Declaration of Independence, US: symbolic importance of, 15, 34; and nationalism of US, 19; Locke's influence on, 63
Defense, in J and US, and manufacturing, 86. *See also* Militarism
Democracy
   In J: and education, 204–205; and

burakumin, 214. *See also* Social mobility, Social structure
   In US: and imperialism, 27–28; and education, 204, 207, 213–214, 216–217, 226; and problem of mediocrity, 204, 207, 218–219; and Jefferson's aristocracy of talent, 207. *See also* Social mobility, Social structure
Denver, Colo., rejects Olympic Games, 35
Depression, in US in *1930*s, and lavish architecture, 175
Descartes, René, and Western thought, 9
Detroit, Mich., 22, 81, 107
De Vos, George, *Socialization for Achievement* cited, 111
Dialectic, in US culture, Lionel Trilling on, 7
Diary of a Mad Old Man, The (Junichiro Tanizaki), erotic themes in, 152
Dickens, Charles, on US, 23
Dickinson, Emily, and Bashō, 76
Dictatorship, alleged influence on character of J, 9–10
Diet, of J, debate in on post–World War II defense budget, 31
Dilworth, David, on William James, 131
Disneyland, and cultural nationalism, 37
Disraeli, Benjamin, 1st Earl of Beaconsfield, on "civilizers of men," 123
Division Street, America (Studs Terkel), cited, 109
Dogen: and materialism, 40; and nature, Kawabata on, 67
Dore, Ronald: on social class of J during Meiji, 88; on advantages of late-developing nations, 88; on psychology of Japanese, 165–166; on education in J, 205, 229; on aims of education, 219, 223; on pragmatic mind in J, 236–237
Douglass, Frederick, on ironies in language in US, 240
Drama, of J, *see* Bunraku, Kabuki, Noh
DuBois, W. E. B.: on irony in US culture, 15; and cultural pluralism, 235
Dumas, Alexandre, in Meiji J, 128

Earhart, Byron, *Japanese Religion* cited, 40, 66
Ecology
   In J: public interest in, 56–57, 119; and political pressures, 81; and

architecture, 200; and education, 204, 231–232, 234
In US: public interest in, 57; and political pressures, 81; and architecture, 200; and education, 204, 234
Economic democracy, in J and US, 85–107. *See also* Social mobility, Social structure
Economic theory
In J and US, 38–57 *passim*, 83–123 *passim*
Western, 10
Economy
Of J: and depression of *1930*s, 29, 33; and workers' share of profits, 33, 99, 100, 106; aided by Korean and Indochinese wars, 33; and materialistic thought, 38–57; and goals of people, 56; rapid changes in, 58; price of land in, and housing problems, 80, 197–198; and organization of work, 83–115 *passim*; and workers at lower levels of, 99, 100, 106; and personal savings rate, 100; as alleged threat to economy of US, 102; and architecture, 197–198; and education, 203, 214–215, 219, 222–223, 225
Of US: and laissez-faire theory, 10, 33, 48, 92; and depression of *1930*s, 33; and materialistic thought, 38–57; and goals of people, 56; rapid changes in, 58; and organization of work, 83–115 *passim*; and workers' share of profits, 99; and education, 203, 214–215, 219, 222–223
Education
In J: "feudal" teaching of medicine, 9; foreign influences on during Meiji, 21, 208; and national politics, 29, 210, 211; and social mobility, 93, 109, 204–205, 210, 215–216; and popular expectations, 106; and economy, 203, 222–223, 225; religious beginnings of, 204; hierarchy of universities, 204, 219; role of Ministry of Education, 204, 223, 226; examination system, 204, 221, 223, 225, 229; Chinese influences on, 204–205;

vocational, 205, 222–223; aims of and curriculums, 205, 208, 216, 221, 222, 227–228; and women, 212–213; local differences in quality of, 214; attendance statistics, 214; teachers' preference for certain schools, 214; student life in universities, 215, 222, 224–225; university attendance, 215; university unrest, 215, 224–225; influences on during US Occupation, 216, 226; teachers' frustrations with large classes, 216, 223–224; hierarchical nature of, 216, 219–220; organization of, 216, 226; "cram schools," 220; and parents' reactions, 221; quality of higher, 222, 224–225; professors' careers, 224; unions of teachers, 225; teachers' role and status, 226–229; debate on moral, 226–228; ultimate importance of, 232
In US: "feudal" nature of medical, 9; and social mobility, 48, 93, 109–110, 204, 207, 211, 215; anti-intellectualism and problem of mediocrity, 48, 204, 212, 216, 218, 226, 227, 228, 229–230; and popular expectations, 106; curriculums of higher, 125, 204, 205, 209; and architecture, 185; and economy, 203, 222–223; aims of, and curriculums, 203–207, 211, 216–217, 222–223, 226–228, 229; vocational, 206, 218, 222–223; and nationalism, 211, 226–227; and women, 212, 213; and training, role, and status of teachers, 212, 214, 217–218, 226–229; power of National Educational Association, 212, 216–217, 218, 223; attendance statistics, 214, 215; and local differences in quality, 214; unrest in universities, 215; local control of, 216, 218, 223, 226, 228; control of universities, 216; examination system in, 221; quality of higher, 222; professors' careers, 224; ultimate importance of, 232
Edwards, Jonathan, as mystic, 64

Eisenhower, Dwight David, image of, 26
Eliot, T. S.: as expatriate artist, 23;
  influence of *The Waste Land*, 156
Ellison, Ralph, *Invisible Man* in tradition
  of seeker, 155
Emerson, Ralph Waldo: *Nature* cited, 11,
  61, 64–65; plea for individualism, 13;
  and cultural nationalism, 129, 209;
  mentioned, 11, 47, 76, 189
Emigration, of Japanese to Brazil,
  Canada, and US, 91
Emperor, of J, *see* Imperial family
Emperor's Birthday, symbolic
  importance of, 34
England: and education of Japanese
  during Meiji, 21, 208; and multifamily
  dwellings, 77, 199; influence on
  colonial America and US, 77, 85, 129,
  172, 173, 175; similarity of culture to
  J's, 165–166; mentioned, 19, 128, 130,
  132. *See also* Great Britain, United
  Kingdom
Enlightenment: and symbolism in US,
  35; and European attitudes toward
  nature in America, 62
Entropy, cultural: in US, 7, 158,
  203–204, 232, 238; in J, 158, 203–204,
  232
"Entropy" (Thomas Pynchon), 159
Escape from Freedom (Erich Fromm),
  cited, 237
Esthetics
  In J: and culture, 10–11, 201; and
    attitudes toward nature, 59–81
    passim; and gardens, 78, 187; and
    familial housing, 78; compared
    with esthetics in US, 130,
    134–135, 139, 183, 202; and
    Sōseki, 133–138; and blank space,
    146; Tanizaki on, 164; and
    architecture, 170, 179, 180–187,
    196–197; and *wabi*, 182, 184;
    Wright on, 190; and popular
    expectations, 201, 237–238. *See
    also* Literature, of J
  In US: and lack of self-confidence,
    22–24, 172–173, 184–185; and
    symmetry, 78; and public space,
    78; compared with esthetics in J,
    130, 134–135, 139, 183, 202; and
    Henry James, 133–138; and
    "plentitude," 146; and
    architecture, 170–201 *passim*; and
    process, 196; and organization of

space, 201; and popular
  expectations, 237–238. *See also*
  "Plain style"; Literature, of US
Eternal Storehouse of Japan, The (Ihara
  Saikaku), and materialism, 41–42
Ethnic groups, of US: and
  neighborhoods, 8, 112; and power
  elite, 15; and jobs, 89–90. *See also*
  Racism, names of national origins
Euclid, and Western architecture, 187
Europe: image of US in, 22–23, 77;
  intellectuals of, and interest in
  colonies and US, 22–23; early isolation
  of US from, 24; and tourism in US,
  77; military tradition of, 127
Everett, Edward, opposes public schools,
  207
Expatriates, US, and American
  self-image, 23

Face of Another (Kobo Ábe), and masks,
  156, 165
Fairs, in US, and leisure, 123
Falling Water–Kauffmann House (Frank
  Lloyd Wright), described, 191–193
Family life
  In J: importance of, 54; and
    housing, 78–80; and
    industrialization, 82, 85, 100;
    compared with that in US,
    116–117; and Imperial Rescript
    on Education, 208–209; and
    population, 231
  In US: importance of, 54; and
    yards, 78; and leisure, 78,
    116–117, 122; and
    industrialization, 85
Farmers
  In J: and government subsidies, 64;
    and preindustrial work habits, 85;
    rank during Tokugawa, 88; and
    architecture, 181
  In US: and "myth of garden," 64;
    English precedents, 84;
    contrasted with industrial
    workers, 85; in industrial work
    force, 86, 89; and "safety valve"
    theory, 91. *See also* Agrarianism,
    Agriculture
Faulkner, William: as innovator, 36; and
  nature, in *The Bear*, 68; humor in,
  140–143, 160, 168; *The Hamlet*
  contrasted with literature in J,
  140–143; compared with Kawabata,

143–147; influence of Hawthorne and Twain on, 143; symbolic mode of, 144, 156; *Light in August* discussed, 144; characterization in, 145; myth in, 156; and masked narration, 166; mentioned, 153

Fenellosa, Ernest: teaches respect for ukiyoe, 21–22; mentioned, 180

Feudalism
   In J: self-stereotype of, 8, 14
   In US: vestiges of, 8; and architecture, 175

Finland, as model for multifamily dwellings, 199

Fishing: in J, 40, 58; in US, 40

Fiske, John T., as advocate of imperialism, 28

Fitzgerald, F. Scott: myth and symbol in work of, 149–150, 151; *The Great Gatsby* compared with Tanizaki's work, 149–150

Flags, of J and US, symbolic importance of contrasted, 26, 34, 37, 226

Florence, Italy, and resistance to skyscrapers, 195

Flying Cloud Pavilion, Kyoto, 192

Folk culture
   In J: renewed interest in, 37, 200, 233; and industrialism, 84; wealth of, 123; and architecture, 171, 179
   In US: and theme of "contrast," 23–24; renewed interest in, 37, 233; and heroes, 39, 97; and industrialization, 84; and influence on literature, 142, 149, 166–167

Football, in US, symbolic importance of, 34

Ford Motor Company, 50, 107

Forster, E. M., *A Passage to India* quoted, 37

Fort Wayne, Ind., 118

Fourth of July, in US, symbolic importance of, 34

France: and education of Japanese, 21, 208; literature favored in J, 128–129; mentioned, 19, 86, 114, 122, 131, 214

Francis of Assisi, as peaceful hero, 25

Franklin, Benjamin: as "archetypical American," 15; and materialism in US, 41–43; and masked narration, 166; and education in US, 206; in textbooks in J and US, 211; as hero during Meiji, 215

Fromm, Erich, *Escape from Freedom* cited, 237

Frontier, in US: passing of, 39, 81; and sense of space, 59; and attitudes toward nature, 60, 65; and influence on thought, 62; and conditions of labor, 91; mentioned, 231

Frost, Robert: influence of transcendentalism on, 11; and cultural nationalism, 36; compared with Bashō, 75–76; on surprise in art, 192

Fuji, Mount, and tourists, 76

Fukuzawa Yukichi, and European languages, 128

Furniture, in US, 177, 183–184

Galahad, as warrior-hero, 25

Gallup Poll, on materialism in US, 56

Gangsters, in J and US, as popular heroes, 25

Gans, Herbert, cited on suburban culture in US, 53, 79, 110

Gardens
   In J: and cultural nationalism, 35, 36; as fine art, 77, 78; and architecture, 187; psychological uses of, 201
   In US: 77

Geertz, Clifford, cited, 34

General Electric Corporation, 84

Geographical features: in J, 25, 38–40, 59; in US, 39, 59

Gergen, Kenneth J., and individualism, 166

Germany: and education of Japanese during Meiji, 21, 208; work force from in US, 91; mentioned, 5, 107, 128

Giedion, Siegfried: *Space, Time, and Architecture* cited, 177–179, 186–187; *Mechanization Takes Command* cited, 177; mentioned, 188, 192

Giri, 136

Gompers, Samuel, 48, 95

Goodman, Paul and Percival, *Communitas* cited on quality of leisure, 112

Government
   In J: and business during Meiji, 92; personnel recruitment, 106, 219; and architecture, 196–198; military budget, 203; and education, 203, 208–209, 212–213, 214, 216, 219, 227–228, 229
   In US: basic documents, 15; and

architecture, 173, 185, 194,
    198–199; military budget, 203;
    and education, 203, 206–207,
    212–213, 214, 219, 226–228, 229
Grant, Ulysses S.: and Noh, 22; as
    popular hero, 26
Great Britain, and easy conquest of
    China, 86
Great Gatsby, The (F. Scott Fitzgerald):
    compared with Some Prefer Nettles,
    149–150; myth in, 151
Greece: and heritage of attitudes on
    nature from, 62, 74; language of, in
    US, 125, 206, 227; as political model
    for US, 173–174; influence of on
    architecture in US, 173–175, 185, 189
Grid system, in US, and attitudes toward
    nature, 59
Grimm, Jakob, and cultural nationalism,
    209
Gropius, Walter: contrasted with
    Wright, 193–194; mentioned, 191,
    193
Guam, and J tourism, 122
Guthrie, Woody, and antimaterialism,
    44

Haiku: paradox in, 14; and seasonal
    tags, 67; Bashō's discussed, 69–75;
    influence on Kawabata, 143
Hamilton, Alexander, encourages
    manufactures, 64, 86
Harada Jirō, The Lesson of Japanese
    Architecture cited, 179–181, 199
Harris, George Washington ("Sut
    Luvingood"), and masked narration,
    167
Harris, Mark, and baseball lore in
    fiction, 120
Harrison, William Henry, image of,
    25–26
Hartford, Conn., 68
Harvard College and University, 28,
    206, 221, 222
Hawaii, and J tourism, 122
Hawthorne, Nathaniel: as expatriate
    artist, 23; The Scarlet Letter mentioned,
    68; pessimism of, 129; as formal artist,
    130; influence on Faulkner, 143;
    psychological themes in, 146;
    distinguishes romance and novel, 150
Hayes, Rutherford B., image of, 26
Health, in J and US, effects of "future
    shock" on, 11–12
Hearn, Lafcadio, 23, 125, 132

Hebrew, and education in US, 125
Hegel, Georg Wilhelm, and dialectic in
    US culture, 14
Heian period: and literature, especially
    by women, 24, 125–127, 212; and
    urban attitudes, 58; architecture of,
    181, 182
Heller, Joseph, and humor in Catch-22,
    160
Hemingway, Ernest: The Old Man and the
    Sea and attitudes toward nature, 68;
    on Twain, 129; compared with
    Kawabata, 139, 147; symbolic mode of
    The Sun Also Rises, 148–150; symbolic
    method in The Old Man and the Sea,
    148; compared with Tanizaki,
    150–151; mythic quality of The Old
    Man and the Sea, 151–152
Henderson, the Rain King (Saul Bellow),
    and attitudes toward nature, 80
Henry V (William Shakespeare), 127
Herder, Johann Gottfried von, and
    cultural nationalism, 209
Heroes
    In J: Shotoku, Genji, samurai, and
        yakuza as, 25
    In US: cowboys, gangsters, peaceful
        generals as, 25, 26–27
Herzberg, Frederick, on job satisfaction,
    98–101
History
    In J: and myth of national origins,
        20; cyclical theory of, 21; study
        of, and best sellers, 119; renewed
        interest in, 200, 233
    In US: and explanation of national
        origins, 20; renewed interest in
        study of, 200, 232–233. See also
        Folk culture, in US
Hitachi, Japan, as company town, 101
Hofstadter, Richard, 6
Holidays: of J, 35, 121, 122–123 (see also
    Leisure, in J); of US, 122–123 (see also
    Leisure, in US)
Homer: warrior-heroes, 25; compared
    with Lady Murasaki, 125–127, 168;
    and literary form, 146
Honda (automobile), 22, 81
Honda Toshiaki, on economic
    nationalism, 45
Hōō-den, at Chicago World's Fair of
    1893, 189–190
Hoover, Herbert, on "rugged
    individualism," 33
Hope, Thomas, on architecture and

"melting pot," 185–186
Household appliances, in J and US, 49
Housing
    In J: crowding in, 16; importance of
        desire for, 49, 51; preference for
        single-family dwellings, 77, 80,
        200; and gardens, 79; inadequacy
        of, 99, 201, 231; rapid changes in,
        112, 113–114; incidence of family
        ownership, 113; and social life,
        117; new plans for, 196; and land
        prices, 197–198. *See also*
        Architecture, of J
    In US: preference for single-family
        dwellings, 77, 172, 200; and social
        life, 79, 117, 118; incidence of
        family ownership, 113; and moves
        to suburbs, 113; for poor, 118,
        176, 195, 198, 201, 232; interiors,
        177–178; capitalism and, 195;
        mobile, 198. *See also* Architecture,
        of US
"How to Tell a Story" (Mark Twain), on
    masks in narration, 166
Howe, Irving, on urban themes in
    American literature, 67
Howells, William Dean, on urban
    themes in American literature, 67
Hughes, Langston, and nature, 65
Human Use of Human Beings, The
    (Norbert Wiener), on cultural
    entropy, 159
Hunt, Richard Morris, and design for
    Biltmore, 175
Hutchinson, Anne, 212

I Am a Cat (Sōseki Natsume), point of
    view in, 132
Ibsen, Henrik, 213
Ikebana, 19, 35, 36, 51, 52, 79
Iliad, The, compared with *Genji*, 126
Irving, Washington, 129
Immigrants, in US: and economic
    attitudes, 39; Lincoln on, and free
    labor, 47–48; and attitudes toward
    nature, 59; in labor force, 86, 89–90;
    and discrimination, 90, 92; and ethnic
    neighborhoods, 112; and education,
    206, 214. *See also* "Melting pot";
    Oriental exclusion acts; Racism, in US
Imperial family of J, symbolic
    importance of, 19, 29, 34, 46, 86, 210
Imperial Hotel of Tokyo (Frank Lloyd
    Wright), 190
Imperial Rescript on Education of *1890*,

29, 208, 210
Imperialism
    In Europe: and Japanese militarism,
        29–30; Meiji leaders' response, 86
    In J: religious sanction for, 20; and
        crowding and poverty, 29, 91
    In US: and Western expansion, 19,
        27; religious sanction for, 20; and
        Japanese imperialism, 30
India, 11, 99
Indians, of US, *see* Native Americans
Individualism
    In J: Chie Nakane on, 13; *Kokutai no
        Hongi* on, 46; discussed, 163–167
    In US: and traditional plea for, 9,
        13; and worker morale, 94;
        discussed, 163–167
Indochinese wars, 22, 29
Industrialism
    In J: and nature, 12, 58, 81, 84;
        rational ordering of, 12, 84;
        history of, compared with US, 83;
        reluctant acceptance of, 86. *See
        also* Business, in J; Ecology, in J;
        Economy, in J; Manufacturing, in
        J; Workers, in J
    In US: history of, 39, 83; and
        economic democracy, 48; and
        nature, 58, 81; reluctant
        acceptance of, 86. *See also*
        Business, in US; Ecology, in US;
        Economy, in US; Manufacturing,
        in US; Workers, in US
Inouye Kaoru, on westernizing Japan,
    210
Intellectuals, European, on American
    culture, 24
Intuition, in J culture, and
    self-stereotypes, 13
Invisible Man (Ralph Ellison), and
    tradition of seeker, 155
Irish-Americans, 89–90, 122
Ise shrine: symbolic importance of, 34,
    36; folkroots of, 36, 171; as prototype
    of J architecture, 178, 186; and
    modern architecture, 186, 196, 199;
    compared with Wright's work,
    193
Italian-Americans, 122
Italian Renaissance, and architecture in
    US, 175
Italy, and holidays, 122
Ives, Charles: and dialectical form, 14;
    and transcendentalism, 65;
    mentioned, 191

Jackson, Andrew: image of, 25; on economic opportunity, 47
Jackson, John Brinckerhoff, on organization of space in US, 201
James, Henry: as expatriate artist, 23; use of theme of "contrast," 23–24; *The American* on materialism in US, 43; and urban themes, 67; and form, 130, 144; compared with Sōseki, 130–134; *The American* discussed, 131; versatility of, 132; *The Bostonians*, 133; *The Ambassadors* discussed, 133–138; and economy of experience, 135; compared with Kawabata, 139; and US innocence, in *Daisy Miller*, 167; mentioned, 168, 235
James, William: and materialism, 41; quoted, 127; "pure experience" in philosophy of, 131
"Japan, Incorporated": popularity of phrase in media, 13; and workers' attitudes, 93
Japan Architect, as reflection of current concerns, 198–200
Japan Here and There (Umemoto Seiichi), cited, 76
Japan Interpreter, cited, 123, 216
Japan the Beautiful and Myself (Yasunari Kawabata), quoted on nature, 67
Japanese-Americans, treatment of in US, 5
Japanese Influence in America, The (Clay Lancaster), quoted, 191–193
Japanese Religion (Byron Earhart), cited, 40, 66
Japanese Society (Chie Nakane), cited, 13
Japanese Tradition and American Literature, The (Earl Miner), cited, 125
Jazz, 19
Jefferson, Lucy, quoted, 108
Jefferson, Thomas: and American sense of mission, 24; and Louisiana Purchase, 27; and symbolism in US, 35; on agrarianism versus industrialization, 45, 48, 64, 87, 88; and economic opportunity, 47; and "aristocracy of talent," 48; egalitarianism of, 90; and architecture, 171–172, 173, 174; on education, 206–207, 212–213
Jesus, 25, 33, 52
Jews, in US: and diminishing racism, 16, 232; and urban literary themes, 67; in work force, 90; impact of immigrants, 193; mentioned, 122, 155. *See also*

Racism, in US; Religion, in US
Jimmu, and myth of J's origins, 20
Jobs, in J and US, *see* Workers
Johnson, Philip, 194
Jōmon culture, of J, 14, 171, 193, 196
Jonathan Livingston Seagull (Richard Bach), as best seller in J and US, 119
Jones, Inigo, and Western architecture, 172

Kabuki, 35, 179, 184
Kahn, Albert, and architecture in US, 195
Kahn, Herman, and stereotypical view of J, 5
Kamakura, Japan, and tourism, 76
Kamikaze, and defeat of Kublai Khan, 28
Kamo no Chōmei, and antimaterialism, 43–44
Kato Shuichi, and cycles in history, 21
Katsura Detached Palace, Kyoto, 171, 181
Kauffmann House–Falling Water (Frank Lloyd Wright), described, 191–193
Kawabata, Yasunari: and cultural nationalism, 36; and attitudes toward nature, 67; compared with James and Hemingway, 139–147; *Snow Country* discussed, 139–140, 147–148; imagery of, 139, 161; compared with Toomer, 140; compared with Faulkner, 141–147; work in European literature, 143; symbolic mode of, 144–145; form in, 144; and psychology, 146; compared with Hemingway, 147; and erotic themes in *The House of the Sleeping Beauties* and *The Sound of the Mountain*, 152–153; use of masks, 165; mentioned, 168
Keene, Donald: on Grant and Noh, 22; on eroticism in literature of J, 66; follows Bashō's travels, 77; on esthetics in J, 127; on international literature, 153; on Dazai, 161, 163
Keiei-kazoku-shugi policy, and organization of work in J, 92, 103
Kennedy, John Fitzgerald, 25
Kenyatta, Jomo, 25
Kesey, Ken, and humor in *One Flew Over the Cuckoo's Nest*, 160
Key, The (Junichiro Tanizaki), and erotic themes, 152
King, Martin Luther, Jr., 89
Kipling, Rudyard, on Chicago, 189
Kirkup, James, 7, 51

Kishimoto, Hideo, 61
Kiyonori Kikutake, and contemporary
    architecture of J, 196, 197
Knights of Labor, goals of, 95
Koestler, Arthur, on culture of J, 9
Kojiki, and myth of J's origins, 20
Kokoro (Sōseki Natsume), discussed,
    133–138, 168
Kokutai no Hongi, on ethics and politics,
    29, 46
Kossuth, Louis, and political thought of
    US, 24
Kouwenhoven, John, on esthetics of
    process, 201–202
Kurokawa Noriaki, and modern
    architecture of J, 196
Kurosawa, Akira, 4

Labor movement
    In J: present strength, 95;
        beginnings, 95; ideological nature
        of, 96; and workers' company
        loyalty, 102; and enterprise
        unions, 105. *See also* Workers, in J
    In US: left-wing suspicion of in J, 6;
        and economic opportunity,
        Lincoln on, 47, 48; social
        importance of, 94; beginnings,
        95; present strength, 95; goals
        after *1890*s, 95, 103; and
        employment practices, 99; and
        retirement, 100; and education,
        207. *See also* Workers, in US
Lancaster, Clay, *The Japanese Influence in
    America* cited, 191–193
Land
    In J, high price of: and gardens, 77,
        79; and cities, 197–198. *See also*
        Gardens, in J; Geographical
        features, in J; Housing, in J;
        Landscape, in J
    In US: and economic attitudes, 39;
        ownership of, and architecture,
        172. *See also* Geographical
        features, in US; Landscape, in US
Landscape
    In J: and attitudes toward nature,
        61; Bashō's use of, 68–75
    In US: and grid system, 59, 63;
        Twain's use of, 69–75; Frost's use
        of, 76; and yards, 77
Language
    Of J: mastery by few Americans, 4;
        ceremonial nature of, 8; and
        culture, 16; and attitudes toward

    nature, 60
    Of US: ceremonial nature of, 8; as
        distinct from British English, 129;
        dialects of, 129; and nationalism,
        209
Lao Tze, Wright on, 190
Last Puritan, The (George Santayana),
    cited, 115
Latin language, in American schools,
    125, 206, 227
Latrobe, Benjamin, influence of Greeks
    on, 173
Lawrence, D. H., on Franklin, 15, 41
Leatherstocking tales, 44, 68, 127, 129
Leaves of Grass (Walt Whitman): as
    innovation, 129–130; and esthetic of
    process, 202
Le Corbusier: on architecture in US,
    193; influence, 193, 196; and
    Ronchamp chapel, 194
Leftists, political
    In J: and labor movement of US, 6;
        and accommodation to society in
        J, 15
    In US, 6
Legal system
    In J: French influence on, 21; and
        complexity of industrialism, 84
    In US: and legalistic mind, 15, 35;
        and business, 92
Leisure
    In J: manner of using, 52, 94,
        112–123; and nature, 80, 81; Ábe
        on, 107–108. *See also* Holidays, in
        J; Mass culture, in J
    In US: manner of using, 52, 94,
        112–123; and nature, 80, 81. *See
        also* Holidays, in US; Mass
        culture, in US
Lesson of Japanese Architecture, The
    (Harada Jirō), cited, 179–180, 181
Letters from an American Farmer (Hector
    St. John de Crèvecoeur), 46
Levittown, N.J., culture of, 53, 79, 110
Liberal Democratic party of J, 38
Life on the Mississippi (Mark Twain),
    68–75
Light in August (William Faulkner),
    144–145, 160
Lincoln, Abraham: image of, 34, 35,
    42–43, 215; and economic
    opportunity, 47
Literacy: in J, 203, 205; in US, 203; in
    nineteenth-century England
    compared with that in J, 205

Literature
    Of China, and J, 126
    Of England, and US, 22, 128,
        129–130
    Of France, and J, 128–129
    Of Germany: and J, 129; and US,
        129
    Of J: in Heian period,24, 125–127;
        heroes of, 25; and materialism,
        39; and nature, 66–67, 90; urban
        themes in, 67; Bashō and
        traditions of, 69–75; portrayal of
        workers in, 96, 97; popular,
        compared with US, 119; Western
        influence on, 125–169 *passim*;
        during Meiji, 128; during
        Tokugawa, 128; and form,
        compared with that of US, 130;
        characterization in, 134, 145–146,
        147; symbolic mode of, 137–150
        passim; moral and intellectual
        nature of, 138, 139; and erotic
        themes, 152; international nature
        of, 153; masks in, 156, 163–167;
        and society, 167–169; and
        architecture, 185
    Of US: European image of, 23; and
        theme of "contrast," 23–24; and
        lack of confidence in US, 24, 25,
        209; heroes in, 25; and
        materialism, 39; and urban
        themes, 67; vernacular tradition
        in, 68–77; and pastoral, 68, 80;
        and portrayal of workers, 96; and
        culture, 119, 120, 124–125, 167;
        moralistic nature of, 125, 132,
        138; and symbolic mode, 129,
        143, 145–150; as distinct from
        British, 129–130; and form, 129,
        130, 138–143; characterization in,
        134, 144, 145–146, 147; comic
        tradition in, 142, 160, 168; folk
        and myth in, 151–152, 156, 168;
        and erotic themes, 152;
        international themes of, 153;
        tradition of seeker in, 155–156,
        157, 159, 167–168; and use of
        masks, 163, 166–167; and
        architecture, 185
    Western, 125, 153
Locke, David Ross ("Petroleum V.
    Nasby"), 167
Locke, John, influence on US, 9, 14, 22,
    63
London, England, 83, 132

Longfellow, Henry Wadsworth, 23
Louisiana Purchase, 27
Lowell, James Russell, on architecture of
    US, 176
Lumber industry, in J, 58
"Luvingood, Sut" (George Washington
    Harris), 167
Lynd, Robert and Helen, on materialism
    of US, 49–50
Lyon, Mary, 213
Lytton, Edward George, 128

MacArthur, Douglas, 23, 26, 32
McCarthy, Eugene, 32
McGovern, George, 25, 32
McGuffey's readers, and aims of
    education, 211, 227
McKim, Mead, and White, eclecticism
    of, 188
McKinley, William, and imperialism of
    US, 28
McLellan, Edwin, on translation of
    Sōseki, 136
Maison Carrée, Nîmes, 173
Malamud, Bernard: *The Natural* cited,
    66, 120, 156; and seeker tradition,
    156; *The Assistant* compared with
    Dazai's work, 156, 161–163;
    mentioned, 153
Manchurian incident, escalation of, 29
Mann, Horace, and public education,
    207, 211–212
Manufacturing
    In J: and workers' attitudes,
        83–106; quality of, 105. *See also*
        Industrialism, in J; Workers, in J
    In US: Hamilton's encouragement
        of, 64; and workers' attitudes,
        83–106; and quality of product,
        104–105; movement of to
        suburbs, 113. *See also*
        Industrialism, in US; Workers, in
        US
Maraini, Fosco, cited, 60, 85
Marketing research, in J and US, 107
Marx, Karl, and industrial workers, 8,
    84
Marx, Leo: and cultural dialectic in US,
    7; and attitudes toward nature in US,
    64, 71
Masamichi Kuru, and Phoenix Hall of
    Chicago World's Fair, 189–190
Maslow, Abraham: and human needs,
    98; and individualism, 166
Mass culture

In J: and that of US, 4; and samurai heroes, 34–35; growth of, 49–50; and attitudes toward nature, 58; and traditional architecture, 182. *See also* Leisure, in J; Television, in J
In US: and that of J, 4; and nationalism, 26; and cowboy heroes, 34–35; and cultural history, 36; growth of, 49–50; and attitudes toward nature, 58; and housing, 79; portrayal of workers in media, 96; and manipulation of expectations, 106. *See also* Leisure, in US; Television, in US
Massachusetts, 201, 206, 211, 212
Materialism
    In J: "economic animal" stereotype, 8, 38–57; and nationalism, 33
    In US: "crass materialist" stereotype of, 8, 38–57; and nationalism, 32–33
Mathematics: in J, 12, 202; and culture, 84, 187
Matsuoka Yosuke, and war aims of J in *1939*, 30–31
Matsushita Konosuke, 4, 53
May, Rollo, and individualism, 166
Mayflower Compact, and "state of nature" theory, 62
Mayo, Elton, study of workers in US cited, 94
Mazda automobile, 22, 81
Mazzini, Giuseppe, 24
Mead, Margaret: and changing family patterns, 85; and vision of internationalism, 234
Mechanization Takes Command (Siegfried Giedion), on furniture of US, 177
Meiji, Emperor, 22, 212
Meiji period: and education, 21, 208, 212; and nationalism, 21, 46; and attitudes toward West, 21, 86, 208; and industrialization, 86, 87–88, 92–93, 94; slogans of, 128, 210, 215; and architecture, 178
"Melting pot," of US, and architecture, 176, 185–186
Melville, Herman: dialectic in, 14; and theme of "contrast," 23–24; and cultural nationalism, 36; and antimaterialism, 44; and attitudes toward nature, 68; pessimism of, 129; and language, 129; and formal innovation, 129–130; mentioned, 191

Merchant marine, of J, and nationalism, 45
Merchants, of J, 11, 88
"Metabolists," in architecture of J, 14, 189, 196–197
Mexican-Americans, and education, 214
Michigan, University of: study of work, 98, 99; mentioned, 106
Mies van der Rohe, Ludwig: contrasted with Wright, 193–194; Seagram Building, 194; mentioned, 191
Militarism
    In J: Asian fear of, 6; and rationalism, 12; crowding and, 16, 29; and acceptance among nations, 18; religious sanction for, 20, 29; education in, 21; after *1945*, 32. *See also* Defense
    In US: fear of in J, 6, 123; religious sanction for, 20, 27–28; and economic growth, 18–30 *passim*; and isolationism, 18–30 *passim*; and heroes, 25–26; "peaceful" goals of, 28; in *1970s*, 32; and political priorities, 81; and neutrality of J, 236. *See also* Defense
Miller, Arthur, and consumerism, 54
Miller, Henry, and erotic themes, 152
Miller, Perry, and symbolic mode, 64
Minami, Hiroshi: and role-playing, 102–103; and "introspection boom," 233
Miner, Earl, *The Japanese Tradition and American Literature* cited, 125
Ministry of Education, of J (Monbushō), 29, 204, 215, 223, 224, 225, 227, 228, 229
Mishima, Yukio: compared with Bellow, 153; traditional quality of, 156; and masks, 156, 164–165; and nationalism, 233–234; mentioned, 4, 31
Mission, sense of national:
    In J, 29. *See also* Imperialism, in J; Nationalism, in J
    In US: as "great experiment," 24; and religion, 30; and idea of progress, 63. *See also* Imperialism, in US; Nationalism, in US
Mississippi River: Twain on, 69–75; and language, 129
Miyakonojo Civic Center (Kiyonori Kikutake), 197
Miyamoto Musashi, as symbolic hero, 35
Moby Dick (Herman Melville): and

nature, 68, 152; form of, 129–130;
    mentioned, 14, 127
Momoyama period, art of, 181
Monarchy, in Europe, 35, 46, 87
Monbushō, see Ministry of Education
Montesquieu, Baron de la Brède et, and
    US Constitution, 63
Monticello (Jefferson house), 171
Morality, in J and US, as seen by one
    another, 3, 11, 12, 15, 183–184
Mori Arinori, 210
Mori Ōgai, 128, 129
Morrill Land Grant College Act of 1862,
    and public tertiary education, 211
Morse, Edward S., on architecture of J,
    180–184, 192
Moses, as hero, 25
Motoori Norinaga, and cultural
    nationalism, 209
Movies, of US, and sense of space, 59
Mumford, Lewis: on industrialization,
    83–84; on United Nations Building,
    194; mentioned, 185
Muncie, Ind., in 1920s, and materialism,
    49–50
Munitions industry, of J, 31
Murasaki, [Shikibu], Lady, The Tale of
    Genji discussed, 25, 36, 126–127
Music, in US, 23, 36
Mutual Defense Treaty, between J and
    US, 5
My Ántonia (Willa Cather), quoted, 201
Myoe, quoted by Kawabata, 67
Mythology: of J, 20, 125–126; of US, 20,
    125–126

Nagai, Michio: on free education in US,
    211; on quality of education in J, 222,
    225–226
Nagai, Yonosuke, 6
Nagasaki, Japan, Dutch in, 128
Nagoya, Japan, appearance of, 197
Nakamura Hajime, on national
    character of J, 10, 40, 66
Nakane, Chie, Japanese Society cited, 13
Naked Lunch (William S. Burroughs),
    erotic themes in, 152
Napoleonic wars, and industrialism in
    US, 87
Nara, Japan, 76
Narrow Road to the Deep North (Bashō),
    compared with Twain's work, 68–75
"Nasby, Petroleum V." (David Ross
    Locke), 167
"National character": concept of

discussed, 7–14; of J, 9–10, 48; of US,
    9–10
National Council of Churches, in US,
    and reform, 52
National Education Association, in US:
    power of, 212, 228; and aims of
    education, 216–219, 229
National Socialist party of Germany, and
    Bauhaus, 193
National Statistical Research Center, in
    J, and goals of people, 55
Nationalism
    In J: military-political form of,
        18–33; Western models for, 19,
        86; cultural, 19, 34; and myth of
        national origins, 20; and religion,
        20; cyclical nature of, 21, 34, 86,
        185; as defined in Kokutai no
        Hongi, 29; and sense of national
        mission, 30; and military success,
        32; and materialism, 33, 34, 93;
        and local and international
        loyalties, 37, 232–235; and ethnic
        homogeneity, 93; and
        architecture, 186; and education,
        208–210; and self-examination in
        1970s, 231–234, 236
    In US: military-political form of,
        18–33; early nature of, 19; and
        religion, 20; and myth of national
        origins, 20; and areas of
        confidence, 22; and sense of
        national mission, 24, 63; and
        military success, 32; economic
        since 1919, 32–33, 34; cultural,
        34, 129, 184, 185–186, 209,
        232–233, 234; and local and
        international loyalties, 37,
        232–235; and architecture,
        185–186; and education, 209,
        211, 226–227; in 1970s, 231–233
Native Americans: and whites' wars
    against, 27, 28; and attitudes toward
    nature, 59; image of, 63; and
    education, 214
Natural, The (Bernard Malamud), cited,
    66, 120, 156
"Natural law," idea of, and US culture,
    66, 172
Nature, attitudes toward
    In J: and materialism, 12, 33–34,
        38, 39; discussed, 58–82; and
        housing, 78–80; and time, 84; and
        architecture, 181, 184, 185
    In US: and materialism, 43–44;

discussed, 58–82; and housing,
78–80, 113; and time, 84; and
architecture, 185, 191–193
Nature (Ralph Waldo Emerson), cited,
11, 61, 64–65
Negroes, US, *see* Blacks, in US
Neighborhoods: in J, 112, 117; in US,
112–113, 117
Nenko, and job satisfaction, 105
Netherlands, and culture of J, 21, 45,
128
New Deal, in US, and labor movement,
96
New England: image of in James,
136–137; and architecture, 172–173,
175; and education, 213
New Orleans, La., 70
New York City, 51, 58, 66, 83, 130, 150
New York State: and housing, 198–199;
and public education, 211; mentioned,
214
Newton, Sir Isaac, and Western culture,
62, 84, 174, 187
NHK, 118
Nietzsche, Friedrich Wilhelm, on masks,
167
Nihon shoki, and national origins of J, 20
Nijō Castle, Kyoto, 171
Nikko shrine, 181, 184
Ninjo, as moral imperative, 136
Ninomiya Sontoku, on religion and
materialism, 40
Nippon Hōsō Kyokai (NHK), 118
Nisei, in US, 5
Nishida Kitaro, and William James, 131
Nixon, Richard M., government of, 56
Nkrumah, Kwame, 25
No Longer Human (Dazai Osamu), cited,
156, 161–163
"Noble savage," idea of, and image of
native Americans, 63
Noboru Kawazoe, 184, 186
Noh, 22, 35, 145, 179
Norinaga, Motoori, and antimaterialism,
45
Northrop, F. S. C., *The Meeting of East
and West* and national character, 10–11
Nuclear weapons, of J and US, 6, 31

Oberlin College, 213
Occupation of J by US: differs from
German, 5; and economy of J, 38; and
education in J, 216, 226, 228;
mentioned, 93

Odyssey, The, 126
Oë, Kenzaburo: compared with Updike,
156–157; mentioned, 80, 153, 161,
168
Office of Education, US, 218
Ogiwara, Ajita, 10
Okakura Kakuzo, *Book of Tea* cited, 3, 4,
35–36
Okinawa, US presence in, 5
Ōkuma Shigenobu, quoted, 241
Old Man and the Sea, The (Ernest
Hemingway): attitudes toward nature
in, 68; myth and symbol in, 151–152
Old Testament, and US literature, 125
Olympic Games, Tokyo and Sapporo, 35
One Flew Over the Cuckoo's Nest (Ken
Kesey), 160
Opium Wars, 86
Optimist's Daughter (Eudora Welty), 119
Ordinance of *1787*, US, 207, 209
"Oriental Calvinists," in J, 112
Oriental exclusion acts, in US, 91
Osaka, image of, 85, 150, 163
Oshio Heihachiro, on individualism, 13
O'Sullivan, John L., and US imperialism,
27, 30
Oxford University, 222
Ozawa Seiji, 4

Pacifism, in J and US, 31, 32, 81, 232
Packaging industry, in J and US, 49
Painting
In J, 135
In US: and nature, 64, 68, 71, 74;
influence of J on, 135
Palladio, Andrea, and Western
architecture, 172, 173, 175
Pantheon, Rome, 174
Paris, France, 130, 133–138, 151
Passage to India, A (E. M. Forster),
quoted, 37
Patton, Gen. George S., 26
Pearl Harbor, Hawaii, 31
Peer's School for Girls, in J, 212
Peking incident, 29, 30
Pennsylvania, and education, 206, 212
People of Plenty (David Potter), cited,
15–16, 39
Perry, Matthew C., 3, 19, 21, 45, 86
Personal Matter, A (Kenzaburo Oë):
compared with Updike's work,
156–157; mentioned, 80, 161
Personal Narrative (Jonathan Edwards),
64

Philadelphia, Pa., 77
Philippine Islands, 28
Phoenix Hall, and US architecture,
     189–190, 192
"Plain style," of US, 35
Poe, Edgar Allan: Lawrence on, 15;
     pessimism of, 129; favored in J, 129;
     psychological themes in, 146;
     compared with Dazai, 161, 162
Politics, in J and US, *see* Government
Pollution, in J and US, 16, 57, 123
Poor Richard's Almanack (Benjamin
     Franklin), 41–42
Population, in J and US, 200, 231
Porter, Katherine Anne, and characters
     in *Ship of Fools*, 156, 163
Portnoy's Complaint (Philip Roth), 152
Portrait of a Lady (Henry James), form
     of, 130
Portugal, and J's culture, 21
Potter, David: on national character,
     15–16; on US materialism, 39
Pound, Ezra, 23, 125
Poverty, in US, 12, 53, 81, 123, 214, 232
"Power elite," in J and US, 15
Pragmatism, in US, and culture, 15
Presidency, of US, heroes in, 26
Progress, idea of, and US culture, 62,
     63, 200
Progressive movement, in US, and
     architecture, 176
Proletariat, in J and US, *see* Workers
Propaganda, in J in *1930*s, 29–31
Property, in Western thought, 9
Prussia, 19. *See also* Germany
Puerto Ricans, and education, 214
Puritanism, in US: and esthetics, 35; and
     work ethic, 41, 42, 88, 89; and nature,
     62, 64, 79; and success, 105;
     Santayana on, 115; and literature,
     129; and architecture, 171, 188; and
     education, 206
Pynchon, Thomas: *Crying of Lot 49*
     compared with Ábe's work, 158–161;
     on cultural entropy, 239, 240;
     mentioned, 153, 156, 168

Quakers, *see* Society of Friends

Rabbit, Run (John Updike), and *A
     Personal Matter*, 156–157
Racism
     In J, 4, 30–31, 210
     In US: and Japanese, 5, 103; and

wars, 6, 27, 28; and social
     mobility, 48, 91; and political
     priorities, 81; and education, 207,
     213–214; mentioned, 16, 118,
     123, 145, 231, 232
Rahv, Philip, and US literature, 138
Railways, in US, and labor force, 90
Reading, in J and US, and leisure,
     118–119
Recreation, *see* Leisure
Reischauer, Edwin O., quoted, 234
Religion
     In J: and nationalism, 20, 24, 27–28,
          29; Chinese influence on, 21; and
          materialism, 39, 52, 111; and
          nature, 59, 60, 78; and myth of
          creation, 60; contrasted with
          Western, 60, 65–66; and
          architecture, 78, 171, 179–181,
          185, 186; and education,
          204–205; mentioned, 10, 11, 54.
          See also Buddhism, Shintoism,
          Tao, Zen Buddhism
     In US: denominationalism of, 16;
          and nationalism, 20, 24, 30; and
          materialism, 33, 39, 52;
          importance of, 54; and nature,
          60; and architecture, 174, 179;
          and education, 206; mentioned,
          10, 16, 112. *See also* Jews,
          Puritanism, Roman Catholic
          Church
     Western, 4, 10, 21, 60, 171
Resources, natural: in J, 38, 39; in US,
     39
Reston, James, 6
Richardson, Henry H., 188, 189
Riesman, David, cited, 13, 53, 113
Risshin shusse, as slogan, 91
Rockefeller, John D., 41
Roebling, John Augustus, 14
Rogers, Carl, 166
Roman Catholic Church: and prejudices
     in US, 35, 90, 206; mentioned, 40, 83
Romanticism, in US, and architecture,
     166. *See also* Transcendentalism
Rome, influence of on culture of US, 62,
     173–175, 185, 189
Roosevelt, Franklin Delano, 48, 106
Roosevelt, Theodore, 26, 28, 48
Roth, Philip, 152
Rousseau, Jean Jacques, 22
Rudolph, Paul, 199
Russia, and war with J, 18, 93, 119. *See*

also Union of Soviet Socialist Republics
Ryoanji garden, Kyoto, 187

"Safety valve": and emigration from J, 91; and migration in US, 91
Saigyo, Bashō cites, 69–70
Saikaku, Ihara, and materialism, 41–42
St. Louis, Mo., 75
Salem, Mass., 180
Samurai: as popular heroes, 25, 34–35, 58; during Tokugawa, 26, 88, 89
Santayana, George: and Puritanism, 115; on "genteel tradition," 167
Sato, Eisaku, 4, 56
Sato Nobuhiro, 45
Scarlet Letter, The (Nathaniel Hawthorne), 68
Science: and industrialization, 84; in J, 86, 208, 210; and architecture, 187, 189; mentioned, 23
Scott, Sir Walter, importance of in US, 128, 129
Scully, Vincent, on architecture in US, 171, 175, 193
Seagram Building (Mies van der Rohe), 194
Sei Shonagon, *The Pillow Book*, 126
Seidensticker, Edward, on literature of J and US, 139
Self-Help (Samuel Smiles), translation of during Meiji, 215
Sendai, Japan, 197
Setting Sun, The (Dazai Osamu), characterization in, 156
Sex roles
    In J: and leisure, 8, 117; and arts, 51–52; and work, 87; and education, 212, 228
    In US: and leisure, 8, 117; and arts, 52; and work, 87; Henry Adams on, 153; and education, 212, 227, 228
Sexuality, and industrialism, 50, 84
Shakespeare, William, 28
Shepard, Paul, on attitudes toward nature in US, 61, 62, 74
Shintoism: as used in *Kokutai no Hongi*, 29; and public symbols, 35, 123; and materialism, 40; and nature, 61; and architecture, 171, 179, 187
Ship of Fools (Katherine Anne Porter), characterization in, 156, 163
Shizuoka Building (Kenzo Tange), 197
Shoda Michiko, 34
Shotoku[-Taishi], Prince, as cultural

hero, 25, 35, 119
Silberman, Charles, on education in US, 223, 226
Skidmore, Owings, and Merrill: and corporate architecture, 195; Air Force Academy campus, 197
Skyscrapers, in US, evolution of, 194
Slavery, in US: and national image, 22; Lincoln and, 47; Twain on, 73; and Greek precedent, 173–174
Smiles, Samuel, *Self-Help* translated during Meiji, 215
Smith, Adam, 9
Smith, Sydney, 23
Snow Country (Yasunari Kawabata), discussed, 143–148, 161
Snyder, Gary, 23
Social Change and the Individual (Kazuko Tsurumi), 13
Social Darwinism, in US, 30, 90
Social Democratic party of J, and labor, 96
Social life: in J, and industrialization, 84, 88, 96, 107–123 *passim*; in US, and industrialization, 84, 88, 96, 107–123 *passim*
Social mobility
    In J: and job satisfaction, 85, 98; and education, 93, 106, 215, 220, 221; and workers' expectations, 110–111; during Meiji, 215
    In US: and industrialization, 85, 88; and success ethic, 91, 110–111; and education, 93, 106, 215, 221–222; and job satisfaction, 98; and community, 113
Social security, in J and US, 50, 100
Social structure
    In J: and nationalism, 19; and income distribution, 33; and materialism, 53; during Tokugawa, 88; and worker morale, 96–98, 104–105; and mass media, 107; and arts, 182, 184; and *burakumin*, 214; and education, 219; and status anxiety, 237; mentioned, 8, 13, 15. *See also* Democracy, in J
    In US: individualism and conformity in, 13, 15, 33; and nationalism, 19; and worker morale, 96–98, 104–105; and mass media, 107; and architecture, 184, 199; and education, 219, 207; mentioned,

8. *See also* Democracy, in US
Socialist party of US, and labor, 96
Socialization for Achievement (edited by
     George De Vos), cited, 111
Society of Friends, in US: and
     architecture, 179; and education, 206
Some Prefer Nettles (Junichiro Tanizaki),
     discussed, 149–150, 163
Song of Myself (Walt Whitman), form of,
     14
Song of Roland, The, and heroes, 25, 127
Sony Corporation, 11, 84
Sōseki Natsume: education of, 128–129;
     compared with Henry James,
     130–134; versatility of, 132; *I Am a Cat*
     mentioned, 132; *Kokoro* discussed,
     133–138; mentioned, 235
Sound and the Fury, The (William
     Faulkner), humor in, 160
Sound of the Mountain, The (Yasunari
     Kawabata), masks in, 165
South, of US, culture of: Twain on,
     68–77; Toomer on, 140; Faulkner on,
     145
South Carolina, and architecture, 173
Space
     In J: shortage of, 16, 231; and
          manners, 16, 117–118; and
          militarism, 29; and gardens,
          77–79; and industrialism, 84; and
          leisure, 117–118; and
          architecture, 186. *See also*
          Geographical features, in J; Land,
          in J
     In US: breadth of, 59; and yards,
          77–80; and leisure, 117–118; and
          manners, 117–118; and esthetics
          and psychology, 201. *See also*
          Geographical features, in US;
          Land, in US
Space, Time, and Architecture (Siegfried
     Giedion): and vernacular, 177–178;
     and space, 186–187
Spain, 27–28, 151
Sports: in J, 107–123 *passim*; in US,
     107–123 *passim*
"Stages of civilization," theory of, 62, 63
"State of nature," theory of, 62
Status anxiety, in J and US: and
     materialism, 50, 53; and architecture,
     184; discussed, 237. *See also*
     Democracy, Social mobility, Social
     structure
Steamboats, in US, 70, 77
Steele, Sir Richard, 132

Stein, Gertrude, 23, 150–151
Stephens, Uriah, and labor movement,
     95
Stereotypes of national character, 4–12
     passim
Sterne, Laurence, 84
Stevens, Wallace, 125
Stevenson, Robert Louis, quoted,
     234–235
Stone, Edward, 194
Strikes, in J and US, causes of, 98
Strong, Josiah, and imperialism, 27–28
Success ethic
     In J: and social mobility, 91; and
          education, 106; and workers, 110;
          and group identity, 112. *See also*
          Social mobility, in J
     In US: and idea of progress, 63;
          and psychic damage, 91, 110; and
          social mobility, 91; and education,
          106; and workers, 110; compared
          with that in J, 112. *See also* Social
          mobility, in US
Sullivan, Harry Stack, cited, 13, 165
Sullivan, Louis, discussed, 65, 187–188
Sun Also Rises, The (Ernest Hemingway),
     and symbolic mode, 148–150
Suzuki, Daisetz Teitaro, 61
Suzuki Shosan, 41
Sweden, 31, 122
Swift, Jonathan, 122
Switzerland, 122

Takamura Kotara, on Pearl Harbor, 31
Takano Fusataro, and labor movement,
     95
Takenishi Hiroko, on nature, 66
Takezawa, Shin-ichi, and workers in J
     and US, 101–102
Tale of Genji, The (Lady Murasaki),
     discussed, 36, 126–127, 152, 213
Tale of the Lady Ochikubo, The, 126
Tama New Town, Japan, 112, 198
Tanaka, Kakuei, 56, 106, 119, 226, 228
Tange, Kenzo: on dialectic in J's
     architecture, 14, 171; on nature, 66,
     78; on traditions in J's architecture,
     178–179, 182, 184, 193, 196; on space,
     180, 181, 186, 191; on Nikko, 181;
     and gardens, 187; Yamanashi Press
     Center, 191; and "metabolism," 197;
     mentioned, 185, 235
Tanizaki, Junichiro: Murasaki's
     influence on, 126; *Some Prefer Nettles*,
     149–150, 163–164; symbolic mode of,

149–150; compared with Hemingway, 150–151; erotic themes in, 152–153; mentioned, 168

Tao, in J, 14

Tawney, R. H., 41

Taxation, in US, 12, 214; in J, and schools, 214

Taylor, Augustine Deodat, and housing, 176–177

Taylor, Frederick Winslow, and "American Plan," 103

Taylor, Zachary, image of, 26

Tea, cult of, 35–36, 184

Technology: in J, 15, 83–84, 87, 194; in US, 22, 83–84, 86, 87, 177, 188, 194

Television
    In J: popularity of, 50, 114, 118; and expectations, 106–107; and leisure, 118
    In US: popularity of, 50, 107, 114, 118; and nature, 58; and workers, 96; and expectations, 106–107; quality of, 118; mentioned, 26, 200

Terkel, Studs, cited, 109, 111

Textile industry, in J and US, and beginning of industrialism, 83, 87

Thoreau, Henry David: influence on US culture, 11, 13, 15, 65; and antimaterialism, 43, 47; and nature, 66–68; compared with Dickinson, 76; and civil disobedience, 89; on quality of life, 108; and language, 129, 166

Thought
    In J: and nature, 66–67; and "pure experience," 131; and literature, 168; and architecture, 186; adaptability of, 236–237; and contemporary problems, 236–237. See also Religion, in J
    In US: "Enlightenment," and nature, 62–77 passim; abstract quality of, 62, 92, 144, 172–173; and William James, 131; and literature, 144, 168; and architecture, 174, 185, 187, 189, 191; and education, 206; and contemporary problems, 237. See also Enlightenment; Religion, in US, Romanticism; Transcendentalism

Tocqueville, Alexis de: and materialism in US, 46–47, 54; and nature in US, 65; and work in US, 91; and social mobility, 91, 115; and connotations of "individualism," 166; and mediocrity in mass democracy, 219, 226

Toffler, Alvin, on "future shock" in J and US, 11–12

Tokugawa Ieyasu, and Nikko, 181

Tokugawa period: economy of, 11, 45, 88, 89; literature of, 128, 152; education in, 204–205, 211, 215, 228

Tokugawa Religion (Robert Bellah), cited, 111

Tokyo, Japan, 49–50, 51, 58, 68–69, 83, 112, 123, 150, 157, 159, 163, 190, 196, 197, 205, 220

Tokyo Metropolitan Government, and housing, 198

Tokyo University, 22, 106, 132, 219, 220, 224

Toomer, Jean: and nature, 68; and Kawabata, 140

Tourism
    In J: and Bashō's model, 76; and destinations, 76–77, 122, 129; and leisure, 114, 117, 121; and transportation system, 121–122; tour groups and, 122
    In US: and destinations, 23, 77, 121, 122; and leisure, 121; and transportation facilities, 121–122

Toyotomi Hideyoshi, in Meiji textbooks, 215

Trade agreements, between J and US, 5

Transcendentalism, in US: influence of, 11, 130, 131, 189; and individualism, 13; and materialism, 47; and nature, 64–65

Transportation, public, quality in J and US, 121–122

Transportation Building, Chicago (Louis Sullivan), 189

Travel literature, of J and US compared, 69–76

Trilling, Lionel, on dialectic in culture, 7

Trollope, Frances, on US culture, 23

Truman, Harry S., 32, 48, 96

Tsurumi, Kazuko, Social Change and the Individual cited, 13, 103, 117

Turgenev, Ivan Sergeevich, during Meiji, 128

Twain, Mark, see Clemens, Samuel Langhorne

Tyler, Royall, and theme of "contrast," 23

Ukiyoe, in J, 22–23, 115

Umemoto Seiichi, Japan Here and There

cited, 76
Unemployment, in US, 50
Union of Soviet Socialist Republics, and education, 218
United Auto Workers, 103
United Kingdom, 118, 214
United Nations Building, critique of, 194
United States Capitol, as architecture, 173
United States Military Academy, 106
United States Steel Corporation, 94
Updike, John: *Rabbit, Run*, and Oë, 156–157; and seeker tradition, 156; and myth, 156

Vanderbilt family, and architecture, 175
Vaux, Calver, and architecture of US, 177
Veblen, Thorstein: on architecture, 176; on education, 228–229
Venturi, Robert, and vernacular architecture, 195
Versailles, Treaty of, 24, 235
Violence, in J and US, 6, 15
Virgil, 25, 62
Virginia, and architecture, 173, 175, 201
Virginia, University of, and architecture, 174
Virginia State Capitol, 173
Vogel, Ezra and Suzanne, on materialism of J, 49–50

Wages
    In J: and job satisfaction, 98–99; compared with those in US, 99. *See also* Workers, in J
    In US: and job satisfaction, 98, 99; and popular expectations, 107. *See also* Workers, in US
Walden (Henry David Thoreau): antimaterialism of, 43; and nature, 68
Wallace, Irving, 119
Wars, of J and US, 5, 16, 21, 25, 26, 27, 28–30, 32, 38, 39, 96, 231, 232, 236
Washington, George, and symbolism of US, 20, 24, 25, 26, 35, 42–43, 211
Washington, D.C., 77, 169
Waste Land, The (T. S. Eliot), influence of, 156
Watergate, 231, 234
Weber, Max, 41
Webster, Noah, and cultural nationalism, 209

Welty, Eudora, 119
West, Benjamin, 23
West, of US: and nationalism, 19; as symbol, 23–24, 63, 77, 150. *See also* Frontier; Mythology, of US
"Western" movies, and nature, 58
Wheatley, Phillis, 212
Whistler, James McNeill, 23, 135
White-collar workers
    In J: status of, 33, 53, 54, 84, 96–97; style of life of, 52, 55, 101, 105. *See also* Workers, in J
    In US: status of, 53, 84, 96, 97; style of life of, 117. *See also* Workers, in US
Whitehead, Alfred North, 220, 224, 225
Whitehill, Arthur M., Jr., 101–102
Whitman, Walt: form in, 14, 15, 129–130; and sense of US mission, 24; influence of, 65, 189; and urban themes, 67
Whittier College, 106
Whyte, William H., Jr., 53
Wiener, Norbert, on cultural entropy, 159
Willard, Emma, 213
Wilson, Woodrow: and US innocence, 24, 167; and business, 48
Woman of the Dunes (Kobo Ábe), compared with Pynchon's work, 158–161; and architecture, 161
Women
    Of J: role of, 8, 51–52, 85; and literature, 125–126; and education, 205, 208, 212, 221. *See also* Sex roles, in J
    Of US: role of, 8, 177; and education, 207, 212. *See also* Sex roles, in US
Wood, Leonard, 25
Work
    In J: organization of, 83–106 *passim*; and education, 219
    In US: and boredom, 50–51; organization of, 83–106 *passim*; and education, 219
Work ethic
    In J: and religion, 40–41, 42; and materialism, 44; strength of, 52, 102, 114, 115
    In US: and materialism, 44; strength of, 52, 103, 115
Workers
    In J: status of, 33, 96–99, 109; during Meiji, 88, 92, 94; and job

security, 93, 105; attitudes toward jobs, 93, 96–98, 109; and social life, 93, 117; image of, 96, 97; and education, 106; and popular expectations, 106–115; and housing, 114; mentioned, 6, 9, 113, 116. *See also* White-collar workers, in J

In US: composition of work force, 39; culture of, 53, 84, 113, 116; and social mobility, 91, 93, 109; attitudes toward, 92; and social life, 93, 117; and attitudes toward jobs, 93, 96–98, 109; and working conditions, 94–95, 99; status of, 97; and popular expectations, 106–115. *See also* Labor movement, in US; White-collar workers, in US

Wouk, Herman, 119

Wren, Christopher, 172

Wright, Frank Lloyd: influence of transcendentalists on, 11, 65; and architecture in J, 80, 190; and space, 178, 190; and international style, 178, 193–194; discussed, 189–193; Falling Water described, 191–193;

mentioned, 14, 235

Yakuza, as heroes, 25

Yale Review, 9–10

Yale University, 175, 221

Yokoi Shoichi, 31–32

Yamamoto Tadashi, and architecture, 199

Yamanashi Press and Radio Center (Kenzo Tange), discussed, 191, 197

Yamanoto Kanae, 135

Yamasaki, Minoru, 194

Yanagida, Kunio, and folklore, 233

Yashiro Yukio, cited by Kawabata, 67

Yayoi culture, 14, 171, 193

Yoshida Shigeru, 4

"Youth culture," in J and US, 11, 56, 65, 116

Yukawa Hideki, and nature in J, 60

Zen Buddhism: Koestler on, 9; paradox in, 14; and materialism, 40; and gardens, 78; and architecture, 182, 184, 186, 187; and esthetics, 194, 201. *See also* Buddhism

Zola, Émile, read during Meiji, 128